INTERNATIONAL PERSPECTIVES ON TEACHING AND LEARNING ACADEMIC ENGLISH IN TURBULENT TIMES

This volume shares proven strategies for Academic English teaching, research, and development in challenging circumstances. Through original first-hand experiences from around the world, the collection reveals how educators in higher education have responded to the specific needs and challenges of teaching second language learners in turbulent times, as seen during the COVID-19 pandemic. Organised thematically, the book covers rapid responses to crises, adapting to teaching online, collaboration and online learning communities, and assessment practices. The volume provides original insights and practical suggestions for a range of practices across English for Academic and Specific Purposes that can address new and unfamiliar circumstances, both now and in future challenging times.

The collection includes a wealth of effective strategies, varied research methodologies, and resources for practice making it an invaluable reference for practitioners, students, and researchers in the field of academic English, ESL/EFL, and online language instruction.

James Fenton is Lecturer in English for Academic Purposes at University of Westminster, UK.

Julio Gimenez is Principal Lecturer and Researcher in Academic Literacies at University of Westminster, UK.

Katherine Mansfield is Lecturer and Researcher in English for Academic Purposes at University of Westminster, UK.

Martin Percy is Senior Lecturer and Researcher in English for Academic Purposes at University of Westminster, UK.

Mariangela Spinillo is Lecturer and Researcher in English for Academic Purposes at University of Westminster, UK.

INTERNATIONAL PERSPECTIVES ON TEACHING AND LEARNING ACADEMIC ENGLISH IN TURBULENT TIMES

Edited by James Fenton, Julio Gimenez, Katherine Mansfield, Martin Percy, and Mariangela Spinillo

Routledge
Taylor & Francis Group

NEW YORK AND LONDON

Cover image: © Getty Images

First published 2023
by Routledge
605 Third Avenue, New York, NY 10158

and by Routledge
4 Park Square, Milton Park, Abingdon, Oxon, OX14 4RN

Routledge is an imprint of the Taylor & Francis Group, an informa business

Library of Congress Cataloging-in-Publication Data
A catalog record for this book has been requested

ISBN: 978-1-032-25479-1 (hbk)
ISBN: 978-1-032-25478-4 (pbk)
ISBN: 978-1-003-28340-9 (ebk)

DOI: 10.4324/9781003283409

Typeset in Bembo
by Apex CoVantage, LLC

CONTENTS

FIGURES

TABLES

CONTRIBUTORS

Diana Akhmedjanova (Khalifa University of Science and Technology in Abu Dhabi, United Arab Emirates) is a postdoctoral fellow in the English department. She has experience of teaching Academic English and education courses in the United States and Uzbekistan. Her research interests include multilingual writing, self-regulated learning, digital education, and formative assessment.

Feruza Akhmedova (Westminster International University in Tashkent, Uzbekistan) is Lecturer in Academic English and a co-editor of the journal *Active Learning and Teaching Foreign Languages in Uzbekistan*. She holds an MA TESL from Webster University in Tashkent. Her research interests include classroom management and learner motivation.

Mirela Alhasani (Dubali) (EPOKA University in Tirana, Albania) is Lecturer in English for Academic/Specific Purposes at the Faculty of Architecture and Engineering. Her research interests include English language programs arising from the socio-cultural dynamics of the EU. She is the author of two books, several book chapters, and journal articles.

Jan Beneš (University of Ostrava, Czech Republic) teaches survey courses in American and British literature and on an academic writing course for doctoral students. He received his MA from Texas A&M University and his PhD from Masaryk University in Brno, Czech Republic.

Averil Bolster (University of Turku, Finland) is a University Teacher of English. Averil's research interest is in teachers' attitudes to student collaboration and she co-authored the ELTons Award-winning "Develop EAP: A Sustainable Academic English Skills Course" in 2017.

Nigel A. Caplan (University of Delaware, United States of America) is Associate professor and the online program manager at the University of Delaware English Language Institute in the United States. His publications include textbooks on grammar and writing as well as research on systemic functional linguistics, collaborative writing, and graduate communication support.

Laura Colombo (National Scientific and Technical Research Council, Instituto de Enseñanza Superior en Lenguas Vivas, Argentina) is Adjunct Researcher for the National Scientific and Technical Research Council, Argentina. Her work focuses on the teaching and learning of academic and scientific writing in first and second language. She has 24 years of teaching experience at various levels.

Katrien L. B. Deroey (University of Luxembourg, Luxembourg) is Assistant Professor in Applied Linguistics and Language Teaching at the University of Luxembourg, where she is Head of English at the Language Centre. She teaches EAP courses for postgraduate students and linguistics. Her main research interests are lecture discourse and lecturer training for English Medium Instruction.

Cara Dinneen (Macquarie University, Australia) has taught, developed, and managed English language programs for over 20 years in Spain, Oman, and Australia. She is Associate Director for Learning and Teaching at Macquarie University College, and the Macquarie University English Medium Instruction Centre. Cara is also convener of the English Australia Assessment SIG.

John Donovan (University of Westminster, United Kingdom) has taught on pre-sessional EAP courses at a number of universities in the UK including Oxford University and University of Leicester. For the past four years, he has been teaching at the University of Westminster supporting undergraduate and postgraduate students in a range of disciplines.

James Fenton (University of Westminster, United Kingdom) has over 25 years' experience of English language teaching in 11 countries. He currently lectures in Academic English at the Centre for Education and Teaching Innovation and has previously lectured in Language Acquisition and Clinical Linguistics. His recent published research explores multilingual language assessment and access to education.

Julio Gimenez (University of Westminster, United Kingdom) is a principal lecturer and researcher in academic literacies at the Centre for Education and

Teaching Innovation. His main interests are in the areas of academic writing and multilingual resources and his work has appeared in international journals and edited collections.

Yan Guoying (Donghua University, Shanghai, People's Republic of China) has been an English teacher for 18 years. Her students are mainly postgraduates, non-English majors. Her research interest falls in teaching English as a second foreign language. Currently she is doing research on using storytelling as a major teaching strategy.

Alena Hradilova (Masaryk University Language Centre, Czech Republic) is an Assistant Professor in English and Vice-director for Education and Quality of Instruction. She is also in charge of internal teacher training and continuing professional development of the Language Centre staff. She specialises in teaching English for Law and Videoconferencing in English.

David Ishii (Massey University, New Zealand) lectures in Applied Linguistics and English for Academic Purposes. His research interests are in teaching English for speakers of other languages, academic writing, and digital learning. He has taught ESOL in New Zealand, Japan, Canada, and the United States of America.

Angeniet Kam (Delft University of Technology, the Netherlands) has taught academic writing for more than 30 years. She co-founded the Dutch Network of Communicative Skills that organises a yearly conference for teachers of academic skills. She currently coordinates the Department of Communicative Skills at the Centre of Academic and Language Skills.

Kathrin Kaufhold (Stockholm University, Sweden) is Associate Professor in Applied English Linguistics at Stockholm University. Her research interests include academic writing across languages and institutional communication. She has published in journals such as *Linguistics and Education*, *Applied Linguistics Review*, and the *Journal of English for Academic Purposes*.

Žana Knežević (University Mediterranean Podgorica, Montenegro) is Assistant Professor at University Mediterranean. Her research focuses on English for Specific Purposes and Computer-Assisted Language Learning. She has participated in and presented at numerous regional and international conferences, and published in academic journals.

Joe Lennon (Masaryk University Language Centre, Czech Republic) is Assistant Professor and coordinator of the Masaryk University Writing Lab. He has taught English, academic writing, and creative writing in the US, China, and the Czech Republic.

Peter Levrai (University of Turku, Finland) is a teacher at the University of Turku and is also undertaking a PhD in Language Acquisition in Multilingual Setting, with a focus on the assessment of collaborative assignments. He co-authored "Develop EAP: A Sustainable Academic English Skills Course", which won an ELTons Award in 2017.

Jing Liu (Donghua University, Shanghai, People's Republic of China) is an associate professor at Foreign Language College, Donghua University. She has a keen interest in TESOL and has been teaching English to non-English majors for nearly 20 years. She got her PhD degree in Western Theatre at STA and her master's degree in second language acquisition at Xi'an Jiaotong University.

Mohammad Manasreh (Qatar University, Qatar) has a PhD in Applied Linguistics from the University of Warwick, has more than 20 years of teaching and training experience and 13 years of TESOL management in institutions inside and outside Qatar. His research interests include general education, TESOL leadership, identity, and teacher training.

Katherine Mansfield (University of Westminster, United Kingdom) is a lecturer and researcher in Academic English at the Centre for Education and Teaching Innovation. She has over 20 years of English language teaching experience in both Spain and the UK. Her research interests include academic writing, ipsative feedback, student progression, online learning, and bi/multilingualism.

Špela Mežek (Stockholm University, Sweden) is Senior Lecturer in English linguistics at Stockholm University. Her research interests include English for Academic Purposes, second-language reading, vocabulary learning, and genre studies. Her work has appeared in *TESOL Quarterly*, *English for Specific Purposes*, and the *Journal of English for Academic Purposes*.

Martin Percy (University of Westminster, United Kingdom) is a senior lecturer at the Centre for Education and Teaching Innovation. He has over 25 years of experience teaching ESP and EAP in Germany, Poland, and the UK. His recent publications have included an exploration of the acquisition of critical writing skills within disciplinary contexts and a comparative exploration of academic writing practices in tertiary institutions in the UK and Uzbekistan.

Gracielle K. Pereira-Rocha (Pontificia Universidad Católica, Chile) is a Fulbright alumna with an MA in TESOL from Central Michigan University. Her area of specialization is academic writing in English. She manages the Academic Writing Center at the English UC Language Center and teaches academic writing to PhD students at Pontificia Universidad Católica de Chile.

Kashif Raza (The University of Calgary, Canada) is currently doing his PhD at The University of Calgary, specializing in Leadership, Policy and Governance. He has previously taught in Qatar, USA, and Pakistan. His research interests include policy development, TESOL, expectations and perceptions in education, legal English, and teacher training.

Elisabeth L. Rodas (University of Cuenca, Ecuador) researches on faculty writing groups. As a member of the Reading and Writing Program and the Academic Writing research group, she has organized writing groups for faculty and university students. She is also an English professor in the University's Institute of Languages.

Naima Sarfraz (Qatar University, Qatar) has an MA in English and an MBA. She is currently working as a lecturer at Qatar University where she manages the university's foundation level writing courses. Naima is a certified teacher trainer and has managed several projects and presented at a number of international conferences.

Irina Shchemeleva (St. Petersburg School of Arts and Humanities at the HSE University, Russia) is the Dean. Her current research interests are in the field of academic ELF and ERPP. She has published on topics related to written ELF and L2 scholars' research writing practises.

Agnes Simon (Masaryk University, Czech Republic) is a political scientist who currently works as an academic developer in the Pedagogical Competence Development Centre at Masaryk University. In addition to researching US foreign policy and undertaking curriculum development, she is committed to teaching English-language academic writing skills to both native and non-native speakers worldwide.

Pragasit Sitthitikul (Thammasat University, Thailand) is an associate professor with a doctorate in Language and Literacy Studies from the University of Illinois at Urbana-Champaign, USA. His research interests include Second Language Literacy, Cognitive and Sociocultural Factors in Second Language Learning, and Intercultural Issues in Second Language Learning.

Jennifer Skipp (Trier University/University of Luxembourg, Germany/Luxembourg) is a Senior Lecturer in the English Department at Trier University, Germany, and an adjunct teacher for the University of Luxembourg Language Centre. Her research focuses on doctoral EAP. Jennifer was awarded her PhD by the University of Leeds and has previously worked at the University of Salzburg.

Natalia V. Smirnova (HSE University, Russia) is an associate professor and the Head of the Department of foreign languages. Her research interests lie in the field of writing for publication in the global context and how scholars work in the times of increasing publication pressure. She draws on academic literacies research and the conceptual frame of geopolitics of academic writing.

Mariangela Spinillo (University of Westminster, United Kingdom) is a lecturer in Academic English at the Centre for Education and Teaching Innovation, University of Westminster. She has taught Linguistics and Academic English at several universities in the UK and her research interests include English syntax and discourse analysis.

Libor Štěpánek (Masaryk University Language Centre, Czech Republic) is Assistant Professor in English and Director of the Masaryk University Language Centre. His research, teaching and teacher training activities focus on Creative Approach to Language Teaching (CALT) and English-Medium Instruction (EMI).

Linda Steyne (Comenius University in Bratislava, Slovakia) is a lecturer at the Department of British and American Studies in the Faculty of Arts, where she teaches English language teaching methodology and English-language academic writing skills.

Tewero Tchekpassi (Indiana University of Pennsylvania-IUP, United States of America) earned a PhD in English Composition and Applied Linguistics and an MA in TESOL from IUP, USA. His experiences include teaching undergraduate writing and ESL courses and advising students. His interests include writing pedagogy, second language pedagogy, educational policy research, and language teacher education.

Eszter Timár (Central European University in Budapest, Hungary) has been teaching academic writing skills for over 20 years. She has participated in various international projects and is a member of the European Association for the Teaching of Academic Writing.

Petra Trávníková (Masaryk University Language Centre, Czech Republic) is Assistant Professor of English, teaching EAP and ESP to students of humanities at the Masaryk University Language Centre. Her long-term research interests are intercultural pragmatics and politeness, student autonomy, and self-reflection. She specialises in teaching presentation skills.

Vorakorn Tuvajitt (Assumption University of Thailand, Thailand) currently works as a lecturer at the Institute for English Language Education. He holds a PhD degree in English Language Teaching and his interests include action research, academic writing, language testing, and alternative assessment in ELT.

Rosemary Wette (University of Auckland, New Zealand). Rosemary is an associate professor at the University of Auckland and has a special interest in second language academic literacy skill development and, in particular, the teaching and learning of source-based writing. She is currently Co-Editor of the *Journal of Second Language Writing*.

Li Zhang (Donghua University, Shanghai, People's Republic of China) is a lecturer at Foreign Language College, Donghua University. Her research interests and publications focus on academic reading and writing, and cross-cultural interaction. She has been teaching college English to non-English majors for 23 years and published more than 20 scholarly articles in Chinese and in English.

Tong Zhang (Indiana University of Pennsylvania-IUP, United States of America) received her PhD degree in Composition and Applied Linguistics from IUP. She is the supervisor of the English tutoring program and an EAP instructor in the American Language Institute at IUP. Her dissertation and recent work examine students' metacognitive development in writing through formative assessment.

ACKNOWLEDGEMENTS

We would like to express our gratitude to the contributors to this volume who, among the challenges posed by the pandemic, found time to write their chapters and share their experiences with us; without their work, this project would have never been possible.

We would also like to thank Karen Adler at Routledge who supported the project and guided us all along. We are equally grateful to Andy Pitchford and colleagues at the Centre for Education and Teaching Innovation for their support.

London, February 2022

James Fenton, Julio Gimenez, Katherine Mansfield,
Martin Percy, and Mariangela Spinillo

ACKNOWLEDGEMENTS

INTERNATIONAL PERSPECTIVES ON ACADEMIC ENGLISH IN TURBULENT TIMES

An introduction

James Fenton, Julio Gimenez, Katherine Mansfield, Martin Percy, and Mariangela Spinillo

Introduction

Since the late 1970s Academic English (AE) has increasingly become a central teaching and learning activity in higher education (HE) contexts, both in English-speaking universities and also in many HE institutions around the world (Jordan, 2002). Although the origins of AE, which developed from English for Specific Purposes (ESP), can be traced back to British universities, it rapidly developed internationally under a range of umbrella terms, such as English for Academic Purposes (EAP), English for Specific Academic Purposes (ESAP), college English and study skills, gradually earning its own place in both language teaching and research (Hyland & Jiang, 2021). Although these terms vary in focus and emphasis, they all refer to the teaching, learning, and assessment of the skills and competences needed to succeed in an academic environment (Hyland & Shaw, 2016).

The contributors to this volume conceptualise AE as a specific register of English used for study, teaching, and research purposes in "formal higher education" (Russell & Cortes, 2012, p. 3). They also highlight its strong focus on academic writing, linked to the key role that written assignments play in HE. This broad definition has a number of different connotations, depending on the purposes for which and the contexts in which the term is used. When asked about the way they conceptualise AE, some of the contributors to this volume mentioned that it:

- is a formal type of language which requires the use of complex grammar and vocabulary that is not commonly used in informal contexts

DOI: 10.4324/9781003283409-1

- implies the writer has a command of the language necessary to convey ideas in an L2 while at the same time dealing with the differences in cultural conventions and expectations
- is a specific use of English for the purpose of communicating ideas, theories, data, and/or perspectives on subject areas in educational settings
- entails teaching learners the specialized registers of AE, particularly in writing but also for speaking
- aims to prepare students to participate in discursive practices in HE
- is English to prepare students for successful matriculation into their major colleges/departments, and
- is a stepping stone for students to succeed in their future university studies.

The 21 chapters in this collection reflect such a range of terms, foci, and emphases in the context of the shift to emergency online learning when the pandemic struck, providing at the same time teaching and learning experiences that may resonate with colleagues working in similar contexts. The changes to teaching and learning AE brought about by the pandemic, the areas of activity that have been mostly affected by it, and the actions that the contributors to the collection took in order to deal with the crisis are the most significant contributions that the volume makes and what we explore here as a way of introduction.

The effects of the Covid-19 pandemic on teaching academic English

The global crisis brought about by the Covid-19 pandemic significantly affected all activities in HE, and teaching and learning AE was no exception. As the chapters in this volume exemplify, an effect of the pandemic was the demand for a rapid transition from face-to-face to online teaching and learning. Almost overnight, lecturers of AE were faced with the unprecedented challenge of having to embrace new pedagogies for online learning, adapt their teaching practices as well as materials, and manage expectations of both their institutions and students.

The contributors to the collection share their experiences of having to incorporate online tools while teaching their students how to make the best of such tools for learning as a social activity (Bolster & Levrai; Ishii; Mežek & Kaufhold). They also highlight the need to support lecturers through professional development so that they felt better prepared for the transition to online teaching and to develop resilience and adaptability (Donovan; Knežević), at the same time taking the local culture into account (Manasreh, Raza, & Sarfraz). Similarly, some contributors recount how they worked hard during the crisis to keep students at the centre of the learning process (Alhasani (Dubali), Colombo; Deroey & Skipp; Pereira-Rocha) and even experimented with new pedagogical approaches (Wette), while others had to take a more conservative approach to teaching and learning (Akhmedjanova & Akhmedova). The introduction of e-tools and online platforms to facilitate learning is another recurrent feature in these narrated experiences (Akhmedjanova & Akhmedova; Bolster & Levrai; Colombo; Knežević; Mežek & Kaufhold). All this had a considerable effect on the workload of lecturers as they established their new online courses, designed new materials for online learning (Deroey & Skipp; Pereira-Rocha; Colombo), as well as motivated their students (Akhmedjanova & Akhmedova; Alhasani (Dubali)).

Institutions, lecturers, and students of AE gradually realised that a greater degree of collaboration was required to recover from the effects of the pandemic. Collaboration was felt to be necessary to manage institutional attitudes and expectations (Caplan), learn from the experiences of other colleagues across institutions and countries (Steyne, Simon, Kam, Timár, & Beneš) and, through explicit pedagogical interventions, encourage students to engage in collaborative learning (Ishii; Rodas) both within and outside the classroom (Ishii; Lennon, Trávníková, Hradilová, & Štěpánek). Coupled with this, institutional support and collaboration, mainly in the form of holistic professional development, was seen as a central endeavour for lecturers to be able to effectively transition from face-to-face to online teaching (Donovan; Manasreh et al.).

The other decisive effect of the transitioning to online learning as a result of Covid-19 was experienced in the area of assessment. As many of the contributors exemplify, practices and procedures for assessing AE had to be revised. Such revision affected not only the nature of the assessment components (Dinneen; Zhang, Jing, & Guoying) but also the formative and summative practices implemented to assess learning (Sitthitiku & Tuvajitt; Smirniova & Shchemeleva; Zhang et al.) whose transformative effects may last longer than expected (Dinneen; Smirniova & Shchemeleva).

Looking forward

The effects of the Covid-19 crisis on AE have been unprecedented in many respects, as demonstrated by the challenges discussed in the previous section and in more depth in the chapters of this collection. However, we cannot be certain that this will be the last time we are faced with such challenges.

Unlike emerging research on teaching AE in times of Covid-19, which tends to emphasise difficulties (e.g., Kohnke & Jarvis, 2021), the contributors to this collection share the strategies and solutions they implemented as responses to the global pandemic in the hope that they would serve as a way forward should we be faced with similar turbulent times in the future.

At the macro level, institutional support and collaboration mainly in the form of culturally sensitive professional development, which includes technology, pedagogy, as well as mental and physical training for online learning, was considered fundamental for an effective response to the crisis (Bolster and Levrai; Donovan;

Knežević; Manasreh et al.). Collaboration is also explored beyond the contributors' own institutional space in the form of cross-cultural and international efforts (Steyne et al.).

At the meso level, context-specific pedagogical responses were seen as the most strategic way of facing the challenges posed by the pandemic. A number of reactions, ranging from trying out new methodologies (Wette) to holding a more conservative teaching approach (Akhmedjanova & Akhmedova), have been shared by the contributors. By the same token, their experiences from experimenting with a wide range of e-tools and online platforms (Akhmedjanova & Akhmedova; Bolster & Levrai; Colombo; Knežević; Lennon et al.; Mežek & Kaufhold) to enhance their students' learning while minimising social isolation (Ishii; Mežek & Kaufhold) are also offered in the pages that follow.

At the micro level, the contributors share their efforts and strategies to avoid learning losing its social quality in the new realities of the virtual classroom. Their efforts resulted, among other things, in a higher level of attendance (Pereira-Rocha), a more dialogic approach to learning (Colombo), a more positive attitude to learning by the students (Alhasani (Dubali)), and a community-based learning experience (Akhmedjanova & Akhmedova). Coupled with this, some authors also provide possible modifications that the assessment of learning may need in similar future turbulent times. The narrated experiences of some of the contributors (Dinneen; Zhang et al.) point to the key role that formative assessment plays in online learning and the ways in which a harmonious relationship and balance between formative and summative assessments can be successfully achieved in AE.

Conclusion

The 21 chapters in this collection represent one of the first attempts to document the experiences of a group of lecturers of AE working in different HE contexts during the time of the Covid-19 pandemic. The authors of the chapters provide readers with a detailed account of how they experienced the effects of the pandemic, the areas of teaching and learning that were most affected by it and, possibly more importantly, which strategies they put in place to deal with the dramatic effects on the teaching and assessment of AE.

The contributors have approached the task by sharing their experiences and strategies from a range of methodologies. Some of them have followed an experimental perspective and used the results of analysing data to complement their lived experiences. Others have used a more experiential way of narrating. Still others have resorted to mixing quantitative data with their personal experiences, their colleagues, and their students in an attempt to provide a richer picture of their situation. Although the contributors have taken different methodological stances to narrate their experiences, they all have one aim in common: to share how they dealt with teaching and assessing AE in turbulent times and point to ways of negotiating similar challenges in the future.

The contents of the volume have been divided into four parts thematically. The first brings together six contributions that recount the responses to the crises. "Adapting to teaching academic skills online", the second part, explores how contributors from five countries adapted their courses to the online environment in order to respond to the global crisis. The chapters in Part III explore collaboration as a conduit for achieving a constructive relationship among the different AE stakeholders and for building possible collaborations in future times of turbulence. The final part of the collection, "Assessing students online", examines the transformative impact on assessment of the transition to online learning in the face of Covid-19.

The choice of chapters for the collection, the authors, and their institutional and geographical locations thus aims at showcasing the experiences, efforts, and strategies for responding to the challenges presented by such turbulent times. We hope that the narrations included in the book will resonate with other colleagues working in similar circumstances.

The chapters in this book provide a detailed description of the key changes that were needed to deal with the Covid-19 pandemic in an attempt to prevent learning being disrupted. We sincerely hope that the volume will constitute a legacy of the experiences and actions of colleagues working in many varied, yet similar, contexts of HE should we find ourselves having to teach AE in turbulent times in the future.

Reference list

Hyland, K., & Jiang, F. (2021). A bibliometric study of EAP research: Who is doing what, where and when. *Journal of English for Academic Purposes, 49*(1), 1–12. https://doi.org/10.1016/j.jeap.2020.100929.

Hyland, K., & Shaw, P. (2016). Introduction. In K. Hyland & P. Shaw (Eds.), *The Routledge handbook of English for academic purposes* (pp. 1–13). Routledge.

Jordan, R. R. (2002). The growth of EAP in Britain. *Journal of English for Academic Purposes, 1*(1), 69–78. https://doi.org/10.1016/S1475-1585(02)00004-8

Kohnke, L., & Jarvis, A. (2021). Coping with English for academic purposes provision during COVID-19. *Sustainability, 13*(15). https://doi.org/10.3390/su13158642

Russell, D. R., & Cortes, V. (2012). Academic and scientific texts: The same or different communities? In M. Castelló & C. Donahue (Eds.), *University writing: Selves and texts in academic societies* (pp. 3–17). Emerald Group.

PART I

Rapid responses to the crisis

Mariangela Spinillo

EAP teaching and learning have been reshaped by the crisis brought about by the Covid-19 pandemic. Although for a number of HE institutions blended and distance learning were not completely unfamiliar, the sudden and full transition to online education presented challenges for EAP lecturers around the world, who had to act quickly, so that their courses could be delivered entirely remotely.

In the six chapters included in this part, EAP practitioners from six different countries (Finland, the United Kingdom, Montenegro, Qatar, Sweden, and New Zealand) share their context-appropriate solutions in response to the challenges caused by the pandemic. They draw upon education theories and evidence-based teaching practices to provide a rapid response to these sudden and unexpected changes in the field of EAP. Shifting expectations and adapting pedagogy to the remote tools are among the suggestions offered here. The way in which these contributors have responded to the crisis shows their commitment to their students and colleagues and to providing quality instruction at all times.

Averil Bolster and Peter Levrai (Finland) examine how the Centre for Language and Communication Studies (CeLCS) at the University of Turku (UTU) in Finland responded to the crisis by incorporating e-tools to facilitate collaborative learning on their EAP courses. Students were introduced to different digital tools to attempt to recreate physical classroom experiences and develop the social aspect of learning in a potentially isolating time. These e-tools and the creation of new channels of communication also offered a means for lecturers to provide and gain support. According to the authors, an acute awareness of student and teacher well-being and mental health underpinned the adaptations made to their EAP courses for the transition to online teaching. Bolster and Levrai show that their immediate implementation of support, and their holistic approach to

DOI: 10.4324/9781003283409-2

teaching, through consideration of the digital, cognitive, and physical aspects of online learning, allowed for a more immediate response when dealing with the unexpected challenges.

Staff development and support are also the focus of the chapter by John Donovan (UK). Donovan describes how the University of Westminster in London dealt with some of the challenges by delivering a four-week induction course online for a team of summer pre-sessional lecturers. The author considers how induction programmes for pre-sessional EAP lecturers can facilitate resilience and adaptability during disruptive times. Donovan highlights the importance of a holistic approach to professional development for teachers transitioning to the virtual learning environment and considers three conceptual frameworks and their relevance to pre-sessional EAP teaching. His chapter identifies characteristics of effective professional development for EAP lecturers on pre-sessional courses to develop resilience during disruptive times. According to Donovan, EAP departments should integrate pedagogy, technology, and research-informed content into professional development. Donovan's experience offers a useful point of reference for those wishing to organise similar professional development events, to enhance staff practice in ways that ultimately benefit student experiences and outcomes.

Zăna Knežević (Montenegro) shows how ESP lecturers and students at two universities in Montenegro were insufficiently familiar with the pedagogical uses of technology and therefore unprepared for the transition to online teaching. Knežević explains that the universities offered little support to their teaching staff and students, and the responsibility for responding to the crisis was initially largely left to the lecturers, who had to explore the technologies for ESP teaching on their own. Knežević also shows how the ReFLAME (Erasmus+) project helped lecturers and students to adapt to remote teaching and was therefore key to their response to the crisis.

Mohammad Manasreh, Kashif Raza, and Naima Sarfraz (Qatar) describe how Qatar University's Foundation Programme Department of English (FPDE) responded to the crisis by providing a strong support system to lecturers and students. The authors show how culturally based strategies facilitated the teaching and learning process during turbulent times. These strategies included teacher and student training for online learning, modification of course content and assessment, exam security, and health and safety measures. For them, professional development was key to overcoming the challenges. They show how, through acquiring the necessary knowledge and skills, teachers could effectively transfer their real-world classrooms into a virtual learning environment. They found that by giving students a two-week break, the teachers had sufficient time for training, which facilitated the transition to online teaching and ensured that everyone had more time to adjust to the changes.

Špela Mežek and Kathrin Kaufhold (Sweden) outline how the Department of English at Stockholm University addressed some of the challenges they faced. Their chapter reports on the experience of teaching an interdisciplinary postgraduate EAP course and describes how the university-wide implemented video conferencing tool and online learning platform were used in line with the pedagogical ethos of the course. The authors explain that while these e-tools provided a space for learning and communication, they also presented challenges for interacting spontaneously, and the additional time needed to organise activities in a virtual learning environment. Considering the advantages and disadvantages of these e-tools, core elements of the course were redesigned through teacher collaboration and co-learning with the intention of reducing students' sense of social isolation.

Rosemary Wette (New Zealand) looks at how the University of Auckland in New Zealand responded to the crisis by implementing flipped learning (FL) on a 12-week graduate academic writing course. Her chapter outlines the benefits and limitations of FL for students and lecturers, and how any negative consequences in terms of student interest and engagement might be mitigated. Wette offers reflections on the effects of FL on students' cognitive and affective/behavioural engagement and explains why she considers this method an effective way of overcoming some of the limitations of online learning, particularly as a way of addressing student passivity and disengagement during online learning.

While each narrative conveys a unique, context-specific solution, there are core threads running through this section. One is the creation of learning and teaching communities to reduce the sense of isolation experienced in online teaching. The accounts here show that an effective response to the challenges posed by disruptive events would not have been possible without close collaboration. Another theme is training and support. To overcome the challenges, institutions need to provide training that supports both staff and students. These six narratives can enable readers to evaluate the transferability of the practices described and potentially adopt good practice examples in their own contexts.

1

FAST-FORWARDING TOWARD THE FUTURE OF EAP TEACHING IN "THE HAPPIEST COUNTRY IN THE WORLD"

Lessons learned in turbulent times

Averil Bolster and Peter Levrai

Introduction

Friday, March 13, 2020, was an ominous day. What had been expected for some time had arrived: notification that all teaching at our university in south-west Finland was to be carried out remotely from the following Monday, March 15. The Covid-19 pandemic that had seemed so far away on the news had reached the "happiest country in the world" (Helliwell et al., 2020). Little did we know at the time that "remote teaching" would become the norm, not only for the remainder of the 2020 spring semester but also for the entire 2020–2021 academic year and is likely to impact teaching and learning for years to come.

While this was disruptive and required us to adapt to a fully virtual learning environment, the transition was eased due to the foundations of remote learning, which already existed as a part of some courses, and an overall course structure which allowed for flexibility. By maintaining a focus on Backward Design (Wiggins & McTighe, 2005, please see Section 2.3) and considering the learning outcomes of courses, changes could be made to course modes and the nature of interactions without compromising course learning outcomes. Reflection over the summer of 2020 and beyond allowed for refinement of the emergency measures taken at short notice, to develop courses which consider the student experience holistically and are robust enough to deal with changing circumstances in these turbulent times. This is important because despite Finland being given the title of "The Happiest Country in the World" for the fourth time in 2021, by the United Nations Happiness Report (Helliwell et al., 2020), it also has amongst the highest suicide rates in Europe for young people aged 15 to 24 years (Official Statistics of Finland, n.d).

DOI: 10.4324/9781003283409-3

Language learning in Finland and the University of Turku

Background: education in Finland

The general level of English language competence is relatively high among tertiary-level students, with most operating at CEFR B2 level and above, with the majority of Finnish pupils learning English from the age of 9 (YLE, 2020). With a population of 5.5 million, Finland has 13 universities and 22 universities of applied science. According to the Universities Act, undergraduate students must complete language studies in Finnish and Swedish, the two official languages, and one other foreign language, most typically English (Tuomi & Rontu, 2011). Finland has a well-respected education system, consistently placing high in the[1] PISA rankings (ThisisFINLAND staff, 2019), which looks to equip students with 21st-century skills (Lavonen, 2020) and embraces technology enhanced learning. Educators have a high level of academic freedom, with autonomy regarding course design and content.

University students study both Academic Finnish and Academic English, which support them in developing awareness of the conventions of academic discourse in the different languages. This is especially important because Academic Finnish tends to be a more reader-responsible language, while English is more writer-responsible, requiring more than direct translation to produce appropriate scholarly work in each of the languages, for example English texts require more metalanguage than Finnish ones (Mauranen, 1993). As such, the teaching of academic discourse, in both Finnish and English, is valued in higher education in Finland and is available for all students. This differs considerably from the more "peripheral role" Academic English courses are sometimes seen to have in inner-circle countries (Ding & Bruce, 2017, p. 107).

Teaching context

The University of Turku (UTU) celebrated its centenary in 2020, albeit in a much more muted style than expected. The CeLCS, an independent unit in UTU, is responsible for language, communication, and intercultural skills courses. The mandatory language courses taught by the centre are Finnish and Swedish, and students must also choose a third mandatory language course, with English being by far the most popular choice. There are a range of other languages also taught as electives, with most language classes having a maximum of 24 students.

Students across faculties are required to take compulsory, credit-bearing English language courses, although the number of credits varies from faculty to

---

[1] "PISA is the OECD's Programme for International Student Assessment. PISA measures 15-year-olds' ability to use their reading, mathematics and science knowledge and skills to meet real-life challenges". – www.oecd.org/pisa/

faculty. For example, in the Faculty of Social Sciences, students are required to take two three-credit courses (English: Academic & Professional Skills I (EAPS I) and English: Academic & Professional Skills II (EAPS II)). In contrast, some of the departments in the Faculty of Technology require students to take one or two two-credit courses (English for STEM A and/or English for STEM B), while others require one three-credit course (English for STEM C). The mandatory courses are discipline specific and targeted towards particular cohorts of students, for example first- or second-year undergraduates. While the global pandemic changed the modality of courses, as will be discussed later, there were no substantial curricular level changes.

Approach to course design

Both authors have a history of course design and curriculum development with an approach which encourages flexibility, adaptation, and localisation. As early as 2013, Levrai (2013, p. 6) was advocating for materials which stepped away from "pre-determined linearity" to materials, while Bolster (2015) explored the feasibility of "gapped" textbooks, which would provide space for teachers to bring in materials or activities tailored to their students' needs. Describing the development of a previous EAP course, Bolster and Levrai (2017, p. 147) emphasised that:

> A course is not a fixed artefact, but rather an ongoing process, involving the identification of strengths, weaknesses and emergent outcomes that can be incorporated into later iterations of the course. This adaptive approach has . . . flexibility and longevity.

The favoured approach to course development was Backward Design (Wiggins & McTighe, 2005), which begins by setting the course objectives, moves through determining how success will be measured and assessed, before moving onto the last stage, that of material development. The benefit of this approach is that it allows for potentially greater flexibility than Forward or Central Design approaches (Richards, 2013). Forward Design begins with materials and moves through to objectives, which means, from the outset, the course is to some extent set by the materials initially selected. Central Design begins by looking at processes, which might favour a particular approach, for example Task-Based Learning, which again serves as a fixed point around which the rest of the course develops (Richards, 2013). With Backward Design, it is the learning outcomes that are fixed and the means by which they can be reached are myriad, allowing for personalisation and tailoring of materials to particular classes or cohorts. Since EAP is goal driven, tending to have clearly defined and focused aims (Alexander et al., 2008), the outcomes-driven Backward Design approach is a good match.

English: academic and professional skills course structure

The EAPS I course is 28 hours, typically delivered in one two-hour lesson per week over 14 weeks. The course is assessed through a portfolio of work, including an initial letter of self-assessment, a glossary, a summary of an academic article, lecture notes, and a critical response and a final learner reflection. This course serves as a prerequisite for the more challenging EAPS II course, which includes essay writing and academic presentations, as well as job application documents. Students are given freedom to source their own articles and lectures for the assignments, after practising the required skills with teacher selected input texts and being given guidance on effective search strategies and suitable repositories.

Prior to 2020, there was some useful grounding already in place for when courses moved fully online. Two main platforms were in use to support the EAPS courses, Moodle and Office365, both operating within the UTU network. Moodle provided an active learning space, operating as an extension of the classroom for asynchronous discussion or to provide input to be reviewed before class or later consolidation. It was also the main repository for course materials, as no textbook was used, but the intention was very much that it was an active learning space rather than a digital filing cabinet. Students also had Office365 accounts linked to their UTU credentials, so Word online and PowerPoint online could also be used as collaborative workspaces when students were working together (e.g. developing a presentation). One or two lessons per course were set up as asynchronous, self-access lessons to allow the students to experience learning, which was not classroom centred or teacher led.

Implementing change

The pandemic pivot

By the middle of March 2020, the remaining five weeks of the English language courses had to be navigated remotely since access to offices and classrooms was prohibited. When the announcement was made on March 13, 2020, that all teaching was to be online, the reaction by our unit, CeLCS, was immediate.

Since much of CeLCS's communication was already conducted via our internal Microsoft Teams platform, this proved an effective space to continue communicating when online lessons suddenly began. There were established Teams channels for all staff, different language teams, and special topics (e.g. research and the "coffee room" channel), but new channels were created to facilitate "Remote Work" and "Well-being". The creation of these new channels provided a means for teachers to provide and gain support.

For the rest of the semester, daily support meetings for all members of the unit were held on Teams to address issues with technology and to share tips about successes, in addition to the features and pitfalls of various platforms.

This immediate implementation of support by the CeLCS Director recognised that some teachers were more comfortable utilising e-tools and technology and established a meeting point so colleagues could benefit from one another's ideas and experiences.

Within the English team, particular attention was given to checking in on each other, providing moral support and highlighting what activities proved effective (or not) online. With the sudden move to remote teaching, holding lessons synchronously or asynchronously was a major talking point. The high levels of trust in Finnish teachers (Schleicher, 2019) meant how to hold lessons was left to the teachers' discretion. Due to an often unfavourable teaching environment at home, an asynchronous approach was preferred by some teachers, but in other cases, a synchronous approach was adopted.

Support for teachers at this time of flux comes not only from staff at CeLCS but also from university management. Although public healthcare in Finland is accessible and comprehensive, some employers provide occupational healthcare. Through the UTU occupational healthcare plan, several services were made available to university teachers to better cope with the physical demands of "The Pandemic Pivot":

- remote ergonomic consultations could provide advice on home workspaces
- funds could be provided for special reading glasses to deal with the increased screen time from online teaching
- up to three appointments could be made with an occupational psychologist for those experiencing anxiety or loneliness due to working in a more isolated context.

Getting on the same page

Colleagues in CeLCS discussed at length the use of a common language around online learning. Terms like "blended" and "hybrid" can be used to talk about quite different course types but can also be conflated and confused so there was a proposal to agree on a nomenclature for the different course options which the virtual environment makes possible. The key variables are modality (*where* the student has to be) and time (*when* the student has to be there). The different course types are outlined in Table 1.1, and Figure 1.1 visualises where course types lie on a matrix of those two variables.

There is no judgement as to which type of course is superior, but it is important to acknowledge how fractured the different course delivery types have become and seek a shared clarity. One challenge is that significantly different courses, for example mixed delivery and hybrid, could occupy the same space on the matrix, despite being significantly different. However, without an attempt to generate a shared language and taxonomy, there can be no meaningful discussion of best practice.

TABLE 1.1 A taxonomy of course types

Course Type	Delivery Method	Delivery Schedule	Defining Characteristics
Contact	Physical	Synchronous	Majority contact lessons, majority synchronous
Hybrid	Simultaneously physical and virtual	Synchronous	Majority synchronous
Mixed delivery	Physical/virtual	Synchronous	Balance between physical and virtual lessons, majority synchronous
Contact blended	Physical/virtual	Synchronous and asynchronous	Balance between synchronous and asynchronous lessons, balance between physical and virtual lessons
Online	Virtual	Synchronous	No contact lessons, majority synchronous
Online blended	Virtual	Synchronous and asynchronous	Balance between synchronous and asynchronous lessons
Fully independent	Virtual	Asynchronous	No synchronous lessons
Guided independent	Virtual (and possibly physical)	Asynchronous (and possibly physical)	Most materials self-access asynchronously, with limited teacher input (e.g. feedback)

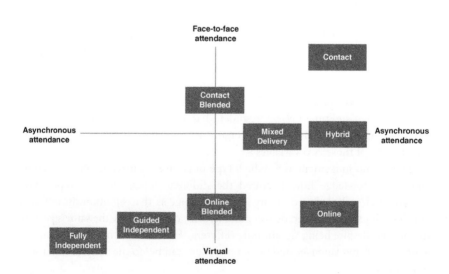

FIGURE 1.1 Course types in time and space

Challenges and solutions in the use of technology

The initial response to the sudden change involved a steep learning curve for all teachers. In some ways, it was a great fast forward, forcing technological innovation to become a core activity, where teachers necessarily taught online. The teaching delivery mode may have fundamentally changed, but the nature of teaching remained unchanged. Student-centred learning is still student-centred learning, albeit with the student having become pixels on the screen. Communication and collaboration are still central, whichever mode and channel they take place. The classroom environment can be mimicked or, better yet, surpassed. For this to happen though we need to expand our view beyond the classroom to the student, taking holistic considerations into account and addressing the digital, mental, and physical aspects of online learning.

One of the challenges in the move to fully digital learning was the competing tools, which offered new ways of doing things or ways of doing new things. There is a plethora of online collaborative spaces (e.g. Google Docs, Word Online, Dropbox Paper, Padlet) survey tools (e.g. Survey Monkey, Webropol, Microsoft Forms), and personal response systems (e.g. Answergarden, Mentimeter, Quizlet, Kahoot). While these all have their uses and can be part of a successful course, there can be an over-elaboration in the use of tools, for example having a lesson where students are following links or QR codes to an endless parade of different tools or requiring them to create accounts across various workplaces. Any use of a tool is a potential point of technical breakdown with teachers and students being unable to access the tool, students (and teachers) needing to learn to use new software effectively. Limiting the variety of e-tools in use helped to mitigate this.

The decision was made to try to keep things as straightforward as possible. The concept of "digital natives" has been challenged in the literature (Kirschner & De Bruyckere, 2017), and while students may be competent social media users, they can still struggle to effectively employ technologies for their learning. The focus was only on those tools that could operate through students' existing UTU credentials or through anonymous guest accounts. This kept student work in the UTU environment and added a layer of security against privacy concerns. Students had access to Zoom through their UTU credentials and it was the preferred location for synchronous teaching to take place. The university purchased a secure Zoom Client package, and this allowed for lessons to remain secure and avoid "Zoombombing" (Lorenz, 2020) and maintain a safe environment for the students. This provided a sense of having "our own" online class environment.

The best way for the tools to work together was also considered. Zoom was set up as a recurring meeting, so each class had its own unique link, valid for the whole course. A folder was shared with each class in OneDrive, where any collaborative documents would be stored. The links to the Zoom meeting and a shared OneDrive folder were in the course information section in Moodle, so access was always clear to students, ease of access being a primary concern.

The learning curve for Zoom for students is relatively easy, and, once students are made aware of reactions, simple personal response systems can be emulated within the Zoom environment, for example. thumbs up for "Yes", crying face for "No", shocked face for "Maybe". However, one of the drawbacks found with Zoom was the monitoring of breakout rooms. A teacher could move from room to room, but discussion was missed. A solution was using Zoom in conjunction with Word Online. A shared Word document (part of the internal OneDrive system) had the task instructions, and members of each breakout room could note their responses in the document, using a different font colour for each group. This enabled the teacher to see what was happening in each room and also served as motivation and inspiration to other groups who could see what the other groups were discussing. Alternatively, each breakout room sometimes had its own Word document it could work on and then share with the whole group after the closure of breakout rooms.

Through this combination of technologies, tasks common to the EAP classroom (e.g. a listening, note-making, and summarising activity or a K–W–L (Know–Want to know–Learned) reading activity) could be followed without major change. Perhaps the greatest challenge came during speaking activities. At first, some students were reluctant to turn on their cameras, negatively impacting oral communication tasks. However, students could be persuaded to use cameras, if the rationale for doing so was given (Castelli & Sarvary, 2021), which greatly facilitated academic speaking tasks like group discussions and presentations. However, nothing can quite replicate the spontaneity of discussions in the physical classroom.

Considering the whole student: mental and physical

The paradox of being a "happy" country with a high rate of youth suicide is recognised in the attention paid to the anxiety and well-being of university undergraduates (McGhie, 2017), and the University and CeLCS had a number of initiatives to continue to address this when going through the massive changes necessitated by the pandemic, as shown in Figures 2, 3, and 4.

From 2014, the University had a "Pylly ylös!" policy, which translates as the "Bottoms Up!" initiative (University of Turku, 2016), encouraging physical movement during lessons and lectures to stimulate mind and body (please see Figure 1.2). This continued into online lessons, with breaks from screen time and stretching. Soothing pictures of natural landscapes were also shared during breaks, and students were encouraged to get up and look out of their windows.

Whenever new students were introduced to CeLCS courses, teachers shared the "Et ole Yksin" or "You are not alone" information (please see Figure 1.3). This was a way of directing students to services which could be of help, be that courses designed to support students who find presenting too stressful or consulting with the Head of Academic and Student Affairs in the Centre or

FIGURE 1.2   A poster for classroom movement from the "Pylly ylös!" Facebook page (Pylly ylös!, 2015)

FIGURE 1.3   Cover slide for the "Et ole yksin" initiative (Nelson, 2019, slide 29)

the University learning psychologists, accessibility officer or student healthcare psychologists.

CeLCS also had a reading dog ("lukukoira") initiative prior to the pandemic (please see Figure 1.4), where students who experienced anxiety could practice reading aloud, speaking, or presenting with a trained service dog, providing a safe and encouraging environment. While this could not continue during the pandemic, pets were welcome during lessons and the unexpected appearance of a cat or large dog helped forge relationships.

A very useful workshop titled "Working from home – viewpoints and tools for motivation and well-being" was run by an occupational health psychologist early in the 2020–21 academic year for all university staff in Finland (Grandell, 2020). It included strategies that were also transferable and relevant to students, including the importance of the rituals we follow to go to work and to leave work behind. This could involve something as simple as going for a short walk to "leave home" and "go to work" or having a dedicated workspace (corner of a table at home) that you leave at the end of work (move to another corner of the table). Another useful tip relevant to students was having a dedicated digital workspace, meaning a browser specifically for university-related work that could be opened when needed and closed when studying was done, for example Google Chrome for study and Firefox for surfing the web. To support them in remote learning, discussion increased with students about *how* they work, and more attention was

FIGURE 1.4   This very good girl is Kaisla, the reading dog (lukukoira) (Nelson, 2019, slide 31)

paid to time management strategies, which students reported as difficult. While some of these issues may not seem immediately relevant to an EAP classroom, it is vital to ensure that the students can derive more benefit from classes through effective learning practices.

It was also important, in an attempt to mitigate the social isolation students could feel, to make use of collaborative assignments. While the authors would typically advocate for collaboration in relation to Sociocultural Theory and the added learning gains and affordances from collaborative tasks (Levrai & Bolster, 2019), there is also an important social aspect to collaboration. For some students, working with peers in their groups could be the only social interaction they had during study periods. Collaboration provides more opportunity for communication and the social care this provided was invaluable. In feedback at the end of courses, this opportunity to work with and talk to other students was highlighted as a strongly positive feature of the course.

Future strategies and applications

A positive take-away from the pandemic is that a number of useful lessons were learnt, and we discovered that fruitful learning can take place in fully online environments. The conjunction of a collaborative document (or documents) with Zoom breakout room discussions was a very effective combination, resulting in a record of discussions that would otherwise be lost in the face-to-face environment, as well as providing motivation and prompts for groups. Presentation rehearsal was also facilitated more effectively and productively through Zoom. Rather than students having to scatter around a building in presentation groups or doing simultaneous reads, two presentation groups could be put into a Zoom room for rehearsal and peer feedback. When this was recorded asynchronously, it was noticeable how students spent more time discussing and acting on feedback than was available in class.

As we emerge from the pandemic and into a future of different challenges, technologies are already developing to provide new opportunities. For example, online gathering tools like Wonder and Gather offer an alternative experience to a static Zoom-like meeting space. Students can control an avatar that moves around to mingle with other students. When their avatars are close to each other, video communication can start. Input texts and videos can be put in the environments, and it can become a more classroom-like experience of students gathering in groups to work on something and a teacher physically moving around and monitoring. As exciting as that may sound, the prime considerations for any new tools will revolve around the following key questions.

Key questions for adopting new technologies

- What affordances does this provide that we do not have already?
- How steep is the learning curve for teachers and students?

- How does this integrate with the tools we already use?
- How much would we have to change the way we do things?
- How does this make the learning experience better for students?
- Do we need it?

Knowing the answer to those questions means that we can ensure technology is being utilised for the benefit of learning rather than just being novel.

Due to the pandemic, we have moved further down the path education was already going, but the journey is not over. The next major foreseeable challenge is how to best facilitate a hybrid classroom, with some students attending virtually while others simultaneously attend in person. There is a clear appetite in the student body for remote learning and the flexibility it gives the students in terms of where they need to be to attend classes. Hybrid learning will require careful thought about interaction patterns and how to be fully inclusive of students, whichever mode the course is utilising. This shows that whatever challenges arrive next, a robust course can respond and adapt, rising to meet the challenge. For us, the key takeaways from the experience of the last year are as follows:

- Any challenge, however unexpected, can be met through dialogue with and support from colleagues
- Using a Backward Design approach to courses provides flexibility so that content and modality can be adapted as needed, while keeping the central integrity of the course stable
- When dealing with a challenge, it is vital to keep the students' and teachers' well-being front and centre, rather than getting lost in the detail of working on a solution
- Less is more in terms of keeping things simple and directly useful
- Education has changed, but does not make former ways of doing things obsolete. We need to marry the best elements of different approaches and ways of doing things together
- Language education is built on the opportunity for communication, whatever the modality
- Collaborative learning can help scaffold students through new ways of doing things.

The Covid-19 pandemic changed the world, but the world constantly changes. There will always be new challenges and new opportunities. This requires agility and flexibility on behalf of teachers to address the current needs of students according to the situation, while maintaining a standard of education. We have learned that change can be positive, bringing with it new options, affordances, and opportunities.

Reference list

Alexander, O., Argent, S., & Spencer, J. (2008). *EAP essentials: A teacher's guide to principles and practice*. Garnet Education.

Bolster, A. (2015). Materials adaptation of EAP materials by experienced teachers (Part II). *Folio, 16*(2), 16–21.

Bolster, A., & Levrai, P. (2017). A slow (R) evolution: Developing a sustainable EGAP course. *The European Journal of Applied Linguistics and TEFL, 6*(1), 147–166.

Castelli, F. R., & Sarvary, M. A. (2021). Why students do not turn on their video cameras during online classes and an equitable and inclusive plan to encourage them to do so. *Ecology and Evolution, 11*(8), 3565–3576.

Ding, A., & Bruce, I. (2017). *The English for academic purposes practitioner*. Palgrave Macmillan.

Grandell, R. (2020). *Working from home – viewpoints and tools for motivation and well-being*. Åbo Akademi University. https://blogs.abo.fi/personalbloggen/kurser/

Helliwell, J. F., Layard, R., Sachs, J., & De Neve, J. (Eds.). (2020). *World happiness report 2021*. Sustainable Development Solutions Network. https://worldhappiness.report/ed/2021/

Kirschner, P. A., & De Bruyckere, P. (2017). The myths of the digital native and the multitasker. *Teaching and Teacher Education, 67*, 135–142.

Lavonen, J. (2020). Curriculum and teacher education reforms in Finland that support the development of competences for the twenty-first century. In F. Reimers (Ed.), *Audacious education purposes*. Springer. https://doi.org/10.1007/978-3-030-41882-3_3

Levrai, P. (2013). The coursebook as trainer. *English Teaching Professional, 85*, 4–7.

Levrai, P., & Bolster, A. (2019). A framework to support group essay writing in English for academic purposes: A case study from an English-medium instruction context. *Assessment & Evaluation in Higher Education, 44*(2), 186–202.

Lorenz, T. (2020, March 20). Zoombombing: When conference calls go wrong. *New York Times*. www.nytimes.com/2020/03/20/style/zoombombing-zoom-trolling.html

Mauranen, A. (1993). Contrastive ESP rhetoric: Metatext in Finnish-English economics texts. *English for Specific Purposes, 12*, 3–22. https://doi.org/10.1016/0889-4906(93)90024-I

McGhie, V. (2017). Entering university studies: Identifying enabling factors for a successful transition from school to university. *Higher Education, 73*(3), 407–422. https://doi.org/10.1007/s10734-016-0100-2

Official Statistics of Finland. (n.d.). Causes of death [e-publication]. ISSN=1799-5078.2019, 7. Fewer suicides than in the previous year. Helsinki: *Statistics Finland* [referred: 25.6.2021]. www.stat.fi/til/ksyyt/2019/ksyyt_2019_2020-12-14_kat_007_en.html

Richards, J. C. (2013). Curriculum approaches in language teaching: Forward, central, and backward design. *RELC Journal, 44*(1), 5–33. https://doi.org/10.1177/0033688212473293

Schleicher, A. (2019). The secret to Finnish education: Trust. *Organisation for Economic Cooperation and Development. The OECD Observer*, 1–3.

ThisisFINLAND staff. (2019). Finland remains among top nations in PISA education survey. *This Is Finland*. https://finland.fi/life-society/finland-remains-among-top-nations-in-pisa-education-survey/

Tuomi, U. K., & Rontu, H. (2011). Discussion note: University language centres in Finland – role and challenges. *Apples-Journal of Applied Language Studies, 5*(2), 37–44.

University of Turku. (2016). *Bottoms up! Sit less, feel better. University of Turku*. https://intranet.utu.fi/index/bottoms%20up/Pages/default.aspx

Wiggins, G. P., & McTighe, J. (2005). *Understanding by design.* Merrill/Prentice Hall.
YLE. (2020, August 13). Finnish schools teach languages earlier than ever, but struggle to move beyond English. *Yleisradio Oy.* https://yle.fi/uutiset/osasto/news/finnish_schools_teach_languages_earlier_than_ever_but_struggle_to_move_beyond_english/11492669

Images

Nelson, M. (2019, September, 5). *Kieli- ja viestintäopintojen keskus.* [PowerPoint slides]
Pyllyylös. (2015, February 16). Did you get out of your seat for a minute? [status update]. *Facebook.* www.facebook.com/534600789981886/photos/a.534609386647693/748020951973201.

2

BUILDING RESILIENCE IN PRE-SESSIONAL EAP COURSES THROUGH PROFESSIONAL DEVELOPMENT

A perspective from the UK

John Donovan

Introduction

Pre-sessional EAP courses play an important role in preparing international students for academic life in UK universities. However, these programmes are vulnerable to disruption due to geopolitical, environmental, and public health crises (Hodges et al., 2020). The chapter explores how the design of induction programmes for pre-sessional EAP teachers can facilitate resilience against future unexpected events. The rapid pivot to online teaching was challenging for higher education faculties (Hodges et al., 2020; Rapanta et al., 2020). In many cases, the emergency transition caused by the pandemic involved rapid improvisations focused on an emergency remote teaching environment (ERTE) model characterised as rapidly developed, temporary instructional support in a crisis (Hodges et al., 2020). Bruce and Stakounis (2021) indicate that in this transition, some EAP teachers experienced an overload of technological information combined with a perceived lack of focus on pedagogical purpose.

This chapter focuses on lessons learned from the induction programme for teachers on a pre-sessional course for international students at the University of Westminster. The review was conducted by analysis of participants' comments on an online forum during the teacher induction course. The needs of pre-sessional teachers are an underrepresented area of study in the literature. Much of the debate about EAP and technology focuses on students' learning experiences, and there is a dearth of literature about EAP teachers' professional development (Breen, 2018). The aim of this chapter is to identify characteristics of effective professional development for EAP teachers on pre-sessional courses in order to develop resilience and enhance ability to navigate unforeseen, disruptive events.

DOI: 10.4324/9781003283409-4

Literature review

The concept of resilience is central to understanding EAP faculties' abilities to respond to unexpected events which may disrupt academic programmes. Resilience is a multi-faceted construct and most of the literature in this field focuses on fostering undergraduate students' academic resilience in terms of emotional and mental well-being (Brammer, 2020) or building resilience at an institutional level (Nandy et al., 2020). However, relatively little attention has been paid to fostering resilience in teaching professionals. Resilience in relation to teachers is defined as "a quality that enables teachers to maintain their commitment to teaching and their teaching practices despite challenging conditions" (Brunetti, 2006, p. 813). A resilient faculty is associated with flexibility, innovation, and collaboration (Wilcox & Lawson, 2017), and teachers' resilience is linked to the academic communities in which they work (Brammer, 2020). Specifically, Rapanta et al. (2020) argue that the facilitation of effective online teaching environments depends on infrastructural support provided by universities in terms of professional development.

The need for professional development in online pedagogies is based on the premise that in the transition to online teaching, some teachers adhere to traditional pedagogies which may not be as appropriate in the digital environment (Baran et al., 2011; Bezuidenhout, 2018; Meyer, 2013). Online learning requires specific skill sets relating to technologies, pedagogical strategies, and communication processes (Baran et al., 2011; Belt & Lowenthal, 2019; Salmon, 2011). There is recognition of the need for training interventions for teaching professionals to develop skills relating to technology, instructional strategies, and communication processes in the context of digital education (Baran et al., 2011; Lowenthal et al., 2019; Magda, 2019). Koehler and Kim (2012) note that technology is not devoid of context and an appreciation of the relationship between technology, pedagogy, and course content is a requirement for effective teaching. A review of the literature indicates three theoretical constructs, which frequently feature in the design of professional development programmes for teachers related to delivery of online learning: (i) communities of practice (Lave & Wenger, 1991; Wenger, 1998), (ii) Technological Pedagogical Content Knowledge (TPACK) (Mishra & Koehler, 2006), and (iii) Salmon's (2002) Five Stage Model for Online Learning.

Communities of practice

A range of literature (Kimble et al., 2008; Lave & Wenger, 1991; Shattuck & Anderson, 2013) espouses the importance of the concept of community in education. This concept is based on the premise that learning is a process where individuals within a learning community share knowledge and experience. The role of collegiate collaboration in pedagogic training is recognised (Vilppu et al.,

2019) and such collaboration results in *communities of practice,* which facilitate discussion with colleagues about teaching and the reduction of academic isolation (Remmik & Karm, 2009). This concept has roots in Vygotsky's (1978) social development theory, which posits that sociocultural interactions are critical to the learning processes which emerge from dialogue in what Vygotsky terms *a zone of proximal development.* The ultimate aim of this process is learner autonomy, which is mutually constructed by participants through a structured dialogue. Wenger (1998) identifies three interrelated structural elements, which underpin communities of practice: (i) mutual engagement, (ii) joint enterprise, and (iii) a shared repertoire. Mutual engagement describes the patterns of interaction between individuals resulting in the creation of shared meaning and understanding. Joint enterprise describes the common purpose in which members are engaged, which creates coherence for their actions. The concept of a shared repertoire refers to the common resources and terms of reference developed by the group members to facilitate learning within the group. The role of communities of practice in times of change and rapid technological transition is recognised (Breen, 2015; Wenger et al., 2002) with emphasis placed on the fostering of collaboration and sharing of pedagogical and technical knowledge.

TPACK

TPACK is a foundational theory for teacher technology professional development; however, it is employed relatively rarely in the context of higher education faculty development (Herring et al., 2016; Koh, 2020). The TPACK framework builds on Shulman's (1986) work relating to pedagogical content knowledge (PCK) and sets out to categorise the knowledge required by teachers to integrate technology in teaching while incorporating the multifaceted nature of teacher knowledge. The model emphasises the integrative relationship between content knowledge, pedagogy, and technology, which should be incorporated into teacher professional development.

Mishra and Koehler (2006) assert that TPACK is a specific body of knowledge required to teach with technology. The TPACK model presents a holistic construct that merges technological, pedagogical, and content knowledge, and it underlines the argument that the integration of digital education requires more than technological skills. Falloon (2020) states that the efficacy of this approach is dependent on "teachers' capacity for flexibility, willingness to update, and readiness to explore how the domains interrelate to support effective technology use in a range of different situations" (p. 2454). There has been limited research into the application of TPACK for professional development of EAP teachers. However, Breen (2018) notes that technological knowledge in the context of TPACK is not exclusively focused on developing detailed knowledge of the functionality of the latest teaching software. Rather, it promotes the notion that technology can be integrated into EAP teaching in an organic way.

Salmon's Five Stage Model

The concepts of socialisation, collaboration, and knowledge construction in online teaching environments are at the centre of Gilly Salmon's Five Stage Model for Online Learning (2002). On the basis of constructivist theory, this model presents a pedagogical scaffold for online learning comprising five stages facilitating students' development of autonomy and agency. There is an emphasis on varying degrees of interaction between participants at each of the five stages of the model, based on frameworks for enabling active and participative online learning *e-tivities*. The five stages are access and motivation, online socialisation, information exchange, knowledge construction, and development. Becoming accustomed to the online learning environment is the first stage. Once participants have completed the first stage, familiarising themselves with the technology and exploring their motivation for participating in online learning, the focus is explicitly on facilitating socialisation. The e-tivities in this stage are designed to facilitate connections and networks. Wright (2015) highlights the similarity between the socialisation stage of Salmon's model and the principles of joint enterprise, mutuality, and shared repertoire in Wenger's (1998) conceptualisation of communities of practice. It should be noted that the emphasis on socialisation is not limited specifically to the second stage of Salmon's model. Socialisation is further evolved in stage three, where participants engage in in-depth cognitive processes and exchange information to achieve co-operative tasks (Wright, 2015). The penultimate stage enables learners to construct knowledge in their online community and the final stage sees the learners build on the ideas acquired through the online tasks and undertaking reflection and meta-cognition. Interestingly, although Salmon's model is now primarily perceived in the context of student learning, it was initially conceived as a framework for the professional development of educators.

Pre-sessional EAP programmes

Pre-sessional programmes for international students are a feature of most UK universities. The courses vary in length from two weeks to one year and the majority are held in the summer months preceding the start of term. In addition to improving academic English across the four language skills, these courses aim to facilitate students' acculturation into their new academic environment and development of strategies to adapt to the UK higher education system (Pearson, 2020). Pre-sessional courses may be perceived as a subset of EAP programmes; however, they have specific logistics and staffing characteristics. The majority of UK universities employ pre-sessional EAP academic staff on a temporary or sessional basis. There is evidence which indicates that sessional staff in higher educational institutions tend to have limited access to professional development opportunities (Ní Shé et al., 2019). Dhillon and Murray (2021) argue that the short duration and limited scope of induction or professional development courses for EAP teachers are insufficient for teachers to meaningfully integrate technology into their pedagogical practice.

Overview of the University of Westminster's EAP teachers' induction programme

The pre-sessional EAP teachers' induction course was of four weeks' duration, comprising ten hours of professional development activities (eight hours online plus two hours home study task) each week. The majority of sessions were delivered synchronously with some optional asynchronous sessions. The course was held immediately prior to the commencement of the summer pre-sessional EAP course. There were 16 participants, all of whom were experienced EAP teachers. Only two of the teachers had previously participated in formal professional development courses at the University of Westminster. The course was developed and coordinated by the Westminster Centre for Education and Teaching Innovation (CETI) and was structured on the basis of a series of workshops facilitated by eight full-time CETI staff members. Two digital learning specialists also delivered training sessions and provided additional online support. Course participants received a certificate of professional development. On a practical level, a limited budget was set aside for teachers to purchase or upgrade technological hardware with the additional option of borrowing university laptops in order to access the induction programme and deliver the pre-sessional course.

The objectives of the programme were to enhance pre-sessional teachers' confidence and skills in pedagogies and technologies in order to transition to online EAP course delivery due to the Covid-19 pandemic. The course included practical sessions on using Blackboard (Virtual Learning Environment) and Microsoft Teams to deliver lectures and seminars and conduct assessments, including guidance on screen sharing, sharing files, and managing breakout rooms. A workshop was also devoted to a study of Salmon's model for online learning with emphasis placed on the stage relating to the concept of socialisation. However, the course diverged from the ERTE model in that the majority of workshops in the first three weeks were not exclusively devoted to utilising technology. Instead, the syllabus provided opportunities for participants to discuss a range of pedagogical-related topics including:

- transition from ELT to EAP
- discipline specific Academic English & Academic Literacies
- engaging students with their disciplinary communities
- Vygotsky's theory of socialisation and the role of social interaction in online learning.

The programme also included an overview of the university's structure and ethos and the role of CETI. Content knowledge was incorporated in the course syllabus with sessions on course materials, assessments, and grading criteria. The final week of the course was primarily given over to online teaching practice with groups of teachers taking part in peer observation and peer mentoring activities. Throughout the course, emphasis was placed on critical reflection relating to changing roles and competencies required for the migration of the pre-sessional EAP programme to the digital sphere.

Analysis of comments on the course's online forum indicates that at the outset most participants placed priority on enhancement of their technology skills. A minority of comments initially expressed scepticism about the benefit of sessions relating to theories underpinning EAP. However, later comments suggest that the integration of theoretical content generated debate and inspired the participants to reflect on their pedagogical practice. A theme running throughout the comments relates to the value of developing technological skills in a context which was specific to EAP as opposed to a generic approach. The teachers were situated in the role of students in an unfamiliar digital learning environment and a number of participants' comments indicate that this provided a deeper understanding and empathy with the experience of international students on the pre-sessional EAP programme. There was also explicit reference to the importance of the concept of socialisation in the context of Salmon's model as it applied to participants' roles both as learners on this course and as online teachers. Using the lens of Salmon's Five Stage Model, the analysis demonstrated that the teachers moved rapidly into the socialisation stage, with participants citing isolation as one of the main challenges of teaching online while social distancing.

The availability of asynchronous sessions was perceived favourably by participants due to the flexibility of access and opportunities for independent learning. On EAP programmes there is emphasis on supporting students to become autonomous learners (Breen, 2015). Teachers had the opportunity to develop their own autonomous learning skills with most participants reporting that they spent time experimenting independently with educational software. The outcome of this independent learning was frequently shared with colleagues in the online chat room in terms of recommendations about online tools such as Padlet or Google surveys. Participants also posted links to YouTube and TED Talks and guides to using relevant educational technology. The majority of participants made independent arrangements to practise using the online learning platforms with their peers. Feedback indicates that these sessions were beneficial in providing a safe environment to learn from errors and to develop coping mechanisms for technological failures. Overall, analysis of the online forum comments indicates that participants' experiences on this course reflect research (Dhillon & Murray, 2021) in which EAP teachers create a community of practice to share learning and tips for surviving and thriving in an online learning environment.

Lessons on building resilience for pre-sessional programmes

Pre-sessional EAP programmes are vulnerable to disruptive events, and higher education institutions across the globe are increasingly aware of the need to develop resilience to face unforeseen crises (Dohaney et al., 2020). The acronym VUCA (volatile, uncertain. complex, ambiguous), previously used in military and business contexts, increasingly applies to strategic planning and risk management in higher education in the post-pandemic era. During the Covid-19 crisis, EAP faculties demonstrated adaptability and resilience. In universities in many countries, a digital transformation which could otherwise have taken years to develop was enacted in a relatively short period of time. Consequently, it can be argued that in times of turbulence and disruption, the migration of pre-sessional EAP courses to the digital sphere on the basis of an ERTE model potentially provides a viable alternative to face-to-face learning. There is a need for longitudinal research, which will emerge in due course, as the emphasis shifts in universities from an emergency rapid response approach to longer term strategic planning. However, case studies such as the analysis of the University of Westminster induction course may provide learning points which can contribute to understanding of the role of professional development of pre-sessional EAP teachers in enhancing resilience and minimising disruption in uncertain times.

There are many examples across the globe of good practice in technology-assisted professional development for educators. It should be noted that the University of Westminster induction training course took place in an environment with reliable and affordable Internet access, which may not always be available. The development of infrastructure and affordable connectivity needs to be a global priority in order to facilitate inclusion and equitable access in a professional development context. Availability of good-quality hardware and access to IT support are also prerequisites for effective participation in professional development. This clearly requires investment and planning. However, this case study supports the assertion that although technology is the medium for online teaching and professional development, it is not the sole solution. The focus needs to be on the human dimension. In many cases, the emphasis is placed on optimising technology platforms; however, a high level of teacher engagement is a prerequisite for effective professional development.

A further key learning point relates to the need to establish institutional structures and strategies to provide appropriate professional development opportunities for pre-sessional EAP teachers. The literature (Ní Shé et al., 2019; Rogers, 2000) indicates that part-time or temporary teachers may not be fully integrated into the EAP faculty and consequently lack access to ongoing professional development on effective pedagogical methods and theories relating to online teaching. Online professional development has the potential to enhance teachers' knowledge and skills through the provision of synchronous and asynchronous learning events. For many pre-sessional EAP teachers, it presents opportunities for more inclusive access to professional development training, previously available only to full-time faculty. Given the important role of pre-sessional courses, it is essential that EAP teachers are provided with guidance and the time and space to enhance competence in using appropriate digital platforms for online learning during times of crisis. However, it is equally important that EAP teacher induction courses are not solely predicated on a tools-based approach, focused on using a specific learning platform. To optimise teachers' resilience and adaptability, the design of induction programmes should aim to incorporate an integrative relationship between technological, content, and pedagogical knowledge (Falloon, 2020; Mishra & Koehler, 2006; Rapanta et al., 2020).

Conclusion

In most higher education programmes, the concepts of academic resilience, independent learning, and digital literacy are emphasised for students and integrated into course delivery. However, the mandated shift in professional practice during the Covid-19 crisis highlights that these concepts apply to teachers as well as students. This case study emphasises the importance of integrating theoretical underpinning in the design and content of pre-sessional teacher induction courses. Analysis of participants' feedback reflects the literature (Baran et al., 2011; Meyer, 2013) highlighting the role of theoretical discussion in facilitating teachers' critical reflection on their changing roles and competencies required for teaching EAP online. The case study also demonstrates that theoretical concepts related to learning such as socialisation, TPACK, Salmon's Five Stage Model, and communities of practice apply as much to professional development of EAP teachers as to pre-sessional students. Contextualisation of theoretical components is important with teachers reporting higher levels of engagement in professional development, which is specifically situated within the pre-sessional EAP discipline-specific context, rather than generic pedagogic theories and strategies.

Finally, one of the greatest challenges faced by EAP teachers during disruptive events is a sense of isolation (Moorhouse & Kohnke, 2021). A key finding from this case study is the importance of facilitating a community of practice among pre-sessional EAP teachers. The concept of socialisation is key to the effective design of pre-sessional teacher induction courses to facilitate meaningful mutual engagement, joint enterprise, and a shared repertoire (Wenger, 1998) and foster innovation and resilience. Although these recommendations emanate from the experience of one professional development course in the United Kingdom, it is worth reminding ourselves of Breen's (2015, p. 16) assertion that as EAP teachers, we are part of a global community of practice:

> We are artisans in a particular field, and are not only part of a teaching community within our own workplace but part of . . . a "broader TESOL

community", indeed a "global community" . . . in both geographic and cultural terms. This is a community of shared discourse and practices, shared histories, and sets of experiences particular to the profession.

In the context of internationalisation, the provision of online professional development training opens up the potential of creating communities of practice beyond a single institution, nation, or region. Whatever disruptive events may occur in the future, the shift to online learning supported by effective professional development can play a role in facilitating resilience in pre-sessional EAP teachers. Whilst there are many challenges, this transition offers opportunities for enhanced collaborative learning and discussion among peers relating to effective EAP pedagogy.

Reference list

Baran, E., Correia, A., & Thompson, A. (2011). Transforming online teaching practice: Critical analysis of the literature on the roles and competencies of online teachers. *Distance Education*, *32*(3), 421–439. https://doi.org/10.1080/01587919.2011.610293

Belt, E., & Lowenthal, P. (2019). Developing faculty to teach with technology: Themes from the literature. *TechTrends*, *64*(2), 248–259. https://doi.org/10.1007/s11528-019-00447-6

Bezuidenhout, A. (2018). Analysing the importance-competence gap of distance educators with the increased utilisation of online learning strategies in a developing world context. *The International Review of Research in Open and Distributed Learning*, *19*(3), 263–280. https://doi.org/10.19173/irrodl.v19i3.3585

Brammer, M. (2020). Faculty resilience in higher education: A review of the literature. *Online Journal of Complementary and Alternative Medicine*, *5*(2), 1–6. https://doi.org/10.33552/ojcam.2020.05.000609

Breen, P. (2015). Letting go and letting the angels grow. *International Journal of Web-Based Learning and Teaching Technologies*, *10*(1). 14–26. https://doi.org/10.4018/ijwltt.2015010102

Breen, P. (2018). *Developing educators for the digital age: A framework for capturing knowledge in action*. University of Westminster Press. https://doi.org/10.16997/book13

Bruce, E., & Stakounis, H. (2021). *The impact of Covid-19 on the UK EAP sector during the initial six months of the pandemic*. BALEAP-funded Report.

Brunetti, G. (2006). Resilience under fire: Perspectives on the work of experienced, inner city high school teachers in the United States. *Teaching and Teacher Education*, *22*(7), 812–825. https://doi.org/10.1016/j.tate.2006.04.027

Dhillon, S., & Murray, N. (2021). An investigation of EAP teachers' views and experiences of e-learning technology. *Education Sciences*, *11*(2), 54. https://doi.org/10.3390/educsci11020054

Dohaney, J., de Róiste, M., Salmon, R., & Sutherland, K. (2020). Benefits, barriers, and incentives for improved resilience to disruption in university teaching. *International Journal of Disaster Risk Reduction*, *50*, 1–9. https://doi.org/10.1016/j.ijdrr.2020.101691

Falloon, G. (2020). From digital literacy to digital competence: The teacher digital competency (TDC) framework. *Educational Technology Research and Development*, *68*(5), 2449–2472. https://doi.org/10.1007/s11423-020-09767-4

Herring, M. C., Meacham, S., & Mourlam, D. (2016). TPACK development in higher education. In M. C. Herring, M. J. Koehler, & P. Mishra (Eds.), *Handbook of technological pedagogical content knowledge (TPACK) for educators* (pp. 207–223). Routledge. https://doi.org/10.4324/9781315771328

Hodges, C., Moore, S., Lockee, B., & Bond, A. (2020). The difference between emergency remote teaching and online learning. *Educause Review, 27*, 1–12.

Kimble, C., Hildreth, P., & Bourdon, I. (2008). *Communities of practice. Creating learning environments for educators* (Vols. 1–2). Information Age Publishing.

Koehler, A. A., & Kim, M. C. (2012). Improving beginning teacher induction programs through distance education. *Contemporary Educational Technology, 3*(3), 212–233. https://doi.org/10.30935/cedtech/6079

Koh, J. (2020). Three approaches for supporting faculty technological pedagogical content knowledge (TPACK) creation through instructional consultation. *British Journal of Educational Technology, 51*(6), 2529–2543. https://doi.org/10.1111/bjet.12930

Lave, J., & Wenger, E. (1991). *Situated learning: Legitimate peripheral participation in communities of practice.* Cambridge University Press. https://doi.org/10.1017/CBO9780511815355

Lowenthal, P. R., Gooding, M., Shreaves, D., & Kepka, J. (2019). Learning to teach online: An exploration of how universities with large online programs train and develop faculty to teach online. *Quarterly Review of Distance Education, 20*(3), 1–9.

Magda, A. J. (2019). *Online learning at public universities: Recruiting, orienting, and supporting online faculty.* The Learning House Inc.

Meyer, K. A. (2013). An analysis of the research on faculty development for online teaching and identification of new directions. *Online Learning, 17*(4), 1–20. https://doi.org/10.24059/olj.v17i4.320

Mishra, P., & Koehler, M. J. (2006). Technological pedagogical content knowledge: A framework for teacher knowledge. *Teachers College Record, 108*(6), 1017–1054. https://doi.org/10.1111/j.1467-9620.2006.00684.x

Moorhouse, B., & Kohnke, L. (2021). Thriving or surviving emergency remote teaching necessitated by Covid-19: University teachers' perspectives. *The Asia-Pacific Education Researcher, 30*(3), 279–287. https://doi.org/10.1007/s40299-021-00567-9

Nandy, M., Lodh, S., & Tang, A. (2020). Lessons from Covid-19 and a resilience model for higher education. *Industry and Higher Education, 35*(1), 3–9. https://doi.org/10.1177/0950422220962696

Ní Shé, C., Farrell, O., Brunton, J., Costello, E., Donlon, E., Trevaskis, S., & Eccles, S. (2019). *Teaching online is different: Critical perspectives from the literature.* Dublin City University. https://doras.dcu.ie/23890/

Pearson, W. (2020). The effectiveness of pre-sessional EAP programmes in UK higher education: A review of the evidence. *Review of Education, 8*(2), 420–447. https://doi.org/10.1002/rev3.3191

Rapanta, C., Botturi, L., Goodyear, P., Guàrdia, L., & Koole, M. (2020). Online university teaching during and after the Covid-19 crisis: Refocusing teacher presence and learning activity. *Postdigital Science and Education, 2*(3), 923–945. https://doi.org/10.1007/s42438-020-00155-y

Remmik, M., & Karm, M. (2009). Impact of training on the teaching skills of university lecturers: Challenges and opportunities. *Haridus, 11*(12), 20–26.

Rogers, J. (2000). Communities of practice: A framework for fostering coherence in virtual learning communities. *Educational Technology & Society, 3*(3), 384–392. www.jstor.org/stable/jeductechsoci.3.3.384/

Salmon, G. (2002). *E-tivities: A key to active online learning.* Routledge.

Salmon, G. (2011). *E-moderating: The key to teaching and learning online* (3rd ed.). Routledge.

Shattuck, J., & Anderson, T. (2013). Using a design-based research study to identify princi-ples for training instructors to teach online. *The International Review of Research in Open and Distributed Learning, 14*(5), 186–210. https://doi.org/10.19173/irrodl.v14i5.1626

Shulman, L. S. (1986). Those who understand: Knowledge growth in teaching. *Educa-tional Researcher, 15*(2), 4–14. https://doi.org/10.2307/1175860

Vilppu, H., Södervik, I., Postareff, L., & Murtonen, M. (2019). The effect of short online pedagogical training on university teachers' interpretations of teaching – learning situa-tions. *Instructional Science, 47*(6), 679–709. https://doi.org/10.1007/s11251-019-09496-z

Vygotsky, L. S. (1978). *Mind in society: The development of higher psychological processes.* Harvard University Press.

Wenger, E. (1998). *Communities of practice: Learning, meaning and identity.* Cambridge Uni-versity Press.

Wenger, E., McDermott, R., & Snyder, W. (2002). *Cultivating communities of practice: A guide to managing knowledge.* Harvard Business School Press. https://doi.org/10.5465/amle.2009.41788855

Wilcox, K., & Lawson, H. (2017). Teachers' agency, efficacy, engagement, and emotional resilience during policy innovation implementation. *Journal of Educational Change, 19*(2), 181–204. https://doi.org/10.1007/s10833-017-9313-0

Wright, P. (2015). Comparing e-tivities, e-moderation and the five stage model to the community of inquiry model for online learning design. *The Online Journal of Distance Education and E-Learning, 3*(2), 17–30. https://doi.org/10.3390/educsci4020172

3

ACADEMIC ENGLISH IN HIGHER EDUCATION IN MONTENEGRO DURING THE COVID-19 PANDEMIC

Institutional impact and lessons to be learned for the future

Žana Knežević

Introduction

The start of the 21st century saw higher education institutions in Montenegro increasingly adapting their curricula to the needs of the labour market. A key competency that the market requires is knowledge of English, particularly English for Specific Purposes (ESP) that meets the particular needs of the discipline or workplace setting. For this reason, all four Montenegrin universities (one state and three private) offer General English and/or ESP courses at different levels. ESP is studied between two and six semesters, and the number of ESP classes varies from two to four per week, depending on the accreditation of the faculty. Teaching takes place mainly in the classroom, although some faculties provide the Moodle platform through which teachers can share teaching materials and communicate with their students. This method is usually optional and mainly depends on the willingness of the teacher to use it. According to Knežević's (2017) research, foreign language teachers in Montenegrin higher education institutions were unaware of the potential and uses of different technologies in teaching, which led to their unpreparedness for the transition to online teaching during the Covid-19 pandemic.

Montenegro is a small country in south-east Europe with just over 620,000 inhabitants and was the last country in Europe to record a Covid-19 case (March 17, 2020). The Government of Montenegro ordered a two-week lockdown on March 13, 2020, and all educational institutions were closed (Vlada Crne Gore, 2020), with none of the four Montenegrin universities having a strategy or contingency plan in place. However, teachers from the state university had an advantage over their colleagues from private universities because the Ministry of Education reacted quickly and provided them with the Learning Management

DOI: 10.4324/9781003283409-5

System Moodle and Zoom (a video conferencing system). In contrast, teachers at private universities were initially largely left on their own to navigate through their digital skills and competencies. ESP teachers working at technology-oriented faculties had a slight advantage because their colleagues were able to offer them professional assistance, which was not always the case with the faculties in the field of humanities.

This chapter describes how ESP teachers in two Montenegrin universities (the University of Montenegro and the University "Mediterranean") initially responded to Covid-19 confinement, the challenges both teachers and students faced along the way, the extent to which the universities supported their teaching staff and students, and the adaptations necessitated by the situation.

Literature review

Technology has been incorporated in language teaching and learning for more than 60 years, with an early well-known example being the PLATO tutorial system introduced in 1960 (Warschauer & Healey, 1998). Technologies have now become an indispensable part of learning General English and ESP. Which technological applications are used are likely to be determined by their specific purposes and the needs of the students. Bonk (2009) claims that modern technologies can meet almost all traditional academic student needs. Also, Kern (2013) indicates the benefits of using technologies in ESP, such as enabling interaction and communicative activities that are representative of professional and academic environments; using task-based strategies and issues that are reflected through tasks in environments and situations related to their discipline; and using authentic materials from specific disciplines. Analysing online learning during the Covid-19 pandemic and other natural disasters, Dhawan (2020) presents its strengths and weaknesses. Some strengths he lists are time and location flexibility, wide availability of courses and content, and immediate feedback; weaknesses are technical difficulties, distractions, frustration, anxiety, and lack of personal attention (Dhawan, 2020, p. 14).

The potential of computers and the Internet is not always adequately exploited in education, as participants often lack the required digital competence. Winston (in Johnson et al., 2014) saw educating teaching staff in the use of new classroom online platforms as the most important future IT mission. Knežević in her research on the situation in Montenegro in 2017 found that 40% of teachers and 9% of students in Montenegrin universities did not feel confident using computers and associated technologies. Presenting a similar situation in Serbia, Šćepanović et al. (2021, p. 4) concluded that "this practice is perceived as a barrier to conducting an effective instructional process".

Although higher education institutions in Montenegro are autonomous and independently organize their own curricula, there are certain national strategies that universities need to implement. However, these strategies are not always feasible. For example, according to the Strategy for the Development of the Information Society 2012–2016 of the Ministry of Information Society and Telecommunications of Montenegro, 100% of teachers in primary and secondary schools and universities should be competent in ICT by 2014 (Ministarstvo za informaciono društvo i telekomunikacije, 2011). However, it was later shown that only 20% of teachers in Montenegro had received computer training (Ministarstvo za informaciono društvo i telekomunikacije, 2016). The new situation arising from the Covid-19 pandemic revealed that the higher education institutions in Montenegro were unprepared, and the responsibility for adequately responding was largely passed on to the teachers. The universities did not have strategies for the implementation of teaching technologies in general, not just for foreign languages or ESP, beyond what might have been gained from the use of Moodle since its introduction in 2009.

Response to Covid-19 at Montenegrin Universities

In contrast to primary and secondary schools, which had classes that were recorded and broadcast through two television channels and the specially developed portal (www.ucidoma.me), the autonomous universities in Montenegro were left to their own devices and largely reacted according to their capabilities. The University "Mediterranean" and the University of Montenegro first released the most relevant information about the organization of lectures on their official websites, but then each faculty conducted communication with their students in different ways, for example, via e-mail or VoIP applications. Switching to the online mode was not welcomed by all teachers (and students) for various reasons: many of them were not digitally savvy enough, they lacked adequate devices and/or internet access, and there were difficulties in implementing some content in an online environment, as was the case with the faculties of arts. The students of arts had been used to practical individual work or work in small groups, alongside in-person meetings with their teachers, so any form of online or blended learning was completely unfamiliar to both teachers and students.

University "Mediterranean"

The University "Mediterranean" first introduced Moodle to support traditional learning at the Faculty of Information Technology (FIT) in 2009. All teachers were initially trained to use it, and since then it has been widely used by both teachers and students. Materials used in the classes are added in the form of a document (Word, PDF, or PowerPoint), alongside additional materials such as video, audio, and internet links. Subject-related information, e.g., homework, tests, and exam preparation are located on the course page. The courses of English for Information Technology include all these types of materials but other faculties do not use this platform to the same extent for different reasons. It usually depends on the readiness and will of the teachers and also on the internal organization of the faculty. For example, at the Faculty of Visual Arts (FVA) which includes English for Visual Arts, teachers believe that Moodle (or any learning platform) is not relevant for the art subjects such as drawing and painting that include traditional techniques and practical individual or small group work to be monitored in a studio, and Moodle therefore remains unused.

During Covid-19 confinement, classes and communication with students from the English for Information Technology course were held synchronously, via Zoom, and asynchronously, via the Moodle forum and email. Since the University "Mediterranean" uses an older version of Moodle which does not incorporate a video conferencing system, the university management decided to use the free Zoom application. Although FIT students are well acquainted with the application of technology in education and regularly use Moodle, the transition to online teaching was not easy. The online environment created a space that differed significantly from the one in which English for Information Technology classes were held. Firstly, the classes were shortened from 45 to 30 minutes which affected the amount of material that could be covered. This shortening also reduced the interaction between teachers and students, as well as between students. The video cameras of many students were constantly turned off, mostly justified by poor internet connectivity which also contributed to reduced interaction. All this affected the quality of work, so the teacher, in agreement with the students, held full classes for 45 minutes (two hours twice a week, with a break of ten minutes between classes). Also, the free version of Zoom frustratingly interrupts the session after 40 minutes, so the teacher invested in the pro version from her own funds. In addition to uninterrupted classes, the option of Breakout Rooms in Zoom was obtained, in which students could work in groups. Students were encouraged to communicate via Chat to maintain interaction. All classes were recorded, with the consent of the students, and the recordings were posted on the Moodle platform. In this way, students could review the recordings to check if something was unclear or catch up if they were absent. However, this also had a somewhat negative impact on class attendance.

Regardless of the new environment, the curriculum and teaching methods did not change. Students did group assignments via the Moodle platform (making videos, writing wikis, and blogs, creating a website) in the same way as before the pandemic. Although the university administration had decided that teachers could replace the mid-term exam with some other form of assignment (seminar paper, project, or similar), the English for Information Technology exam was online via the Moodle quiz in real-time. Students were able to take the test at a precisely defined time and had a specified length of time to complete. They were required to turn on the cameras in Zoom and share their screen. In this way, the teacher could monitor the work of students on two screens, using the Extend screen option, and ensure students were not cheating. Article 85 of the Law on Higher Education (2017) stipulates:

> Teaching may also be organized remotely (distance learning), whereas exams shall be held at premises of an institution.
>
> Conditions and manner of teaching organization and exam taking, referred to in paragraph 1 of this Article shall be prescribed by the Ministry, following the prior opinion of the Council.

As a result, the final exam was held at the end of the semester at the faculty, in adherence to prescribed measures – in small groups, keeping recommended distance and wearing medical face masks. The overall results achieved by the students in the exams corresponded to pre-pandemic attainment (Knežević & Tripković-Samardžić, 2020). Subsequent interviews with students showed that their knowledge of the use of technology in teaching, as well as earlier assignments in English for Information Technology that involved the application of technology, was helpful for navigating the new situation, but this was not an advantage shared by Visual Arts students.

As mentioned, due to the nature of the discipline, teaching at the Faculty of Visual Arts usually takes place in studios, and online teaching is less suitable for the practical nature of the classes. This also applied to the English for Visual Arts courses, which is why the transition to online teaching presented a greater challenge for both the teacher and the students. After the university decided to use Zoom and/or Moodle at all faculties, English for Visual Arts classes were held regularly according to the earlier set timetable, that is two 30-minute classes twice a week. Zoom was used for synchronous teaching, which the teacher and students adapted to easily, although interrupting a session after 40 minutes sometimes meant disrupting a video or group work. Asynchronous communication was maintained via e-mails. The emerging teaching environment imposed a change in the curriculum and the implementation of some new activities, such as additional audio and video materials, essay writing, discussion, and peer-reviewing student presentations (Knežević & Tripković-Samardžić, 2020). This kind of work kept the students' attention and they were more involved in group discussions, which contributed to critical thinking which is one of the main skills needed by artists. Due to the formative assessment, students were motivated to attend classes regularly by increasing the points assigned for attendance. The mid-term exam was done in a defined term via the Google Classroom platform with student tracking via Zoom. The final exam was held on faculty premises when circumstances allowed. The overall exam results were better than before the lockdown. This can be explained in two ways: either the new methods and strategies applied in the online classroom improved student motivation or students cheated on the exam, despite the monitoring measures (Knežević & Tripković-Samardžić, 2020).

University of Montenegro

Before the Covid-19 pandemic, the Moodle platform was used at five faculties of the University of Montenegro, but only by teachers who requested it (Zarubica et al., 2021). There were no ESP teachers among them. Teachers of English for Art and English for Mathematics and Computer Science explained that the transition to an online model was stressful since they had never used Zoom or Moodle before. One week after the government's decision to close educational institutions, the University of Montenegro started assigning Moodle accounts to all its teachers and students. Also, the use of the Zoom pro version was enabled because the Moodle they used at the time did not have the BigBlueButton system used for video conferencing. However, teachers and students had to study how to use these platforms by themselves, relying on the manual provided by the IT administrators.

English for Mathematics and Computer Science classes were held once a week and lasted 90 minutes. Due to the problems with devices and internet connections that students reported, students' presentations were cancelled, and class attendance was not graded. The online environment enabled greater use of video material, which was not possible in a traditional classroom because some rooms lacked the necessary equipment. The advantage of online teaching was also shown through reduced costs for the teaching staff – it was not necessary to print the handouts usually used in all ESP classes, and there were savings in travel costs and time. Some shortcomings indicated by the teachers included less willingness of students to participate in discussions, probably for fear that classes would be recorded and that they might be embarrassed if they made a mistake. Also, the majority of students had their cameras and microphones turned off, further supporting the impression that the students were sometimes unwilling to interact. Finally, there were often e-mails from students indicating that they could not cope with the Moodle platform. Mid-term and final exams were held in small groups in the classroom with strict adherence to the protocols. The results achieved by the students differed little from the previous semester, despite lower student activity in class.

The experience of an English for Arts teacher was similar despite differences between English for Arts and other ESP courses. Firstly, art subjects imply individual or small group work and, as stated before, rely on face-to-face teacher-student interaction. Secondly, English for Arts at a state university is taught as a common subject for numerous departments (the Faculty of Drama, the Faculty of Fine Arts, and the Music Academy) which do not necessarily have much in common. The diversity and specificity of each department make the English for Arts course complex and demanding, especially for the teacher, because the classes need to adapt to all students and their needs. Thirdly, a further problem for both the teacher and the students of art is mixed-level classes – not only do the students come from different departments, but they also have different knowledges of English.

Despite these difficulties, the teacher tried to take advantage of the situation and use technology to aid the students by providing easy access to authentic video and audio recordings, class discussions, and individual and group presentations that made it possible so all students could follow the lessons. Although students' involvement was much lower, the teacher reported a better ability to adapt to students' needs, as the technologies allowed easy and fast sharing of different materials on the Moodle platform.

The examples given earlier from the Montenegrin universities show the same view towards online learning. As reported by both the teachers and the students, the advantages of online learning are largely the same: the adaptability to the needs of a wide audience, student-centeredness, a collaborative learning environment, and a variety of content aimed at lending a human touch to the lectures and providing immediate feedback, which coincides with Dhawan's (2020) conclusions. The students and teachers were unanimous about the disadvantages: poor adaptability to the usage of Learning Management Systems, the lack of practice and effective learning, technical problems, differences in students' performances, inefficient time management, and low willingness to adapt to online teaching.

REFLAME project

The initial experience of online learning in higher education institutions in Montenegro demonstrated that both the teachers and students required training in this area. Such an attempt was made with the training on blended learning, organized within the Erasmus+ project ReFLAME (Reforming Foreign Languages in Academia in Montenegro) in June 2021 (www.reflame.ucg. ac.me/blended_teaching.html), where the teachers improved, consolidated, and exchanged their knowledge and experiences on a number of topics. The participants learned how to adapt face-to-face courses into online teaching and learning, apply a blended learning approach to ESP courses, utilize technology in LSP classes, assess students' achievements in the blended course, develop interactive/collaborative activities online, and motivate students in blended classrooms. They also shared their own experiences and helped each other solve problems they encountered during online classes. It is expected that blended or fully online learning will become increasingly popular, and the knowledge and skills acquired in training will serve to improve the ESP teaching and learning in Montenegrin universities.

Global trends

Shortly after Covid-19 emerged, the first papers appeared on its impact at all levels of education, with universities mostly opting for online teaching or blended teaching and learning. Luporini (2020) claims that online learning has three positive aspects: attendance, the number of students attending classes did not decrease during online classes, as opposed to face-to-face classes when attendance typically decreased; interactivity, as "more students interacted more frequently" (Luporini, 2020, p. 7); and informality, for example using emoticons to react to comments.

The latest research by Duraku and Hoxha (2020) and Luporini (2020) pays special attention to the mental health of students because, in some cases, isolation led to a loss of motivation to learn and even depression. Purwanto and Nurhamidah (2021) suggest that motivation in ESP online teaching could be improved by adapting the curriculum and teaching methods to the virtual environment. In addition to the previously mentioned strengths and weaknesses of online learning during the Covid-19 pandemic, Dhawan (2020) highlighted some opportunities that arose including the scope for innovation and digital development, designing flexible programmes, encouraging problem-solving, critical thinking, and adaptability. Some challenges included unequal distribution of ICT infrastructure, digital illiteracy, technology costs, and obsolescence.

In line with the latest research results and their own experience, ESP teachers at the University "Mediterranean" and the University of Montenegro have learned certain lessons. First, they have realized that online teaching and learning is applicable at all faculties no matter what the field of study is. ESP teachers must also be ready to apply new technologies to future extraordinary situations. In support of this is the fact that digitally savvy ESP teachers more easily switched to a new teaching model. Teachers have also learnt that they can apply the digital skills acquired during the pandemic in regular classes so that they can practice blended learning in future. ESP teachers found that advanced Moodle and Zoom options could be further explored for the benefit of collaborative and student-centred learning. Finally, online teaching has shown that teachers must monitor the behaviour of their students and continuously motivate them.

Conclusion

ESP teachers at Montenegrin universities were generally not sufficiently familiar with learning and communication platforms, such as Moodle and Zoom, and were forced to explore the potential of technologies for ESP teaching on their own. Without institutional support in providing quality devices and internet connections, teachers changed curricula, teaching methods, strategies, and activities, all in order to meet learner needs and encourage their autonomy. A special challenge for teachers was to encourage student motivation and assess knowledge. Evidence of the successful implementation of ESP courses in the new situation was the achievements of students, which generally did not differ from levels achieved before the pandemic.

As new strains of coronavirus emerge and there is a threat of re-closure of educational institutions, the universities in Montenegro should adopt positive practices and jointly, with the support of the line ministry, prepare a permanent strategy on online teaching to maintain quality at the level of in-person teaching. Therefore, institutional support (training for both the teachers and the students, quality devices, reliable internet infrastructure), reorganization of curricula, and creating a national strategy for blended and online learning can lead to improved ESP teaching.

Reference list

Bonk, C. J. (2009). *The world is open: How new technology is revolutionizing education.* Jossey-Bass.

Dhawan, S. (2020). Online learning: A panacea in the time of COVID-19 crisis. *Journal of Educational Technology Systems, 49*(1), 5–22. https://doi.org/10.1177%2F0047239520934018

Duraku, Z. H., & Hoxha, L. (2020, May). *The impact of COVID-19 on higher education: A study of interaction among students' mental health, attitudes toward online learning, study skills, and changes in students' life.* ResearchGate. www.researchgate.net/publication/341599684_The_impact_of_COVID-19_on_higher_education

Johnson, L., Adams Becker, S., Estrada, V., & Freeman, A. (2014). *NMC horizon report: 2014 higher education edition.* www.learntechlib.org/p/130341/

Kern, N. (2013). Technology-integrated English for Specific Purposes lessons: Real-life language, tasks and tools for professionals. In G. Motteram (Ed.), *Innovations in learning technologies for English language learning* (pp. 89–115). British Council.

Knežević, Ž. (2017). *Savremeni trendovi u nastavi engleskog kao jezika struke u oblasti IT* [Doctoral thesis, University of Belgrade].

Knežević, Ž., & Tripković-Samardžić, V. (2020). Modalities of learning assessment in the context of COVID-19 (a case study). In S. Gupta (Ed.), *Online education challenges and opportunities* (pp. 14–20). Excellent Publishing House.

Luporini, A. (2020). Implementing an online English linguistics course during the Covid-19 emergency in Italy: Teacher's and students' perspectives. *ASp. la revue du GERAS,* (78), 75–88. https://doi.org/10.4000/asp.6682

Ministarstvo za informaciono društvo i telekomunikacije. (2011, December). *Strategija razvoja informacionog društva 2012–2016: Crna Gora – digitalno društvo.* Ministarstvo za informaciono društvo i telekomunikacije. www.gov.me/dokumenta/5f51bacf-25f6-46c5-91a3-d8c71ac442cf

Ministarstvo za informaciono društvo i telekomunikacije. (2016). *Strategija razvoja informacionog društva Crne Gore do 2020- godine.* Ministarstvo za infomaciono društvo i telekomunikacije. www.gov.me/dokumenta/cc172acc-d7a7-4cf0-ba12-e3023ce721b2

Ministry of Education, Science, Culture and Sports. (2017, September 22). *Law on higher education.* Retrieved from Government of Montenegro: www.gov.me/en/documents/45683d7c-1b7b-4747-bbba-4dd0439d2ef6

Purwanto, S., & Nurhamidah, I. (2021). Digitizing English for specific purposes in the era of COVID-19 pandemic. *Parole: Journal of Linguistics and Education, 11*(1), 57–72. https://ejournal.undip.ac.id/index.php/parole/article/view/31303/19262

Šćepanović, D., Korać, I., & Lazarević, B. (2021). The readiness of teachers for implementing information and communication technology in Serbian higher education institutions. *Teme, XLV*(1), 19–32. https://doi.org/10.22190/TEME200509002S

Vlada Crne Gore (Government of Montenegro). (2020, April 21). *www.gov.me/ dokumenta/20d6c0bf-fa1b-4233-84dd-05bb15f320ca.* Retrieved from the official website of the Government of Montenegro: www.gov.me

Warschauer, M., & Healey, D. (1998). Computers and language learning: An overview. *Language Teaching, 31*(2), 57–71. https://doi.org/10.1017/S0261444800012970

Zarubica, M., Filipović, L., Terzić, J., Milosavljević, L., & Gazivoda, V. (2021). Digitalizacija i unapređenje distance learning platforme na Univerzitetu Crne Gore tokom COVID19 pandemije. In B. Krstajić (Ed.), *INFORMACIONE TEHNOLOGIJE – sadašnjost i budućnost 2021* (pp. 10–13). IT društvo.

4

LANGUAGE EDUCATION DURING THE PANDEMIC

Qatar University foundation programme's responses for teaching in future difficult circumstances

Mohammad Manasreh, Kashif Raza, and Naima Sarfraz

Introduction

As the unpredictable recent Covid-19 pandemic has disrupted the world's normality and brought upheavals to educational systems around the world, some contexts were more affected than others due to their levels of preparedness, the availability of contingency plans, and the severity of the pandemic in the local setting.

Founded in 2004, the Foundation Programme Department of English at Qatar University (FPDE) is one of the largest TESOL institutions in the Arabian Gulf region with more than 130 full-time faculty members teaching 15,000 students annually. Through offering 16 different EAP undergraduate and foundation-level courses, the department facilitates students' enrollment onto their majors across the ten colleges of Qatar University (QU). The sudden transitioning to online teaching has posed challenges to the department's administration, faculty, and students. Examples of these challenges included the immediate need for technical training on learning portals like Microsoft Teams and Blackboard Collaborate Ultra, more preparation time for online lessons, and the unavoidable impact on mental health.

Although the aforementioned challenges may echo the experiences of other EAP practitioners around the world, the department's response was shaped by the societal and cultural norms of the local context. For instance, students, and particularly females, were not allowed to turn on their cameras. In addition, the high incidence of large household structures in the local society did not provide a quiet and conducive learning atmosphere for many students. Fortunately, connectivity and the availability of devices did not pose a major hurdle due to the reliable

DOI: 10.4324/9781003283409-6

infrastructure in the country and the commendable efforts by the university and the Ministry of Education to provide devices to those who could not afford them. Unlike many contexts, online fees were not a concern to students since education is free for Qatari nationals.

Similar to the efforts made by other higher education EAP institutions in Qatar, the department's response was centred on activating the available emergency plans and devising more for the areas that lacked these plans. For instance, we have always had a subscription to Blackboard Collaborate Ultra as part of our contingency plans for special needs students, but we had never used this with other students until we were forced to call off face-to-face teaching. Likewise, our Microsoft subscription included enough Teams licenses. Therefore, we were able to move to remote teaching within days; albeit, the transition was primarily technical in the early days and lacked a proper pedagogical grounding. Another key element of the department's response was the decision to hold more important course assessments, for example, midterms and finals, on-campus with the mandated social distancing measures and to increase their weighting to 70% to uphold the reliability of student grades. Despite these challenges, the department experienced a surge in student enrolments, which was attributed to the flexibility offered by the online mode of teaching and the university's decision to waive deferments and attendance requirements. An example of this surge was the increase in the number of summer groups by 65% between 2020 and 2021.

The pandemic was a lifelong learning opportunity for all stakeholders. Students complimented online teaching for its flexibility and described online lessons as dynamic, personalized, and accessible. Faculty also had their views of the advantages, in spite of the challenges. For example, teaching from home was often found to be more compatible with their domestic circumstances. Likewise, the emergency response in higher education dictated urgent technical and pedagogical training for faculty. While these programmes were demanding at the beginning, faculty were appreciative of the new skills they gained from these programmes and of the impact on their online classes. On-campus presence was mandatory only for the department head who had to provide support to confused students, faculty stranded outside the country, and others at home due to ill health or the lockdown. To mitigate the situation, the department decided to continue its regular academic support services online, which was helpful for both students and faculty. In addition, a team of volunteers was established to help colleagues who were in quarantine or needed mental health support, and regular updates were shared with faculty on academic and non-academic issues. Unfortunately, the pandemic did not provide sufficient time for preparation, reflection, and improvement. The FPDE experience is an example of an emergency response, with relevance to EAP teaching, that may provide guidance for better performance should we face a similar situation in the future.

Literature review

Language education and context

The two main processes that tend to dominate EAP are course planning (e.g., student learning outcomes, curriculum development, textbook selection, and assessments) and delivery (e.g., weekly plans, content delivery, test administration, student engagement, and office hours). Although these two processes may differ between courses (e.g., EAP or ESP; beginner or advanced level) or programmes, they are central to EAP practices globally. One factor that often influences these two processes is the educational context in which the English course is being developed and delivered (Raza, 2018; 2020). The context, which often defines what student learning outcomes (SLOs) will be included in the syllabus, depends upon the type of course, that is, EAP or ESP, and determines what resources will achieve these outcomes (Kramsch & Hua, 2016). EAP programme administrators often attempt to align the aims and objectives of their courses with the educational context in which their programme is located. This not only increases the effectiveness and relevance of the courses but also ensures programme success.

Researchers (e.g., Harper & Jong, 2004; Raza, 2018; 2020; Raza & Coombe, 2020) argue that the alignment of the English courses with the educational setting or context is crucial to their effectiveness. In times of premeditated and unforeseen changes in curricula, the context becomes even more visible because curricular reforms should align with the contextual requirement(s) to increase their effectiveness and feasibility. Challenges posed by the Covid-19 pandemic to EAP practitioners in the local Qatari context are a good example of how changes in instruction, content selection, delivery, and teacher-student engagement may affect teaching practices if the changes are not in line with the socio-cultural expectations and practices (Crabtree, 2010; Raza, 2018, 2020; Raza et al., 2020; Weinstein et al., 2004).

Language education in times of crisis

Research on education during times of crisis outlines strategies that leadership and educators can adopt to maintain quality learning and accessibility. These strategies outline how challenges created by a crisis should be identified, determined, and addressed, and which resources should be considered to accommodate student needs (Raza et al., 2020). For instance, the Covid-19 pandemic requires physical distancing and limits opportunities for face-to-face interaction. Although educational technologies that can provide alternatives to these limitations are available, a successful transition from a face-to-face classroom to a completely remote or blended mode would require changes in policies that address issues of financial support, teacher and student training for online learning, assessment modification, waivers of certain policies, transparency and quality check, and how faculty and students can keep abreast of the changes (Raza et al., 2020).

Although a considerable amount of work has been done on innovation and development in the field of EAP (e.g., see Carless, 2013; Tribble, 2012; Waters, 2009), one major limitation of this body of literature is *time* and *context*. In an urgent situation like the Covid-19 pandemic, where the situation may change rapidly and contingency plans may be required, (re)adjustments and/or policy changes to accommodate contextual requirements, the existing literature on innovation and development becomes somewhat irrelevant as there is insufficient time to ponder and devise strategies. Similarly, the proposals from the literature on language innovation and development do not always coincide with the local teaching and learning practices. For instance, during a webinar organized by Qatar University in July 2020 to discuss the challenges posed by the Covid-19 pandemic, Raza et al. (2020) discussed the limitations of existing resources for EAP and highlighted the need for continuous revisiting these materials to adjust to changing situations and students' needs. The speakers stressed that as universities are continuously switching between online, blended, and on-campus instruction, curriculum and assessment decisions have to be made carefully so quality and consistency are maintained and supported.

Challenges posed by the Covid-19 pandemic

The World Health Organization has urged people to keep a 1.5-metre distance so that Covid-19 transmission can be decreased. This has affected face-to-face interaction and physical presence in the classroom. Although the use of educational technologies in language classrooms is nothing new, in-class instruction is still common in globalized contexts, especially in places where internet and digital resources are not well-developed. With physical distancing being a requirement for stopping the pandemic, language classrooms had to go completely online irrespective of previous practices. This transition has posed challenges for all stakeholders in the field of EAP. Though these challenges may not exist in every context, their existence in the field draws the attention of researchers, policy analysts, curriculum developers, and language teachers. These challenges include teacher and student training for online learning; modification of course content and assessments; learner motivation and engagement; questions related to plagiarism and exam security; macro and micro-level planning; alignment as well as frequent (re)adjustments; accommodating (gifted) student needs; professional development of instructors and course developers; health and safety issues because of longer hours in front of computers; and teacher-student-leadership burnout (Raza & Chua, 2021; Raza et al., 2020).

Different EAP contexts have been responding to these challenges in various ways. In this chapter, we provide a descriptive case study of how an EAP department (FPDE) affected by the challenges posed by the Covid-19 pandemic addressed these challenges to devise contextually effective strategies and implemented initiatives to maintain successful teaching and learning.

Local practices

The sudden Covid-19 outbreak has presented educators with various professional and instructional challenges. At FPDE, teacher preparation, student readiness, curriculum design, and assessment were some of the immediate challenges in March 2020 almost halfway through the spring semester. In response, Qatar University announced a two-week break for students and provided the faculty with necessary training and resources to facilitate the transition to online teaching through Qatar University's Center for Excellence in Teaching and Learning (CETL). Further professional development (PD) was provided by the FPDE's Academic Excellence and Professional Development Committee (AE&PD), which helped the department to switch to online teaching within a short period.

Teacher preparedness

Recognizing the urgent need to maintain "physical distancing", the university mandated that all courses should be delivered via Blackboard Collaborate Ultra (BBCU) or Microsoft Teams (MS teams). This rapid shift presented faculty with a significant challenge as they had little to no prior experience of teaching full-fledged online classes without piloting or a clear theoretical framework. The two-week break in March 2020 offered an opportunity for mitigation through multiple in-person and online sessions on the use of learning platforms. In addition, the department's E-Learning committee scheduled helpdesk hours throughout the semester to help faculty and students with specific questions related to online learning supported by these platforms. Using the online set up proved to be a relatively manageable task because faculty were not only already familiar with several features of BBCU but most of them were also experimenting with other tools such as OneNote, OneDrive, and Zoom for class assignments and office hours meetings. Therefore, learning to master the online features of BBCU did not pose a major challenge to faculty.

While shifting to the digital platforms, the real challenge was to help faculty transfer their real-world classrooms into a virtual learning environment through acquiring the knowledge and skills relevant to using the different applications of these platforms. Going online, the department decided to blend in-class tools and tasks with independent study tools and tasks to help students achieve their academic goals without compromising the quality of their learning. The AE&PD committee was tasked with providing a reliable support system to faculty, in liaison with different training bodies inside and outside QU, through offering training sessions on topics related to the mechanics, challenges, solutions, and best practices in online teaching. Furthermore, the AE&PD committee focused on disseminating information about public webinars that were designed to give educators practical tools to cultivate a greater sense of well-being and pedagogical confidence in the virtual classroom. Information about around 50 such webinars, conferences, forums, and other events by world-renowned publishers and speakers was widely shared with the faculty. In-house PD also thrived during the pandemic, for example, in spring 2020, 10 in-house professional development workshops were conducted by members of the department to share what worked and what did not in their lessons. With 100-plus participant teachers, these workshops were remarkably effective in bringing forth and brainstorming issues related to student engagement and the pandemic impact on learning and teaching. In sum, with a specific focus on meeting the learning needs of students enrolled in the FPDE, these workshops actively supported faculty, offering them ideas on how to achieve the approved learning objectives for the various courses through online teaching.

In addition to webinars, over 20 in-class online demonstration lessons by the faculty teaching different courses were organized by the end of 2020 to foster faculty confidence in their online teaching skills. Attending these demonstration lessons also allowed faculty to know more about the different ways other faculty teaching different courses were using to achieve their lesson objectives using online platforms. Another notable professional development initiative in the department was the organization of swap-shop presentations, where instead of a complete lesson, various genre-specific short activities were shared. Each presenter shared one activity with attendees, which were recorded so they were readily available to faculty. The committee also shared relevant articles from other EAP contexts and held a major conference online with participants from all over the world to learn about how other colleagues were coping and what techniques they used.

Cultural restrictions of not turning on the camera for female students posed another challenge for faculty, influencing students' engagement in the lessons and teachers' ability to gauge their understanding. This challenge is unique to the region and many of the international webinars failed to address this specific issue. In an effort to address such issues, an event was organized where department heads of local universities in Qatar were invited to share their views on topics relevant to EAP with a special focus on using the online platform for learning. Their input was not only at par with the latest research in EAP during the pandemic, but also very relevant to QU context and culture.

Student preparedness

Digital literacy and using the latest laptop or cell phone for basic communication are two different things. Our student body generally had access to the Internet and the latest technological gadgets; however, it became immediately obvious that many did not know how to use those technological tools for learning purposes. As a result, teachers during the crisis have had to play the dual role of training students on using the different tools such as how to interact in breakout rooms, upload documents and present information, use Turnitin to check similarity index, and the like. This became a daily nuisance, and it was eventually decided to create instructional videos for different tasks and assignment submission for students in English and Arabic.

However, since many courses across the university had already utilized different E-Learning tools prior to the pandemic, going online was not a completely alien task for students. Examples of these tools in the classroom include Quizlet, Memrise, ReadTheory, Mreader, Kahoot, EdPuzzle, and Socrative; hence, students had a reasonable sense of familiarity with online learning tools.

In fact, what concerned students more was the modification of assessment weightings to be more skewed towards the midterm and final assessments which it was decided should be held on-campus. Initially, our student body was apprehensive of the changes made to the weightings on BBCU for student grades; however, these changes were well-received when detailed information explaining the rationale of the percentage adjustments was shared with them in both English and Arabic. Fostering this awareness ensured that students could make informed decisions about continuing with or dropping the semester. This partnership with students contributed to a 30% increase in student enrolment in the FPDE courses in the spring 2021 semester, which was announced as a completely online semester.

Curriculum design and assessment

When the university made the decision to cancel on-campus attendance and switch to online classes, we were almost halfway through the semester with only seven more weeks to go. The biggest challenge facing the department was carrying out the pending assessments. The inability to efficiently monitor online quizzes and assessments meant that several changes had to be made to the remaining assessments and the BBCU grade centre to ensure the assessment criteria were met. After consultation with faculty members, the value of some of the previous assessments and tasks were increased, an "online participation" mark was added, and the "Performance Now" and "Final Grade" calculations were adjusted in the corresponding grade centre columns. These changes were made so that the grade percentages were more responsive to the nature of online teaching but without prejudicing the quality of these assessments, and the students were informed of these changes in writing.

With the aim of developing our students' competencies for the new platform, faculty groups were created to work on adapting the curriculum to students' technological learning curve and the learning objectives of the different courses. This metamorphosis helped the department create a curriculum focusing more on developing students' capabilities rather than on content. Higher order thinking-based questions and open-book assignments were chosen for most assessments to ensure that students were allowed to work both synchronously and asynchronously and would ensure that they had more time to adjust to the changes. In addition, faculty were asked to create videos and record all lectures and to make them available for students on BBCU.

Initially, there were issues for many teachers related to remote communication with students. Prior to the pandemic, students met with their instructors during office hours and e-mail was not favoured by students. Faculty were also advised not to share their social media information with students. In addition, several students did not have internet access or a suitable device at home to use for their online lessons. With the whole campus shut down, both faculty and students needed an effective means of communication that could allow content sharing and synchronous interaction. While the university's IT department was testing possible platforms, students were given extensions for their deadlines and the university provided loaner laptops to those who needed them.

In some cases, changes were made to projects that required students to visit the QU library or meet in person. As visits to the library and campus, became inadvisable and eventually discontinued, we switched to online projects. For instance, instead of using M-reader, a quiz application based on library-borrowed books, we chose ReadTheory, which provides online reading comprehension activities without the need to borrow books from the library. In the absence of in-class peer support with English language comprehension, the translation committee of the department provided, on faculty's request, Arabic translations of important messages and announcements, which the faculty could share with low-level English language students.

Finally, surveys were conducted for different courses to assess the efficiency of our online teaching and gain feedback on what was successful and what was not. In addition to ascertaining the level of student satisfaction, the survey sought to identify issues related to materials, impact on attainment, and student preferences. On the basis of the feedback, subsequent changes to the curriculum for the 2020 autumn and 2021 spring semesters were made. For example, more oral assessments were introduced and assignments that required group work were dropped. During the 2021 spring semester, the feedback indicated that students and teachers generally seemed satisfied with the transition. Teachers were able to implement the required changes without much further assistance, suggesting that the directions, training manuals, and QU and FPDE organized PD sessions were effective. In general, the professionalism of faculty, administrators, and IT support staff at Qatar University helped make the quick transition to online learning a meaningful and successful endeavour.

Global trends

Although the FPDE's response was wrought to fit the local context, it was moulded out of the shared experience of the international EAP community. Our local practices during the pandemic have yielded a number of generalizable lessons. For example, our experience showed that for technology to be utilized effectively in EAP, it should have solid infrastructure, stable connectivity, supportive management, and prompt technical support.

Another learned lesson is about the value of online professional development, provided that it is engaging, practical, and relevant. Platforms like Teams and Zoom have facilitated the opportunity to hold events that would have been unattainable and expensive in normal circumstances. An example of that is the annual conference of the department, which previously attracted 300–400 participants. Instead of cancelling it, we decided to hold it online, which allowed us to have world-renowned speakers such as Stephen Krashen and Rod Ellis, and it attracted more than 18,000 participants from over 50 countries. Finally, the decision to hold major assessments on-campus has helped the department tackle the assessment security and integrity issues faced in other contexts. Although it was logistically challenging to hold on campus exams over multiple days with social distancing, the rationale was sufficient to gain the faculty's support.

It is worth noting that the department is still working on addressing several issues, too. Fewer opportunities for informal interaction and learning from peers in mixed abilities classrooms have left a void that seems challenging to bridge. Most importantly, faculty have found it difficult to comprehensively meet the needs of special needs learners in the new online learning environment.

Conclusion

This chapter outlined the initiatives taken and the strategies employed by Qatar University's FPDE to address the challenges posed by the Covid-19 pandemic, including teacher and student training for online learning, modification of course content and assessments, learner motivation and engagement, and student needs, health, and safety issues. The experience of FPDE has highlighted the key role of involving faculty in decision-making during the pandemic to gain their trust and support of the initiatives. It also has been evident that online teaching provided new venues for PD and assessment that require further investigation. On a positive note, going online provided the department and its faculty with an extraordinary learning opportunity while the drastic change in the learning mode gently forced students to continue to make progress more independently and at their own pace. We hope the benefit of this experience will be more visible in similar circumstances in the future.

Reference list

Carless, D. (2013). Innovation in language teaching and learning. In C. A. Chapelle (Ed.), *The encyclopedia of applied linguistics* (pp. 1–4). Blackwell. https://doi.org/10.1002/9781405198431.wbeal0540

Crabtree, S. A. (2010). Engaging students from the United Arab Emirates in culturally responsive education. *Innovations in Education and Teaching International, 47*(1), 85–94. https://doi.org/10.1080/14703290903525929

Harper, C., & Jong, E. D. (2004). Misconceptions about teaching English-language learners. *Journal of Adolescent and Adult Literacy, 48*(2), 152–162. http://dx.doi.org/10.1598/JAAL.48.2.6

Kramsch, C., & Hua, Z. (2016). Language, culture and language teaching. In G. Hall (Ed.), *Routledge handbook of English language teaching* (pp. 38–50). Routledge. https://doi.org/10.4324/9781315676203-5

Raza, K. (2018). Adapting teaching strategies to Arab student needs in an EFL classroom. *Journal of Ethnic and Cultural Studies, 5*(1), 16–26. http://dx.doi.org/10.29333/ejecs/93

Raza, K. (2020). Differentiated instruction in English language teaching: Insights into the implementation of Raza's teaching adaptation model in Canadian ESL classrooms. *TESL Ontario Contact Magazine, 46*(2), 41–50. http://contact.teslontario.org/wp-content/uploads/2020/08/Kashif-Raza.pdf

Raza, K., & Chua, C. (2021, March). *What is next during and after the pandemic?* Guest Speakers as part of 'ELT Practices during the pandemic: Let's get Edu-Vaccinated'' in Turkey.

Raza, K., & Coombe, C. (2020). What makes an effective TESOL teacher in the Gulf? An empirical exploration of faculty-student perceptions for context-specific teacher preparation. *Journal of Ethnic and Cultural Studies, 8*(1), 143–162. http://dx.doi.org/10.29333/ejecs/538

Raza, K., King, M., Reynolds, D., & Abrar-ul-Hassan, S. (2020, June). *Language education during the COVID-19 pandemic.* Webinar organized by Qatar University. Recording available at: www.youtube.com/watch?v=yMJwSgtG3dE&t=311s.

Tribble, C. (2012). *Managing change in English language teaching: Lessons from experience.* British Council. www.teachingenglish.org.uk/sites/teacheng/files/B330%20MC%20in%20ELT%20book_v7.pdf

Waters, A. (2009). Managing innovation in English language education. *Language Teaching, 42*(4), 421–458. https://doi.org/10.1017/S026144480999005X

Weinstein, C. S., Tomlinson-Clarke, S., & Curran, M. (2004). Toward a conception of culturally responsive classroom management. *Journal of Teacher Education, 55*(1), 25–38. https://doi.org/10.1177/0022487103259812

5

ENABLING STUDENT ENGAGEMENT IN AN ACADEMIC ENGLISH WRITING COURSE

Emergency remote teaching at a Swedish University

Špela Mežek and Kathrin Kaufhold

Introduction

Student engagement and dialogue around writing are central to a genre-based academic writing pedagogy. Adapting these principles to remote teaching would usually require time and planning. However, in response to the coronavirus pandemic, Swedish universities were required to switch to digital learning mid-term, and teachers had to adapt their courses to emergency remote teaching (ERT) in a matter of days. ERT is "a temporary shift of instructional delivery to an alternate delivery mode due to crisis circumstances" (Hodges et al., 2020, para. 1). It is different from what is generally referred to as online learning in many aspects. Online learning typically has a long design process, where every part of the course is considered and fits to the tools available. However, the switch to ERT was sudden, so there was very little time to prepare, learn, and adapt to the available tools to serve the pedagogical aims of the course. Much of online learning also happens asynchronously, whereas much of ERT conducted in Sweden was synchronous, which meant that many of the approaches and best practices of online learning and teaching could not be included. The teaching during the crisis also differed from typical synchronous digital learning, as most of our students participated in what can be characterised as virtual, interactive, real-time, instructor-led (VIRI) learning (Francescucci & Foster, 2013), something which is not always the case in synchronous digital learning.

Experiences from around the globe have shown that ERT offers both challenges and opportunities (see, e.g., Bruce & Stakounis, 2021 in the United Kingdom; Moorhouse, 2020 in Hong Kong; Lin & Gao, 2020 in China). Technical challenges and lack of knowledge about the tools used are not the only

DOI: 10.4324/9781003283409-7

challenges. Long silences (Moorhouse, 2020), screen fatigue (Abashidze, 2020; Lin & Gao, 2020), and lack of non-verbal clues (Abashidze, 2020; Moorhouse, 2020; Bruce & Stakounis, 2021) have also been reported as problematic. Student engagement was also a challenge; some reported feelings of isolation and lack of community (Bruce & Stakounis, 2021) and less willingness by students to speak in class (DiMarco, 2020; Moorhouse, 2020). In some cases, an attempt to mitigate one issue such as minimising background noise by muting participants, worsened another such as student engagement (DiMarco, 2020), as muting participants can result in a lack of natural interaction and willingness to respond. ERT not only presented challenges, however. The use of technology also provided opportunities, such as increased student autonomy, and, paradoxically, increased interactions between teachers and students (Bruce & Stakounis, 2021).

In this chapter, we report on the experience of teaching an EAP writing course during the coronavirus pandemic in Sweden. The course is an interdisciplinary postgraduate course, where student engagement and dialogue around writing are two of its central aspects. The emergency remote teaching of this course brought challenges and also opportunities. We discuss what these were, as well as what we have learnt from this experience that can inform our future practice.

Literature review

Student engagement and teaching academic writing

Student engagement and dialogue around writing are central to teaching academic writing from a genre-based perspective, as informed by insights from English for Specific Purposes (ESP) and Academic literacies (McGrath & Kaufhold, 2016). ESP pedagogy focuses on supporting students in gaining awareness of genres by analysing text samples and applying these insights to their own writing (Swales, 1990; Devitt, 2015). The aim is to help students develop an understanding of discipline-specific rhetorical and lexical features in research-based genres, such as master's theses and research proposals (Hyland, 2013). These features are discussed in relation to their rhetorical function rather than merely their textual form so students can transfer this knowledge to other contexts. An academic literacies approaches stresses the importance of dialogue in the process of knowledge production alongside the influence of students' prior knowledge and aims (Lillis & Tuck, 2015; Paxton & Frith, 2014). To enable students to acquire genre knowledge (Tardy, 2009) and develop as academic writers, a high level of student engagement is required. This is expressed in the need to become active in selecting and analysing texts from their discipline and adapting insights into their own writing (Flowerdew, 2015), as well as discussing the functions of patterns in academic writing and recognising how alternative approaches may be transformative (Lillis, 2019).

Engaging students in active learning is central to EAP course design. In contrast to monologic teaching, based on a pedagogical model of information transfer, students need to be involved in dialogic interaction around their texts (Lillis, 2006). Research on tertiary pedagogy suggests that there are three dimensions of student engagement which teaching needs to target: cognitive, relating to deep learning and self-regulation; behavioural, referring to participation and effort; and affectual, encompassing interest and connectedness (Steen-Utheim & Foldnes, 2018). A switch to ERT required an adaptation of teaching alongside these dimensions, that is, to use the given virtual learning environment in ways that facilitate deep learning (e.g., through task design), active participation (e.g., through ease of access), and connectedness (e.g., through community building). The following section discusses relevant studies on teaching online with regard to these dimensions.

Student engagement and teaching online

Most studies on student engagement in online learning have focused more on the differences between synchronous and asynchronous learning and less on the differences between VIRI and face-to-face (F2F) learning. However, the challenges discussed in the literature resemble those mentioned by teachers doing ERT. For example, one study examining the differences in VIRI and F2F learning found that while there were no differences in student performance (related to the cognitive dimension of learning), students in the F2F classroom were more engaged in terms of behaviour and affect: they attended more classes, participated more, and showed more attention and interest (Francescucci & Foster, 2013). Related to the affectual dimension of engagement, community and connectedness have also been in focus (Trespalacios et al., 2021).

Interaction is central in promoting engagement and the sense of community and connectedness in a VIRI classroom. Student-student interactions, in particular, require additional attention, as "student-student rapport and connectedness play a more integral role in reducing perceptions of loneliness in the online classroom than interactions and connections with the instructor" (Kaufmann & Vallade, 2020, p. 8). Facilitating engagement at the behavioural level with, for example, frequent student-student interactions is therefore key in fostering student engagement and a sense of community (Trespalacios et al., 2021).

How we design and structure our courses can also affect student engagement and counteract social isolation. We cannot assume that online interaction will occur online in the same way as in a physical learning environment, the reduction in spontaneity being one reason. Teacher-student, and in particular student-student interaction and collaboration, therefore need to be planned in advance (Kaufmann & Vallade, 2020). Collaboration and peer reviewing are activities that should be promoted, as they can foster the sense of community and connectedness (Trespalacios et al., 2021). These types of interactions should be carefully planned to ensure that students know what is expected of them, how they are supposed to engage with and participate in activities, and when these should be done. Pre-planning the activities can prevent confusion when students are participating in synchronous online learning (McBrien et al., 2009). Finally, pre-planning activities also enables the teachers to monitor these activities to ensure students stay on task, another important aspect of engagement (Kaufmann & Vallade, 2020).

The local practices

The course

The cross-disciplinary EAP course is obligatory for master's students in the Humanities department at our university and aims to prepare students for writing their thesis. The students are multilingual and use English as an additional language. The course comprises six, three-hour seminars. Its design is based on pedagogical principles drawn from ESP and Academic literacies in the following ways: students are introduced to ESP move analysis by first discussing a sample text, for instance an introduction paragraph to a master's thesis, and identifying typical rhetorical and lexical patterns to advance the text's argument. Second, students apply this analysis to self-selected sample texts from their disciplines (Cheng, 2008; Kuteeva & Negretti, 2016). The aim is to develop a metalanguage to talk about the students' texts and become aware of discipline-specific discourse patterns and effects of discursive choices for readers (Swales, 1990). Students apply and transform their insights to their own writing throughout the course as they work towards their final assignment in the form of a research proposal for their thesis project. Engaging in dialogue around the students' draft texts also supports the development of their research proposal (Badenhorst et al., 2015).

Cycles of analysing other texts and developing a metalanguage, writing, and dialogue around students' texts are essential components of the course (see Kaufhold, 2017). Students' engagement and active learning are thus crucial. The original course design relied heavily on in-class, small-group discussions and some asynchronous online forum posts on the virtual learning platform. Student feedback has shown that students appreciate the group discussions. They also use discussions to reflect on the differences between the disciplines, which develops their understanding of their own field. Thus, through discussions in class, students develop a sense of not only community but also their academic identity.

Changes to the course for ERT and implications for future challenges

ERT requires teachers to quickly adapt their courses to a new, online, mode in line with the pedagogical principles of the course. Adjusting a course that has been designed for predominantly F2F communication to an online version entails not only a redesign of learning tasks but also a familiarisation with the technical functionality. On the basis of our experience, we demonstrate how such adjustments for both teachers and students can be facilitated. We focus on the measures we tested to engage students in peer discussion as an essential component of EAP course design. In this section, we discuss the changes to course design and structure and their implementation in class, and what they have taught us about teaching practices in ERT for use in the future.

Course design and structure

Different modes, face-to-face or online, provide different affordances to facilitate discussion and engagement. The introduction of VIRI teaching can pose an initial challenge as teachers and students need to acquaint themselves with the new mode and the technology. To facilitate participation (i.e., the behavioural dimension of engagement), teachers and students have to be well informed about the technology. In our course, the teachers mainly learned from each other, but eventually resources were provided from the university centrally, which will be helpful for future challenges. Instead of presuming that students would be able to orient intuitively in the new environment, the teachers demonstrated in the first meeting how the students could use the online environment (Zoom – the video conferencing tool used for seminars, and the online learning platform) and where to find information and materials. These precautions address potential technical challenges and at the same time create more favourable conditions for engagement, as they remove potential obstacles to participation, lower students' stress levels (Bruce & Stakounis, 2021), and save time for discussions.

Appropriate use of the technological affordances has implications for the overall course structure and can be a catalyst for pedagogical innovation. The introduction of short pre-recorded lectures was inspired by flipped classroom pedagogy. The pre-recordings also fostered student autonomy (Bruce & Stakounis, 2021; McBrien et al., 2009), as students could themselves decide when to watch the recordings. Importantly, this freed time for active discussion. However, a few teachers did not feel comfortable with producing such lectures, which can be time-consuming. Innovation comes at a cost and future EAP developments need to take this aspect into account.

Not all adjustments to the course structure need to be substantial, however. For example, when it comes to task instructions, a simple change implemented in our ERT to facilitate learning (cognitive dimension) entailed making instructions available to the students before the seminar in a document they could download and have open on the screen during class. Another change was related to opportunities for peer reviewing, something our course previously included as a way of facilitating the dialogue around text that is fundamental to EAP and Academic literacies (e.g., Tardy, 2009). In the ERT version of the course, we organised these activities in much more detail and allocated more time for them. We set up peer review groups before each seminar, so that the students read each other's drafts before class and then gave each other feedback during class time in group 'breakout rooms'. The students were also given clear instructions about what to focus on. These kinds of changes help the students to focus on their task (McBrien et al., 2009) and make it possible for the teacher to monitor what they do. Our teachers unanimously reported that the peer review seemed to be more thorough. Finally, in ERT, how feedback is given also requires re-organisation, as giving feedback in person is more time consuming in a VIRI classroom than F2F. For this reason, our ERT students received written feedback on their drafts, which could also be discussed with the teacher in a breakout room during the seminar.

The informal dialogue with the teacher that spontaneously occurs in the F2F mode in breaks or after class is difficult to replicate in VIRI. These types of more informal interactions, however, can help foster the feeling of connectedness and community (Trespalacios et al., 2021); they facilitate the affective dimension of engagement. In our ERT we therefore created a forum on our learning platform where students could ask questions, which would then either be answered in the forum or discussed in class. We also decided to stay on after class and create extra breakout rooms for one-to-one student meetings, thus attempting to reintroduce some of the "human element" (Bruce & Stakounis, 2021, p. 6).

Implementation in class

As in any EAP course, irrespective of the teaching mode, adjustments need to be made with respect to the composition and needs of the specific groups in order to facilitate engagement in the behavioural dimension. In our ERT, we made the following adjustments. Considering that speaking in a foreign language (Dewaele, 2018) online in front of strangers can be daunting, we used the chat function for student responses to some tasks. In this way we aimed to foster different ways of participation, especially since communication via chat has been found to help shyer students participate (Bruce & Stakounis, 2021, p. 39). For the teacher, VIRI generally reduces the scope for spontaneity, but once we were more confident in the use of Zoom, we also added quick polls during a break to get a show of hands and continue to engage students. The use of breakout rooms in Zoom was fundamental to ensuring student activity and their engagement in the plenary, as they could test ideas in smaller, less intimidating groups which were similar to group work in F2F learning. Since video conferencing tools like Zoom reduce the possibility to pick up on non-verbal cues (Bruce & Stakounis, 2021; Moorhouse, 2020), ensuring broad student participation by providing the opportunity to contribute is crucial. Similar to F2F teaching, calling on students directly and asking for their contribution can result in activating these students who would then continue to volunteer perspectives.

The VIRI mode requires that some decisions, which in the F2F classroom would typically be taken by students, are taken by the teachers, thus reducing student autonomy. For example, in the F2F mode students on our course have the opportunity to select their discussion partners (as long as they are from a different discipline), which was technologically more complicated in the VIRI mode. Nevertheless, the possibility to allocate students to breakout rooms enabled teachers to monitor cross-disciplinary work for both text analysis tasks and peer feedback. It also facilitated frequent changes in group composition so that the students worked with and discussed texts with a range of peers throughout the course. Thus, while the teacher assigning discussion partners reduced student autonomy, it also positively affected other aspects of the course.

Course design has to be the guiding principles in all modes, whether F2F or VIRI, which in our EAP course means creating opportunities for students to develop their projects with peers who might not share their discipline-specific knowledge of academic texts. This is typically done in small groups where all students are required to talk and engage with each other. In ERT, it is important to keep this as it facilitates student engagement. In our VIRI classroom, students could be unmuted and take turns more spontaneously in small groups than in the plenary. This meant that we could counteract some of the negative effects of the technology which required a strict protocol of hand raising and unmuting to minimize unwanted disruptive noise. In addition, we noticed an increased level of autonomy and self-organisation (Bruce & Stakounis, 2021) when visiting the groups: different students took on the role of moderator by, for example, suggesting to move on to a different text or encouraging others to add their views.

To support the affective dimension of active learning, small groups are also vital as spaces for social support and help to break isolation (Bruce & Stakounis, 2021). Part of this affective dimension is the development of a sense of belonging. Besides developing a sense of disciplinary identity in the multi-disciplinary interaction (Badenhorst et al., 2015), most groups in our ERT also seemed to develop a sense of group community through getting to know each other in small groups and plenary discussions. This was evident when more students began to contribute in the plenary and students increasingly left their cameras on when returning to the main room. ERT also has to take into account student expectations more broadly. As in our case, students might not be willing to engage in a different teaching mode and choose to postpone their studies. In our experience, however, this applies to the minority.

Global trends

As in most countries, the switch to ERT brought with it a range of challenges but also opportunities for learning and course improvement. Ensuring student engagement has been an important issue (Bruce & Stakounis, 2021). This was certainly the case for our course, as remote teaching through Zoom cannot fully recreate co-presence as would be possible in a physical classroom. Due to the fact that students had to take on the responsibility of producing course material in the form of selecting texts for discussion and continuously drafting their own texts, the course design provided ideal preconditions for activating students. The fact that students become to some extent discourse analysts of their own texts (Badenhorst et al., 2015) entails that students learn not only to identify textual patterns and rhetorical functions of research-based writing but also to apply these to their own writing, thus encouraging deep learning (cognitive dimension). These general EAP principles formed the basis for the VIRI version of our course.

Neither students nor teachers were prepared for ERT (cf. Bruce & Stakounis, 2021). The sharing of experiences among teachers and information from the central higher education pedagogy unit helped the teachers to react to these challenges. Besides learning how to use technology to support the behavioural dimension of engagement, the affective dimension had to be taken into account which been described as the major challenge of recreating the "human touch" (Bruce & Stakounis, 2021). This was seen as the case by our students and staff. However, some of this could have been alleviated by working with small groups and providing opportunities for students to take responsibility for their own learning (by drafting texts on their own projects) and peer learning (preparing for feedback sessions). Besides the opportunities for cognitive engagement, this work also supported the affective side of community making.

Our changes in course design also meant that the teachers were required to engage with recent developments in higher education pedagogy, such as flipped classroom pedagogy (Abeysekera & Dawson, 2015). The element of pre-recording short lectures helped to prepare the in-class activities and might be one of the features that can be carried over to F2F teaching. As has been widely reported, ERT meant many teachers worldwide were thrown into teaching online and some of the lessons learnt are likely to be carried over into a post-coronavirus higher education.

Conclusion

The switch to ERT in response to the coronavirus pandemic brought challenges and opportunities. In our academic writing course, which builds on student interaction, our course adaptation focused on addressing student engagement by modifying the design and structure of the course, as well as its implementation in class.

Our experience of ERT has shown that continuously developing teachers' knowledge of different technical tools is crucial, so that when they are needed, teachers can focus on how to apply them instead of learning how to use them. Our experience also showed us how the affective side of learning is important in an EAP course, especially when the course is given in the VIRI mode. It is thus important that EAP pedagogy focuses more on how to best support the affective dimension of student engagement to facilitate peer-learning (cf. Vygotsky, 1978) also develop writer and disciplinary identities. The affective dimension is therefore also something future EAP research should investigate further. The future higher education landscape may strive for more remote teaching elements to free up resources and respond to student mobility. At the same time, the need for genuine co-presence and the "human touch" will need to be taken into consideration to respond to students' desire for more dialogue around their texts.

Reference list

Abashidze, A. (2020). Education in the condition of "a total lockdown". *The Quarterly Review of Distance Education, 21*(3), 5–8.

Abeysekera, L., & Dawson, P. (2015). Motivation and cognitive load in the flipped classroom: Definition, rationale and a call for research. *Higher Education Research & Development, 34*(1), 1–14. https://doi.org/10.1080/07294360.2014.934336

Badenhorst, C., Moloney, C., Rosales, J., Dyer, J., & Ru, L. (2015). Beyond deficit: Graduate student research-writing pedagogies. *Teaching in Higher Education, 20*(1), 1–11. https://doi.org/10.1080/13562517.2014.945160

Bruce, E., & Stakounis, H. (2021). *The impact of Covid-19 on the UK EAP sector: An examination of how organisations delivering EAP were affected and responded in terms of academic delivery and operational procedures.* BALEAP. www.baleap.org/wp-content/uploads/2021/06/BALEAP-Report-Covid-and-EAP-May-2021.pdf

Cheng, A. (2008). Analyzing genre exemplars in preparation for writing: The case of an L2 graduate student in the ESP genre-based instructional framework of academic literacy. *Applied Linguistics, 29*, 50–70. https://doi.org/10.1093/applin/amm021

Devitt, A. (2015). Genre performances: John Swales' genre analysis and rhetorical-linguistic genre studies. *Journal of English for Academic Purposes, 19*, 44–51. https://doi.org/10.1016/j.jeap.2015.05.008

Dewaele, J. M. (2018). Why the dichotomy 'L1 versus LX user' is better than 'native versus non-native speaker'. *Applied Linguistics, 39*(2), 236–240. https://doi.org/10.1093/applin/amw055

DiMarco, D. (2020). Shifting to online instruction in the epicenter of a U.S. pandemic: A professor's strategies, struggles, and successes. *The Quarterly Review of Distance Education, 21*(3), 23–37.

Flowerdew, J. (2015). John Swales's approach to pedagogy in genre analysis: A perspective from 25 years on. *Journal of English for Academic Purposes, 19*, 102–112. https://doi.org/10.1016/j.jeap.2015.02.003

Francescucci, A., & Foster, M. (2013). The VIRI (virtual, interactive, real-time, instructor-led) classroom: The impact of blended synchronous online courses on student performance, engagement, and satisfaction. *Canadian Journal of Higher Education, 43*(3), 78–91. https://doi.org/10.47678/cjhe.v43i3.184676

Hodges, C., Moore, S., Lockee, B., Trust, T., & Bond, A. (2020, March 27). The difference between emergency remote teaching and online learning. *Educause Review.* https://er.educause.edu/articles/2020/3/the-difference-between-emergency-remote-teaching-and-online-learning

Hyland, K. (2013). *Disciplinary discourses: Social interactions in academic writing* (2nd ed.). University of Michigan Press.

Kaufhold, K. (2017). Interdisciplinary postgraduate writing: Developing genre knowledge. *Writing & Pedagogy, 19*(2), 251–274. https://doi.org/10.1558/wap.30568

Kaufmann, R., & Vallade, J. I. (2020). Exploring connections in the online learning environment: Student perceptions of rapport, climate, and loneliness. *Interactive Learning Environments.* https://doi.org/10.1080/10494820.2020.1749670

Kuteeva, M., & Negretti, R. (2016). Graduate students' genre knowledge and perceived disciplinary practices: Creating a research space across disciplines. *English for Specific Purposes, 41*, 36–49. http://doi.org/10.1016/j.esp.2015.08.004

Lillis, T. (2019). 'Academic literacies': Sustaining a critical space on writing in academia. *Journal of Learning Development in Higher Education, 15*. http://doi.org/10.47408/jldhe.v0i15.565

Lillis, T. M. (2006). Moving towards an academic literacies' pedagogy: Dialogues of participation. In L. Ganobcsik-Williams (Ed.), *Teaching academic writing in UK higher education: Theories, practices and models* (pp. 30–45). Palgrave Macmillan.

Lillis, T. M., & Tuck, J. (2015). Academic Literacies: A critical lens on writing and reading in the academy. In K. Hyland & P. Shaw (Eds.), *The Routledge handbook of English for academic purposes* (pp. 30–43). Routledge.

Lin, X., & Gao, L. (2020). Students' sense of community and perspectives of taking synchronous and asynchronous online courses. *Asian Journal of Distance Education, 15*(1), 169–179.

McBrien, J., Cheng, R., & Jones, P. (2009). Virtual spaces: Employing a synchronous online classroom to facilitate student engagement in online learning. *International Review of Research in Open and Distributed Learning, 10*(3). https://doi.org/10.19173/irrodl.v10i3.605

McGrath, L., & Kaufhold, K. (2016). English for specific purposes and academic literacies: Eclecticism in academic writing pedagogy. *Teaching in Higher Education, 21*(8), 933–947. https://doi.org/10.1080/13562517.2016.1198762

Moorhouse, B. L. (2020). Adaptations to a face-to-face initial teacher education course 'forced' online due to the COVID-19 pandemic. *Journal of Education for Teaching, 46*(4), 609–611. https://doi.org/10.1080/02607476.2020.1755205

Paxton, M., & Frith, V. (2014). Implications of academic literacies research for knowledge making and curriculum design. *Higher Education, 67*(2), 171–182. https://doi.org/10.1007/s10734-013-9675-z

Steen-Utheim, A. T., & Foldnes, N. (2018). A qualitative investigation of student engagement in a flipped classroom. *Teaching in Higher Education, 23*(3), 307–324. https://doi.org/10.1080/13562517.2017.1379481

Swales, J. M. (1990). *Genre analysis: English in academic and research settings.* Cambridge University Press.

Tardy, C. (2009). *Building genre knowledge.* Parlor Press.

Trespalacios, J., Snelson, C., Lowenthal, P. R., Uribe-Flórez, L., & Perkins, R. (2021). Community and connectedness in online higher education: A scoping review of the literature. *Distance Education, 42*(1), 5–21. https://doi.org/10.1080/01587919.2020.1869524

Vygotsky, L. S. (1978). *Mind in society: The development of higher psychological processes.* Harvard University Press.

6

FLIPPED LEARNING ONLINE AND FACE-TO-FACE AS A WAY OF SUPPORTING STUDENTS' COGNITIVE AND EMOTIONAL ENGAGEMENT DURING PERIODS OF FRACTURED INSTRUCTION

Rosemary Wette

Introduction

One benefit of the campus closures caused by the Covid-19 pandemic was that it brought into focus the need to reflect on the benefits, limitations, and challenges of interactive, student-centred pedagogies such as flipped learning (FL). This chapter reports on the implementation of an FL approach in two occurrences of a credit-bearing, 12-week graduate academic writing course at a university in Auckland, New Zealand, in 2020–21 that was offered simultaneously to on-campus and online students and was obliged to shift in and out of fully online learning. It outlines the study context, explains how FL was implemented, and reflects on my experience, as the teacher of the course. It includes reflections about the effects of FL on students' cognitive and affective/behavioural engagement and why I consider FL to be a pedagogically sound approach. I also offer suggestions for how university authorities, teachers, and students can maximise its chances for success during periods of disrupted instruction.

Context

In 2020, New Zealand's initial response to Covid-19 was dramatic and comparatively swift – a reaction facilitated by its isolation (approximately 2,500 kilometres to its closest neighbouring countries) and relatively dispersed population (18 per km²). National borders were closed to everyone except citizens and permanent residents, who were required to complete two weeks of managed quarantine before being allowed to enter the community (McGuinness Institute/ Te Hononga Waka, 2021). After the country went into a strict nationwide lockdown, the university closed its campus for the whole of the first teaching semester

DOI: 10.4324/9781003283409-8

of the academic year (March–June). The second semester began with on-campus teaching, but due to another compulsory city-wide lockdown, teaching moved online for part of the semester, and also in March for part of the first semester of 2021. Campus closures were strictly enforced and the first lockdown so speed-ily implemented that staff training was available for only a day or so; however, I was already reasonably familiar with the Zoom video-conferencing programme supported by the university, and this was used throughout as the main tool for synchronous communication with students, together with PowerPoint slides and course content documents uploaded onto the university's digital learning man-agement system (Canvas). All students were provided with a 220-page text that I had written for the course (in print or in electronic format). This chapter reports on my experience in 2020–21 of teaching courses to students who were enrolled for either on-campus or offshore study, and that shifted in and out of fully online teaching.

Online and flipped learning

This section outlines what is currently known about the benefits and limitations of online versus face-to-face (f2f) teaching and implementing FL in synchro-nous online and f2f learning environments. In this regard, it is useful to keep in mind the conclusions of a recent large-scale international study compar-ing online, face-to-face, and blended learning options during school closures (Education Endowment Foundation, 2021): that teaching quality (e.g., clear explanations, scaffolding, and feedback) is more important than how lessons are delivered (e.g., synchronous, asynchronous, or mixed), and that peer interac-tion and support for independent learning are crucial in online options. Recent related studies have examined the particular difficulties that online instruction can present, including the additional workload for teachers to prepare appro-priate materials or devise ways of using existing materials in a different way (Watson Todd, 2020), the need to achieve effective communication with stu-dents to explain and check on their understanding (Delahunty et al., 2014; Watson Todd, 2020), and the desirability of building a class community where students interact constructively (Delahunty et al., 2014). These authors point out that online learning programmes need to go beyond participation (which may involve little more than posting on discussion boards) to achieve a more engaged, synchronous interaction that breaks down the separation created by the online environment and builds rapport in the class group, as well as between students and the teacher. However, recent studies on online learning experi-ences from students' perspectives have also revealed a number of negative aspects such as problems with broadband connections, difficulties mastering new tech-nology and managing Zoom in domestic settings (Adedoyin & Soykin, 2020), and emotional issues for students who may feel isolated, demotivated, and una-ble to concentrate (Besser et al., 2020).

The term "flipped learning" describes an instructional approach where the teacher scaffolds an initial understanding of core skills through information and guided practice that students complete independently before applying what they have learned in class sessions through collaborative discussions and writing tasks. In FL, instruction is "flipped" or overturned in the sense that basic concepts involving the development of declarative knowledge (DeKeyser, 2007) and the less sophisticated skills of remembering and understanding (Krathwohl, 2002) are introduced through recorded lectures and self-study tasks, while students develop procedural skills through the utilisation of order cognitive skills such as analysing, synthesising, and evaluating, during interactions that take place in class sessions (Flipped Learning Network, 2014). The principles underpinning FL are similar to those on which constructivism and communicative language teaching are based: student-centred knowledge creation, the importance of interaction, deep processing of new content, and the teacher as facilitator rather than regulator of students' learning. Researchers have identified many advantages of FL for students and teachers, including greater opportunities for students to work through the first phase of instruction independently at their own pace, and then to interact with peers and the teacher, drawing on creative, higher order thinking skills to respond to meaningful input (Bauer-Ramazani et al., 2016; Chuang et al., 2018; Doman & Webb, 2017). Students who are motivated and have a strong sense of self-efficacy are likely to thrive in FL courses (Chuang et al., 2018), while teachers can benefit from the shift to new roles that require less teacher-talk and teacher control, and allow more time for devising interactive tasks (Doman & Webb, 2017; Hung, 2017) and providing formative feedback (Bauer-Ramazani et al., 2016). However, students with weaker engagement and self-discipline, who do not complete pre-class study or whose attendance is poor, may not do so well (Chuang et al., 2018; Doman & Webb, 2017), and less proficient learners may struggle during the initial pre-class phase if no teacher is available to explain and answer questions. This group might well need additional scaffolding and guided tasks (Zou et al., 2020). Both teachers and learners may face technology-related difficulties (e.g., camera and microphone malfunctions; Internet outages; difficulties with new technology), particularly if support and training are inadequate (Hall & DuFrene, 2016). Teachers report that devising self-study and in-class FL tasks is time-consuming and that monitoring students' interactions on Zoom is tiring (Hall & DuFrene, 2016).

As a way of overcoming student passivity and disengagement during online learning, Marshall and Kostka (2020) proposed a synchronous online FL approach (SOFLA) that utilised core FL principles. It comprised class sessions that prioritised interaction, which were preceded by teacher-devised self-study tasks to develop an initial knowledge base, and then consolidated through post-class self-study revision and extension tasks. In so doing, their aims were for teachers to take on active roles of facilitator of tasks in online sessions and supplier of support, explanations, and formative feedback, while students were helped to overcome demotivation by interacting with teachers and collaborating with peers to complete online tasks. The main roles of the teacher were to provide direction and assistance, monitor students' interaction, give feedback, and "maintain a presence [online] that offers support and validation of student efforts" (Marshall & Kostka, 2020, p. 4). However, they and another team who adapted FL for online use (Jia et al., 2021) noted a number of additional SOFLA requirements: careful planning and materials preparation for self-study by teachers, conscientious preparation, and focussed attention by students in class sessions. Weaker students and those who were used to receiving instruction verbally from the teacher were less likely to be satisfied with FL courses.

Online and on-campus flipped learning in my graduate writing course

These accounts of the principles, benefits, and limitations of online and FL resonated with my personal experience of teaching over the past year, since my main concerns were the effects of online and fractured instruction on (1) students' ability to meet the learning outcomes of the course and (2) their motivation and engagement with the course. To declare my positionality, I was less keen on trialling the potential of new forms of online technologies than in achieving a good-quality course that would maintain the same levels of student commitment and skill development that I have facilitated over the 15 years or so that I have taught this course. My focus was very much on pedagogy and how I might maintain students' engagement, as well as ensuring that they were comprehending course content and developing skill in relevant areas. In this section, I report on the experience of two occurrences of the graduate writing course: in 2020 (27 students on campus; seven students offshore in three time zones in Asia and the Middle East; a total of 34) and in 2021 (12 students on campus and nine students offshore in two time zones in Asia; a total of 21). Eligibility requirements for admission to the MTESOL and MA programmes that students were enrolled in were a bachelor's degree in a relevant subject and, for the MTESOL, at least two years' teaching experience.

During the period when classes were permitted on campus, there was one two-hour teaching session per week comprising mini-lectures using PowerPoint slides to check on pre-class familiarisation tasks, question and answer exchanges (Q&A), group and individual tasks, and class discussions. The teacher's voice was audio-recorded and this recording was uploaded, along with PowerPoint slides, onto the university's learning management system. Offshore students studying online were provided with an additional video-conferencing session every one to two weeks lasting 60–80 minutes that comprised a summary of the main teaching points by the teacher, Q&A exchanges, and whole-class and small-group tasks. All groups were assigned core, extension, and revision tasks for self-study as well as course readings from published articles and book chapters. Course content

TABLE 6.1 Writing course core content and assignments

Unit	Course content & assignments
1	Approaches to academic literacy instruction; Anglo-western writing practices
2	Evaluative book reviews. *Analysis of a published book review (500 words) & review of a recently published book about academic writing (700 words)*
3	Argumentation, stance, and engagement
4	Paraphrase and summaries in citations
5	Composing processes
6	Synthesisng and citing source texts
7	Writing a research report (RR): Introduction and literature review. *Literature review (1000 words); peer review of draft review*
8	RR: Reporting on methodology
9	RR: Presenting and commenting on results
10	RR: Discussions and conclusions. *Discussion session of a research article (600 words)*

and skills development was the same for all students irrespective of the mode of delivery and following the course outline that students received on enrolment. An outline of core content and assessments can be found in Table 6.1.

Table 6.2 provides a summary of fractured instruction in the two courses. They encompassed fully online and blended online/on campus options to meet campus closure requirements and the needs of students enrolled offshore and on campus. As can be seen from the table, core principles of FL were evident in the way declarative knowledge was developed in the pre-instruction phase and consolidated post-instruction, while in-class work on campus and through Zoom prioritised active learning through student-student and student-teacher interaction. As part of their literature review assignment, students carried out a peer review of a final draft of a classmate's work, providing another opportunity for them to connect and interact with classmates, and to benefit from giving and getting peer feedback.

In video-conferencing sessions, strong encouragement for students to turn on their webcams and dismissing the option of a waiting room allowed for social chat with individual students as they came online, while breakout room sessions and whole-group chat at the end of each session helped the group to get to know each other. I believe that my presence as teacher, conveyed through direct eye contact, small-talk, and humour as well as openness to question-and-answer exchanges about any aspect of the course, was particularly important in Zoom sessions, since they provided invaluable chances for students to carry out discussions with classmates from their home country and other countries, with native speakers of English, and with the teacher in New Zealand. Two 15–20-minute breakout room interludes took place in each session during which groups of two

TABLE 6.2 Course summary

Course	Pre- and post-class self-study	In-class sessions
Fully online: 60% Course 1 20% Course 2	*Online (asynchronous component)* Pre-class • Familiarisation with course text unit • Unit readings (articles/chapters) • Review of session recording • PowerPoint slides Post-class • Extension tasks from course text • Writing tasks (for teacher feedback) • Readings guided by focus questions in course text	*Synchronous (weekly Zoom video-conferencing sessions)* • Social chat & general discussion • Q&A about pre-class tasks and current assignment • Teacher-led Q&A and discussions • Group discussion and tasks to analyse & apply new learning (breakout rooms) • Group reports to the class • Feedback and discussion
Online & on campus: 40% Course 1 80% Course 2	*On campus (asynchronous component)* Pre-class • Familiarisation with course text unit • Unit readings (articles/chapters) Post-class • Extension tasks from course text • Writing (for teacher feedback) • Readings guided by focus questions in course text *Offshore/online students* Pre- and post- class As for online students (see earlier)	*(i) On campus (weekly synchronous class sessions)* • Explanations of core concepts • Independent and group tasks to analyse & apply new learning; teacher feedback • Students' work shared with class (whiteboard or document camera) • Q&A exchanges • Class discussion • Presentations (individually/in pairs) *(ii) Offshore/online students (synchronous zoom sessions every 1–2 weeks; recording of class session in (i))* • Social chat & general discussion • Recap of core concepts & Q&A • Tasks for groups (breakout rooms, monitored by the teacher) • Report back & class discussion

to four students completed tasks relevant to the specific content and writing skills that were the focus of the course unit. Small groups were used to maximise participation opportunities. I visited each room at least once during the session – not to take over the interaction, but as an observer-participant who was available to facilitate discussion, respond to queries, and give feedback on request.

From my experience of using FL for online and blended online/on campus teaching, I have made the following observations and reflective comments. Firstly, with regard to students' learning achievement or cognitive engagement with the course, I found no evidence of differences on coursework assignments with a similar level of difficulty and the same assessment criteria between groups receiving f2f FL in 2017–18 courses, or blended online/f2f FL courses (2020–21) compared with previous cohorts (before 2016) that had received more traditional EAP instruction. The average course mark for these six cohorts (2016–21) in classes of 22–50 students was 72–75% (B/B+). Nor were there any real differences between the achievements of groups studying in different modes. This provides further support for conclusions from reviews of research (Hall & DuFrene, 2016; Zou et al., 2020) that FL has no negative impact on learning outcomes. It supports research evidence provided by Jia et al. (2021) that FL online delivers similar learning gains to conventional FL. Students appeared entirely capable of working independently of their classmates, and used higher order thinking to achieve an understanding of course content and develop advanced academic writing skills. Their cognitive engagement with the course therefore appeared to be largely unaffected by the teaching approach or mode of delivery.

However, I believe that the affective and behavioural/participatory aspects of engagement were negatively impacted by students' isolation from the classroom. The importance of teacher-student and student-student relationships has long been recognised (e.g., Frymier & Houser, 2000), as has the need for effective student-student and student-teacher communication and support by the teacher of students' development of self-efficacy and need for connection. During this period, a small number of students did not attend regularly (on campus) or at all (online) despite encouragement. Some did not complete pre-class work very thoroughly (or at all), so they were scarcely able to participate in the class sessions. Others were resistant to turning on webcams, and although I followed the University's guidelines that students' privacy needed to be respected, I admit to having difficulties relating to blank screens if students were unwilling or unable to turn on their cameras. This group of students also tended to be resistant to participating in group or class discussions, or even in responding to direct questions from the teacher. In written course evaluations, comments in response to a prompt about what was challenging about online study, some reflected that they had very much missed opportunities to interact with classmates: "it made it hard for me to feel a part of the class"; "learning by myself is lonely – I feel helpless"; and "sometimes I feel frustrated . . . that I'm struggling alone". However, they noted the usefulness for self-study of the course-specific text that included information for reference as well as practice tasks, and that "the teacher set a discussion for each zoom session and there was time to ask questions". However, some expressed a wish to hear all the in-class interactions (which would have been impossible unless all students had been provided with microphones).

In response to requests for PowerPoint slides to be made available in advance of class sessions, I shifted answers to self-study tasks to a separate set of slides so students could work through tasks without being distracted by seeing answers and model versions. Online students commented that group activities were very intensive and tiring, given that the other courses they were taking also involved video conferencing. In my Zoom sessions I alternated group and whole-class tasks, assigned no more than two tasks for breakout room work per session, and made sure to allow adequate time for reporting back, general discussion, and Q&A about course content or assessments.

Looking forward and outward

My most pressing concern with regard to the use of FL in f2f or blended courses is that cognitive and affective engagement does not appear to be well aligned, particularly when online study is involved. While students managed to achieve comparable learning outcomes irrespective of mode, the affective and behavioural engagement of some students who were isolated from classmates appeared to be negatively affected. I have no idea whether improvements in affective engagement would boost learning achievement, and this needs to be kept in mind when reading the following observations and suggestions, which are based on my recent experience. For students to engage cognitively and achieve well academically in a FL course, particularly if delivered online to students who are offshore:

- It is important that self-study materials for the pre-class phase be sufficiently clear and comprehensive, that teachers do not step back entirely from their important responsibility as a source of explicit instruction. Examples can be helpful for students who are anxious about being "on the right track"
- If PowerPoint presentation formats and tasks use similar patterns that become familiar to students, this is likely to reduce their cognitive burden
- It might well be necessary to reiterate core learning points at the beginning of class sessions, and to offer, regular Q&A on assignment requirements throughout the period in which students are working on them
- Formative feedback during class sessions and on written work, as well as summative feedback on assessment achievement, is as important as ever
- To the fullest extent possible, in-class work needs to draw on higher order thinking skills that extend what has been learned in the pre-class phase
- Not all students will be proficient in using new technology or in knowing how to interact in breakout rooms and plenary discussion on Zoom, and taking time to develop protocols with students may be useful

- It is helpful if Zoom sessions have a clear plan and if this is circulated to students in advance of the teaching session
- Assignment tasks need to be distinctive for each student (e.g., a particular book or literature review topic) to reduce the temptation to download content from the internet or for shared assignment preparation

Working with the affective issues that can result from online study is a more challenging issue, and I realise that this may be only partially mitigated by the use of FL.

- The importance of attendance and participation needs to be emphasised. While recognising that some students have less than ideal domestic environments, it needs to be pointed out that interaction with peers in class sessions is an important part of learning, and that each online session will make this a priority, that is, online sessions are not for the delivery of more explicit content instruction
- Group assessments and presentations in online courses would certainly help to establish relationships; however, the usual unevenness of participation might well be compounded when students have no social contact with each other. However, in my course, peer review on a draft assignment was handled well by both on-campus and online students
- Teachers need to be flexible in their availability for students living in different time zones, and offer contact through synchronous office hours, chat sessions or time allocated at the end of Zoom sessions, as well as asynchronous email exchanges. Frequent communication, even if just brief announcements, reminders, and sharing of queries and problems, posted on the learning management system, is useful for maintaining contact and building a class community.

Lest this be taken as a counsel of perfection, teachers need to have realistic expectations and not be disheartened by less than optimum student engagement, or the impossibility of knowing whether or how thoroughly pre- and post-task work is being completed. In the case of students who attend or participate infrequently or not at all, the teacher cannot know what or how much they are learning. Being mindful that online teaching and FL generate more work than single-mode f2f instruction, teachers also need to avoid exhaustion by placing limits on the amount of time they can devote to each course. University authorities can assist teachers to manage periods of fractured instruction by offering support to staff in the form of ongoing training, resources, and workload release in recognition of the additional workload that mixed course delivery entails, and both university authorities and teachers need to manage online/offshore students' expectations about what can be provided for them.

Conclusion

This chapter has reviewed and reflected on face-to-face and online FL in a graduate writing course during a period of fractured instruction. With regard to the consequences for students' cognitive and emotional engagement, it appears that online learning and fractured instruction may adversely affect motivation and interest more than students' knowledge and skill development. FL is an effective way of offsetting some of the limitations of online learning through class sessions that are more engaging, and that offer more contact with lecturers and interaction with classmates. I have made some suggestions for how some of the issues arising from this experience might be resolved by university authorities, teachers, and students, since periods of disruption are likely to recur in the near future. Future investigations in this area could continue to collect evidence on the benefits of FL, and on how any negative consequences on student interest and engagement might be mitigated.

Reference list

Adedoyin, O. B., & Soykin, E. (2020). Covid-19 pandemic and online learning: The challenges and opportunities. *Interactive Learning Environments*. https://doi.org/10.1080/10494820.2020.1813180

Bauer-Ramazani, C., Graney, J. M., Marshall, H., & Sabieh, C. (2016). Flipped learning in TESOL: Definitions, approaches and implementation. *TESOL Journal, 7*(2), 429–437.

Besser, A., Flett, G. L., & Zeigler-Hill, V. (2020). Adaptability to a sudden transition to online learning during the COVID-19 pandemic: Understanding the challenges for students. *Scholarship of Teaching and Learning in Psychology*. http://dx.doi.org/10.1037/stl0000198

Chuang, H-H., Weng, C-Y., & Chen, C-H. (2018). Which students benefit most from a flipped classroom approach to language learning? *British Journal of Educational Psychology, 49*, 56–68. https://doi.10.1111/bjet.12530

DeKeyser, R. (2007). Skill acquisition theory. In B. Van Patten & J. Williams (Eds.), *Theories in second language acquisition* (pp. 97–113). Lawrence Erlbaum.

Delahunty, J., Verenikina, I., & Jones, P. (2014). Socio-emotional connections: Identity, belonging and learning in online interactions – a literature review. *Technology, Pedagogy and Education, 23*, 243–265. https://doi.org/10.1080/1475939X.2013.81305

Doman, E., & Webb, M. (2017). The flipped experience for Chinese university students studying English as a foreign language. *TESOL Journal, 8*(1), 102–141.

Education Endowment Foundation. (2021, May 8). *Remote learning: Rapid evidence assessment*. https://educationendowmentfoundation.org.uk/public/files/Publications/Covid-19_Resources/Remote_learning_evidence_review/Remote_Learning_Rapid_Evidence_Assessment.pdf

Flipped Learning Network. (2014). *Flipped learning*. https://flippedlearning.org/definition-of-flipped-learning/

Frymier, A. B., & Houser, M. L. (2000). The teacher-student relationship as an interpersonal relationship. *Communication Education, 49*, 207–219. https://doi.org/10.1080/03634520009379209

Hall, A. A., & DuFrene, D. D. (2016). Best practices for launching a flipped classroom. *Business and Professional Communication Quarterly, 79*, 234–242. https://doi.org/10.1177/2329490615606733

Hung, H-T. (2017). Design-based research: Redesign of an English language course using a flipped classroom approach. *TESOL Quarterly, 51*, 180–192. https://doi.org/10.1002/tesq.328

Jia, C., Hew, K. H., Bai, S., & Huang, W. (2021). Adaptation of a conventional flipped course to an online flipped format during the Covid-19 pandemic: Student learning performance and engagement. *Journal of Research on Technology in Education.* https://doi.org/10.1080/15391523.2020.1847220

Krathwohl, D. R. (2002). A revision of Bloom's taxonomy: An overview. *Theory into Practice, 41*, 212–218.

Marshall, H. W., & Kostka, I. (2020). Fostering teaching presence through the synchronous online flipped learning approach. *Teaching English as a Second Language Electronic Journal (TESL-EJ), 24*, 1–14.

McGuinness Institute/ Te Hononga Waka. (2021, May 7). *New Zealand COVID-19 timeline.* www.mcguinnessinstitute.org/projects/pandemicnz/covid-19-timeline/

Watson Todd, R. (2020). Teachers' perceptions of the shift from the classroom to online teaching. *International Journal of TESOL Studies, 2*, 4–16. https://doi.org/10.46451/ijts.2020.09.02

Zou, D., Luo, S., Xie, H., & Hwang, G-J. (2020). A systematic review of research on flipped language classrooms: Theoretical foundations, learning activities, tools, research topics and findings. *Computer Assisted Language Learning.* https://doi.org/10.1080/09588221.2020.1839502

PART II

Adapting to teaching academic skills online

Katherine Mansfield

Around the world, HE institutions offer courses which aim to develop AE skills of which, listening and speaking, and writing are the most common. These courses enable students, academics, and researchers to communicate more effectively in academia. Part II explores how five countries (Luxembourg, Chile, Argentina, Albania, and Uzbekistan) adapted such courses to the online environment as their way of responding to the crises brought about by the global pandemic. Each chapter provides insight and ideas on teaching a particular skill online, whilst at the same time demonstrating how the lessons learned from the pandemic will or are already being incorporated into skills-based courses available in either blended or online form. Although the authors of these chapters refer to commonly cited problems faced by those involved in emergency remote teaching (Hodges et al., 2020), the main issues pertaining to teaching academic skills online were (1) an increase in workload for instructors setting up, managing, and giving feedback on their courses; (2) the difficulty in mirroring the face-to-face environment; and (3) the lack of student socialisation and motivation in and outside the online classroom.

An increase in workload was mentioned by most of the authors as they strove to develop their academic skills courses online in the face of the pandemic. Wanting to avoid digital fatigue and overcome possible technological problems, Katrien Deroey and Jennifer Skipp (Luxembourg) and Gracielle Pereira-Rocha (Chile) sought ways to reduce synchronous contact by making videos to be used asynchronously, which gave summaries of a particular theory, skill, or practice. Laura Colombo (Argentina) took a highly personalised approach sending a survey to her students to discover their preferred class time, personal situation, and working space available, and with this information designed the course. All the contributors found a variety of online platforms and websites (WhatsApp,

DOI: 10.4324/9781003283409-9

Instagram, WebEx, Zoom, Doodle, Edmodo, BigBlueButton, Discord, Moodle, Quizlet, Padlet, and Tedx) they believed to be pertinent to enriching the online experience and giving students the opportunity to practise their skills. *Padlet* was used by Diana Akhmedjanova and Feruza Akhmedova (Uzbekistan) and *Edmondo* by Colombo as a space for students to share their ideas and practise their writing. However, with such a variety of resources on offer, the contributors found it extremely challenging and stressful not only managing, keeping track of, and negotiating the different channels, but also giving summative and formative feedback on written tasks. On reflection and having analysed student feedback, many of the authors have reduced the number of channels to prevent this from happening again.

Due to the unpreparedness of institutions to move online and wanting to mirror in class teaching, many reconsidered their typical teaching approach. Akhmedjanova and Akhmedova transitioned from Communicative Language Teaching to a teacher-centred approach due to time constraints, whereas Mirela Alhasani (Albania) endeavoured to keep a student-centred approach. Wanting to enhance the student-led approach, Deroey and Skipp, Colombo and Pereira-Rocha chose to make their courses more personalised and adopted a highly humanistic approach whereby the instructors were inherently more flexible, helpful, supportive, and available. They acknowledged this approach was more time-consuming but discovered it empowered the students and increased their confidence, particularly in writing and speaking.

The contributors recognised that teaching online meant students missed out on the vital socialisation that occurs during breaks, in the hallway and after class. As they mention, students need to get to know each other so they do not feel uncomfortable communicating in an open class and they need their own dialogic spaces where they can discuss what they have learnt and air their concerns. Wanting to address this issue, Pereira-Rocha requested students work in small groups where they were encouraged to express their opinion, and Colombo asked her students to set up a WhatsApp group, but still acknowledged this was not enough. Akhmedjanova and Akhmedova's research found that their students often lacked motivation and focus online. They believe that by offering a more personalised approach that considers the appropriate learning styles of the learners, students will be more motivated and focused online.

Each chapter in Part II adds value to the body of knowledge surrounding the teaching of academic skills online in turbulent times. Dereoy and Skipp, in a bid to mitigate the time constraints and somewhat isolating experience of doctoral writing, transformed their writing course to ensure it was interactive, personalised, flexible, and sustainable. Their research shows that the students appreciated the convenience of writing collaboratively online and the quantity of time online pedagogy saved them. As online learning was not novel in Chile, Pereira-Rocha was consciously aware of the requirements of her students. Her research revealed higher student attendance during uncertain times, students receiving the same quality of pedagogy, but slightly lower academic performance. Colombo demonstrates how by adopting a highly personalised humanistic approach and using numerous online platforms, she was able to deepen the dialogues she had with her students and expose the complexities of writing for publication. Alhasani's research shows that despite being unprepared for the digital shift, students were overwhelmingly positive regarding the quality of the online teaching and reported the acquisition of both listening and speaking skills. Akhmedjanova and Akhmedova reveal the importance of "communities of practice" (Wenger, 1998) as the lecturers met every week to discuss upcoming sessions, which not only aided their confidence in teaching academic reading, writing, and listening online, but also improved the quality of their seminars. All the contributors have developed successful and sustainable online academic skills courses that will continue to run post-pandemic. They have all learnt from this novel method of pedagogy and their lessons will feed into future versions of their courses, either fully online or in a blended format.

The opening chapter in Part II, by Deroey and Skipp, takes place in Luxembourg and reports on the design, delivery, and evaluation of an online research article writing course for PhD students. Following Deroey and Skipp's observations, adaptations, and lessons learnt, the second chapter shows the research findings of Pereira-Rocha on a similar Doctoral Writing Course in the Chilean context, which focuses on how to write a research article in the STEM disciplines. Continuing with the theme of Doctoral writing, Colombo offers further insight into the teaching of situated-learning writing workshops for publication in Argentina which focus on a dialogical approach. Alhasani, in the fourth chapter, focuses on different skills through the exploration of postgraduate academic reading and writing course in Albania, a country which was somewhat unprepared for the Covid-19 digital shift. The final chapter in Part II, written by Akhmedjanova and Akhmedova, lands us in Uzbekistan where an academic English module focusing predominantly on academic writing, reading, and listening skills is discussed.

Reference list

Hodges, C., Moore, S., Lockee, B., & Bond, A. (2020). The difference between emergency remote teaching and online learning. *Educause Review*, 27, 1–12.

Wenger, E. (1998). *Communities of practice: Learning, meaning and identity*. Cambridge University Press.

7

DESIGNING AND DELIVERING AN ONLINE RESEARCH ARTICLE WRITING COURSE FOR DOCTORAL STUDENTS IN LUXEMBOURG DURING COVID-19

Katrien L. B. Deroey and Jennifer Skipp

Introduction

This chapter describes the development, delivery, and evaluation of an online research article writing course for doctoral students at the multilingual University of Luxembourg. The shift to online delivery followed the university's closure due to Covid-19. The adaptation of the course for "emergency remote teaching" (Hodges et al., 2020) provided experiences and feedback, which allowed us to better meet PhD students' needs during Covid and beyond.

Doctoral students are under increasing pressure to publish in English early in their PhD (Paré, 2010). Apart from potential linguistic issues, the challenges and needs these novice research writers experience can be manifold. This may include a lack of academic writing training (Caffarella & Barnett, 2000), limited understanding of the publication process and efficient writing practices, a lack of awareness of "Anglophone" writing conventions (Angelova & Riazantseva, 1999), as well as discipline and genre-specific conventions and anxiety caused by inexperience (Caffarella & Barnett, 2000). Furthermore and importantly, doctoral candidates have substantial research duties and additional work and family commitments (Caffarella & Barnett, 2000; Casanave, 2010) since about 60% are aged between 26 and 37 (OECD, 2019). During the pandemic, some students had to additionally cope with Covid-related challenges, such as homeschooling, attending virtual conferences or meetings, teaching online, working from a different time zone, and reduced contact with research colleagues.

The online course described here adopts a flexible, interactive, and personalised approach. It considers the affordances and challenges of the online teaching environment, as well as doctoral students' contextual needs and aptitude for independent work.

DOI: 10.4324/9781003283409-10

Context

The University of Luxembourg is a small university founded in 2003 with three official languages (French, German, English) and three faculties located at campuses in two cities. It forms part of a network of "Greater Region" universities located across the borders from Luxembourg in France, Germany, and Belgium. Its doctoral student population is unusual in that no single language or geographical origin predominates. The English section of the language centre has one permanent lecturer (the first author, Katrien Deroey), who heads a small team of hourly paid adjunct lecturers (including the second author, Jennifer Skipp).

Pre-Covid, the local context already created several challenges in course design and delivery.

- The course demand far outstripped our offer due to difficulties recruiting teachers locally and the need to work with small groups so that interactive, personalised learning was possible. This also led to disciplinary heterogeneous groups.
- Some students lost considerable time travelling between campuses to attend the course and students from the Greater Region could not participate.
- The course concept and materials developed by the first author had to be teachable by (new) adjunct teachers and the associated workload fair.

However, there were also significant contextual affordances.

- The existing course had fully developed course materials, was credit-bearing, and had been taught several times.
- On the basis of the submission of a research article (draft), students were admitted to the course only if their language proficiency would allow them to benefit from it and they had writing to apply their learning to.
- The university has well-developed online learning facilities and our PhD students tend to have good computer skills and Internet access.

Course reorganisation at the start of the pandemic

Pre-Covid, the summer semester course (February-May) was run in its usual ten-week format by the second author with a group of 13 students. It consisted of (1) five 1.5-hour theory "input" sessions and five three-hour writing "output" sessions, (2) mandatory independent tasks from the e-book, (3) periodic submissions of article drafts and a writing log, and (4) optional writing consultations. Class sessions and writing consultations were held face-to-face, while coursework was managed through the virtual learning environment, Moodle. When the university closed mid-March 2020, the course needed to continue as scheduled, but the face-to-face sessions had to be replaced. The university chose the video-conferencing platform WebEx for remote teaching and prohibited the use of Zoom due to security concerns. WebEx training videos and IT support were provided centrally.

Emergency remote teaching created several challenges. First, some students could not attend scheduled sessions due to their children's home schooling or altered work schedules. Second, contact with colleagues to provide writing feedback was reduced. Third, WebEx could not be used for the essential small group work since at the time it did not have breakout rooms. Fourth, both the lecturer and students had very little time to familiarise themselves with the online teaching environment, adding sudden extra work and affecting the efficiency of classes. Finally, we had to be mindful of digital fatigue due to the increase in online work.

To meet these challenges, the lecturer made the following adaptations, considering what was feasible for herself and the students, while trying to maintain quality. Instead of the input sessions, she made short video summaries of the theory, which students watched in their own time and submitted the accompanying tasks as evidence of their learning. In 45-minute online follow-up sessions, findings were discussed and learning consolidated through small group work using Discord (an online gaming platform which hosts breakout rooms). Writing sessions were done independently and the texts were submitted on Moodle along with a writing journal. These course adaptations, as well as students' difficulties in attending sessions and submitting tasks on time, meant a significant sudden increase in the lecturer's workload. Fortunately, students remained highly motivated, were able to process the theory independently, and completed assignments well.

The new online research article writing course

Following emergency remote teaching during the summer semester of 2020, the course was redesigned for continued remote teaching beyond Covid during the academic year 2020–2021. This was done to make it more time-efficient for students and to enable participation by Greater Region students. The online course described here was first delivered in the winter semester (October–December) of 2020. The course concept and e-book were developed by the first author, drawing on her experience teaching research article writing, knowledge of the relevant (research) literature, and previous in-house materials and publications, for example, Deroey (2011).

The course concept was built on the following premises:

- PhD students are usually self-motivated and capable of independent learning (Flowerdew, 2015). This allows for a flipped classroom approach and unsupervised work.

- Given the many demands on their time (Casanave, 2010), classes should be limited in number and should constitute "added value" by focusing on issues that benefit from interaction.
- Students' linguistic, writing, and disciplinary needs vary, necessitating some degree of personalised and discipline-specific learning (Hyland, 2002).
- Peers and disciplinary experts are important additional learning resources (Cho & MacArthur, 2010; Zhu, 2004).
- Learner autonomy and continuous learning benefits from an ability to analyse and improve one's own writing in terms of linguistic accuracy as well as genre and discipline-specific conventions (Charles, 2018; Yasuda, 2011).

The e-book contains theory and tasks on the writing and publication process, paragraphing and coherence, constructing clear sentences, reducing wordiness, and the structure and associated language of research article sections. It was written to allow "self-directed" learning (cf. Fenton-Smith et al., 2018) by a mixed-discipline audience, with the teacher acting as a learning facilitator. To this end, the theory is accompanied by awareness raising tasks that focus on their own writing and research articles using a genre-based pedagogy (cf. Yasuda, 2011) and data-driven learning approach (e.g., corpus work, Charles, 2018).

The redesigned course described was run twice in the winter semester of 2020 (WS20) and twice in the summer semester of 2021 (SS21) for groups of ten to 15 students. Feedback was obtained through an online survey from all 48 students (see "Student feedback and teachers' experiences"). Class sessions were held on WebEx, which by WS20 allowed breakout rooms, while Moodle was used for materials and coursework.

The course comprised five interlocking components, illustrated in Figure 7.1. Synchronous classes, consultations, and peer review meetings provided opportunities for teacher and peer interaction. Asynchronous coursework consisted of independent learning tasks, writing submissions, and peer review reports. Coursework was reviewed by the teacher but not graded; there were no formal assessments.

For the **independent learning tasks (ILTs)**, students read chapters from the e-book at home, did the generic exercises with answer keys, and submitted tasks from the chapters in which they applied the theory to their writing. This writing was then incorporated into corresponding classes to generate collaborative tasks. This flipped classroom approach limited the number of classes and promoted personalised learning. For instance, to prepare for the session on conciseness in the following week, students would read the e-book chapter on "Reducing wordiness" and submit the task in Figure 7.2. In the subsequent session, the teacher would use examples from this task to recap and illustrate key theory points and to create (small) group work tasks.

In addition to tasks on features of academic writing such as conciseness, students completed tasks on the writing and publication process, analysed article

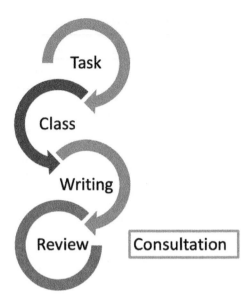

FIGURE 7.1 Course components (WS20–SS21).

Read approximately 500 words of your own text. Paste that text here.

a) Bold instances of wordiness.

b) Use the 'review' 'track changes' function in Word to show how you have made those passages more concise.

c) In the list below, bold the most common source(s) of wordiness in your writing.
-Including information that is not really necessary or relevant
-Adding text in brackets or footnotes because I don't know how important it is or because I can't work out how to incorporate it into the running text
-Repetition (points or words)
-Stating the obvious
-Wordy phrases
-Indirect structures

FIGURE 7.2 Example of an independent learning task from the e-book chapter "Reducing wordiness".

sections from their disciplines, and practised using corpus tools to solve lexico-grammatical and stylistic questions (e.g., AntConc, the British National Corpus (BNC), the British Academic Written corpus (BAWE), the Hong Kong Research Article corpus (HKRA), LexTutor). As Flowerdew (2015) notes, a corpus-based pedagogy can be particularly appropriate for motivated and independent learners,

TABLE 7.1 Course overview for WS20 and SS21.

	WS20	SS21
Credits (ECTS)★	Three	Two
Independent learning tasks	Eight	Seven
Classes	1.5 hours/session, six sessions, participation in minimum four	Three hours/session, six sessions, participation in minimum four
Writing	Text representing 15 hours of work, five submissions, separate writing log	Texts of minimum 500 words, three submissions, in-text reflections on writing
Peer review	Peer review meetings (four–five students/group), review of min. Two peer texts, peer review report summarising reviews received	Unchanged
Consultation	Optional, 45 minutes	Mandatory

Table 7.1 Course overview for WS20 and SS21.
★Following Bologna Agreement guidelines, one ECTS (European Credit Transfer and Accumulation System) represents roughly 25 hours of work, including attendance.

as doctoral students often are. Our students were indeed interested in these tools and able to use them, but few compiled their own corpora for use with AntConc (not mandatory).

Class sessions used WebEx for teaching and group work. Following students' positive feedback on these sessions (see "Student feedback and teachers' experiences"), they were increased to three hours in SS21 from 1.5 hours in WS20. The slides and activity sheets for the sessions were provided beforehand on Moodle. As described earlier, students' ILT submissions were used to illustrate and practise the theory. Breakout rooms were used for small group work on students' examples, groups were asked to prioritise their own examples, and one member shared her/his screen with the activity sheet. Cameras had to be on during breakout rooms and the teacher "dropped in" and provided input if necessary. In the subsequent plenary, the teacher shared her screen and students reported the outcome of their small group work, asking additional questions in the chat or unmuting themselves. Students generally engaged well, obviously in no small part due to the use of their examples. Many sessions additionally integrated proofreading work with corpus tools. The teacher performed the initial queries through a shared screen with students mirroring the process. Participants then performed their own searches and shared their results and evaluation of the tools.

The **writing** component consisted of periodic submissions of draft extracts from a research article together with notes on how the text reflected learning (see Table 7.1). Pre-Covid, writing happened in "output" sessions, but during Covid they wrote in their own time, periodically submitting evidence of their writing along with questions and reflections. In WS 20, they had to submit five texts documenting 15 hours of writing with a log. However, some students asked to submit fewer times with longer texts and the log was poorly performed. In SS21, we therefore required three submissions each of c. 500 words and asked for reflections on the writing to be added in the text.

Peer review was a new component and was largely managed by the participants, who in their mixed-discipline peer groups of four to five members arranged meetings online and shared their texts on Moodle. Each member received one round of peer reviews and had to review the text of at least two others. Meetings were unsupervised but the rationale for peer review was explained in the first class session and detailed in writing (steps, timeline, maximum size of texts, conduct, and sample questions). To document the peer review, students submitted the reviews together with a summary of the peer feedback and what they had learnt from it.

Peer review is a relatively non-threatening way of obtaining feedback that can be especially useful for less confident, novice research writers and to supplement teacher feedback. In the online environment particularly, peer review also promotes a sense of community by "integrat[ing] writing into a social context, providing readers who have more time and patience than the teacher, and who probably have reasonable insights into the writer's difficulties" (Breeze, 2012, p. 145). Caffarella and Barnett (2000) found that giving and receiving feedback from peers and professors was the most effective in improving doctoral students' insights into academic writing and producing better texts. By receiving feedback from several peers, writers gain multiple perspectives on their texts, improving audience awareness, while giving feedback helps develop self-evaluation writing skills (Cho & MacArthur, 2010).

Consultations addressed personal writing issues. Students used Moodle's "scheduler" to book a 45-minute consultation slot and submitted their texts with questions 48 hours ahead of the meeting. In WS20, not all students requested a consultation, but those who did found it useful (see section (5)). Hence, we made consultations mandatory in SS21.

Student feedback and teachers' experiences of the online delivery

This section summarises course feedback and our experiences, along with changes made in response. Feedback about course delivery and components was obtained anonymously from all 48 students (four cohorts: WS20 = 30, SS21 = 18) using an

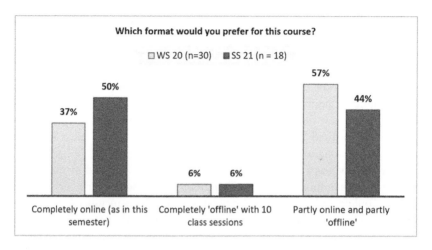

FIGURE 7.3   Preferred course delivery format (N = 48).

online Qualtrics survey with a five-point Likert scale, multiple choice, and open-ended questions. Minor changes were made to the SS21 survey to reflect course adaptations.

Regarding the choice of course delivery format (Figure 7.3), students overwhelmingly dispreferred fully face-to-face ("offline") delivery (3/48), preferring instead a completely online (20/48) or blended format (25/48).

Reasons cited for completely online delivery were the convenience of working with others through online platforms and time saved travelling to the course site. The increase in this choice in SS21 could have been because students had grown more accustomed to online learning and possibly also reflects improvements we had made to online coursework and communication. Of those who chose blended delivery, most selected peer review discussion as the activity they would like to happen face-to-face. This suggests the importance of these interactions to doctoral students, particularly in challenging times. As we can see in Figure 7.4, all course components were perceived as useful.

Independent learning tasks were rated as very useful in both semesters. An additional question in the SS21 survey asked about the least and most useful ILTs. It showed that over 50% found no ILT "least useful". Depending on the specific topic, between c. 72 and 83% found the ILTs on general features of academic writing (coherence, clarity, conciseness) most useful, compared to the ILTs on article sections or the writing/publication process, rated as most useful by c. 22%. This is in line with findings from another SS21 question revealing that half the students enrolled to improve their academic writing generally. Importantly, the popularity of the academic writing ILTs was likely also due to students being

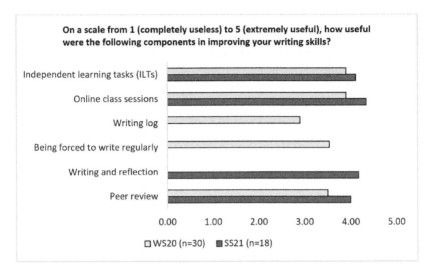

On a scale from 1 (completely useless) to 5 (extremely useful), how useful were the following components in improving your writing skills?

Independent learning tasks (ILTs)
Online class sessions
Writing log
Being forced to write regularly
Writing and reflection
Peer review

0.00   1.00   2.00   3.00   4.00   5.00

☐ WS20 (n=30)   ■ SS21 (n=18)

FIGURE 7.4   Perceived usefulness of course components (N = 48).

*Items with single bars represent differences between components across semesters.

able to identify these issues as areas for personal improvement, especially after being confronted with their examples in class:

> I found a lot of mistakes' by doing these tasks.
>
> *(SS21)*

> These were my weaker points (I feel), and a guided protocol helped me improve them.
>
> *(SS21)*

Online **class sessions** were considered especially useful (Figure 7.4). All students believed they were "a useful addition to the ILTs". A SS21 question further revealed that being able to absorb theory before class was rated important to extremely important and offered "the right balance between theory and practical exercise". Most WS20 students and all SS21 students found "reserving class time for exercises and discussion rather than theory" (extremely) important. They also found working on their own examples (extremely) important even if no ready-made keys could be provided. These findings confirm the benefits of the flipped, personalised approach.

Following WS20 feedback, we increased session lengths from 1.5 hours (WS20) to three hours (SS21), with two breaks of five minutes and one of 15, thus providing more time for students to discuss and share their text revisions.

By WS20, students were familiar with WebEx, so there were no persistent technical issues. Participation remained consistent throughout the plenary and break-out sessions, but as with any course regardless of delivery mode, the same few participants contributed comparatively little.

Students appear to have negotiated the writing components of the course well and clearly saw the benefits of "being forced to write regularly" (Figure 7.4). Their texts and reflections suggest an application of their learning from ILTs and classes. All rated "being able to choose when I write" as important or extremely important. This underlines the key doctoral writer "want" of independently setting the time for writing.

In WS20, many comments regarding the course workload concerned the frequent text submission deadlines and the log. The log was regarded by some as "forced", "a poor use of time" and "an unnecessary addition" to their writing. The instructors found logs to be poorly completed and lacking adequate reflection. In SS21, we thus required fewer submissions, spaced them more evenly, and asked students to reflect on their writing in the text. This improved the score for workload manageability and eliminated negative comments about deadlines. Importantly, in-text reflection made it clearer how students were integrating e-book theory and class learning. For example, in the WS20 survey, one student highlighted how the course "introduces very useful linguistic [corpus] tools that I was not aware of", but writing logs yielded little evidence of their use; by contrast, track changes and notes in in-text reflections showed more evidence of corpus searches.

> Students largely regarded **peer review** as a success.
>
> *(See Figure 7.4)*

> I think it helps to become aware of your communication and linguistic limits.
>
> *(WS20)*

In particular, the benefit of working with peers from outside their field and the comparative element this offered was noted by approximately a third of the students in both semesters:

> Useful to get feedback from people from various backgrounds (scientific, nationalities, studies).
>
> *(SS21)*

> We could observe how different research fields "require" different styles and/or writing strategies/structure.
>
> *(WS20)*

Indeed, not working in the same discipline was sometimes perceived as useful to judging writing more holistically, especially for clarity and coherence:

> When people who are not from my research group read my writing, they can see details my colleagues may skip due to the accustomness of the words and concepts.
>
> *(WS20)*

> Getting feedback from colleagues in different fields helped me to improve the clarity of the sentences. This helps to spread the message of my research to a broader audience besides my specific field.
>
> *(SS21)*

The very few students who did not find peer review useful cited reasons such as the time involved and the perception that some members did not provide adequate feedback due to insufficient effort or different disciplinary affiliations. In the future, peer groups may meet face to face and we will provide more details in class about effective peer review to ensure all members are engaged and give useful feedback.

The coursework (ITLS, writing, peer review) was substantial with almost weekly deadlines. In WS20, around a quarter of students criticised the number and management of submissions and deadlines:

> There was a lot to do regularly (writing log, ITL exercises, peer review, courses sessions) in parallel of the usual PhD tasks.
>
> *(WS20)*

In SS21, we therefore reduced coursework and the ECTS. This caused comments about insufficient credits for the workload, which highlights the importance of credits as a "pay off". This workload/ECTS balance needs to be monitored as we may have underestimated the time needed to complete coursework, perhaps especially by "weaker" students. However, regardless of the number of credits, a few students in both semesters invested limited effort in ILTs. Returning sub-standard work initially increased our administrative burden but often prevented subsequent poor efforts.

Consultations received a mean usefulness score of 4 in both semesters (1= completely useless, 5= extremely useful). Following this high score in WS20 and positive comments about targeted, personalised suggestions, they became mandatory in SS21. They also helped us build rapport with the participants in the online environment. Personalised feedback and the opportunity to consult a writing expert were what most students rated as the main benefits:

> Suggestions were very detailed and specific.
>
> *(WS20)*

> It helped me to develop awareness on other issues I face when I write.
>
> *(SS21)*

> I find it useful because I had the occasion – for the first time in my academic career – to receive insightful comments exclusively on the formal aspects of my scientific writing.
>
> *(SS21)*

Overall, course feedback and experiences show that an online research article course can engender convenience and flexibility and can maximise various productive interaction patterns. However, coursework and deadlines need to be carefully planned and commensurate with the allocated credits.

Pedagogical implications and lessons learnt

Remote teaching during the pandemic led to a successful reconceptualisation of our doctoral research article writing course as an online course. Three course features were key in its success: flexibility, interactivity, and personalisation.

Flexibility was created through the online format and flipped classroom approach. Independent work with limited online class sessions gave students greater flexibility in managing their work schedules and avoided time spent travelling to classes. In the post-pandemic world envisaged by Gomez and Collela (2020), digitalisation would enable students to choose from a wide range of content, building their own curricula at different institutions as the credit system is unified. Our course model allows this.

Interactivity was established through group work in class sessions, peer reviews, and consultations. Research on the efficacy of online interactions in distance learning suggests that a mixture of student-content, student-student, and student-teacher interaction promotes learning (Bernard et al., 2009). Moreover, interacting with peers and teachers can mitigate the often isolating experience of PhD life and offer students regular engagement that can "help them through a difficult time" (Gomez & Collela, 2020, p. 11). In our course, working with mixed-discipline groups did not pose significant problems and was sometimes even highlighted as useful by students. It may also constitute an advantage in the current interdisciplinary research climate by raising awareness of how the (writing) conventions of one's discipline differ from those of others and by creating interdisciplinary networks. As Thomson and Allan (2010, p. 423) note, "in multi-disciplinary and inter-disciplinary research it is more important than ever for doctoral students to form and use networks not just in their own discipline but across disciplines".

Personalised learning was key in the perceived usefulness of the course. This is not surprising as areas for improvement will vary with disciplinary, writing, publication, and language backgrounds. Since this diversity to a greater or lesser extent may also exist in similar courses at other institutions, a personalised approach deserves careful consideration despite potentially involving more work for teachers.

Apart from these strengths, we will also consider attested weaknesses for future course improvement. First, a flexible, multi-component format with substantial independent work requires extremely clear course materials and communication as well as constant monitoring of task completion. The online environment necessitates "more individual follow-up and a strengthened engagement of and communication with students" (Gomez & Collela, 2020, p. 11). Clear and efficient communication was even more important than usual. However, even small adaptations, such as visualising the course format (Figure 7.1) and explaining the coursework schedule in the first session, proved effective.

Second, both student and teacher workload have to be carefully monitored in such a multi-faceted format with extensive independent work. Although students proved capable of independent work and appreciated this study mode, comments on the heavy and persistent workload and ECTS were common. It is thus worth stressing that it might be difficult to get students to engage with a similar course format without credits. Moving forward, we will reconsider the number of ECTS and/or reduce workload, for instance by setting fewer but more substantial tasks. For teachers, class preparation using students' work constituted a significant recurrent time investment. In fact, maintaining the highly valued personalised input while reducing teaching preparation time remains our biggest challenge and one we have yet to find a solution for.

In conclusion, emergency remote teaching during Covid-19 led to a redesigned course, which better addresses the needs of doctoral students. Given its success, we foresee continued online or blended delivery post-Covid. The new online format has in the meantime allowed us to offer the course to more PhD students because it facilitates the recruitment of staff based abroad and enables students from different campuses and Greater Region universities to participate. This widening participation is an extremely positive effect given the direct relationship between writing output and academic status (Aitchison & Guerin, 2014), which is important in "negotiating a professional academic career" (Hyland, 2013, p. 53), securing research funding, and ultimately generating further research.

Reference list

Aitchison, C., & Guerin, C. (2014). *Writing groups for doctoral education and beyond: Innovations in practice and theory*. Routledge.

Angelova, M., & Riazantseva, A. (1999). "If you don't tell me, how can I know?" A case study of four international students learning to write the US way. *Written Communication, 16*(4), 491–525. https://doi.org/10.1177/0741088399016004004

Bernard, R. M., Abrami, P. C., Borokhovski, E., Wade, C. A., Tamim, R. M., Surkes, M. A., & Bethel, E. C. (2009). A meta-analysis of three types of interaction treatments in distance education. *Review of Educational Research, 79*(2), 1234–1289. https://doi.org/10.3102/0034654309333844

Breeze, R. (2012). *Rethinking academic writing pedagogy for the European University*. Rodopi.

Caffarella, R. S., & Barnett, B. G. (2000). Teaching doctoral students to become scholarly writers: The importance of giving and receiving critiques. *Studies in Higher Education, 25*(1), 39–52. https://doi.org/10.1080/030750700116000

Casanave, C. P. (2010). Dovetailing under impossible circumstances. In C. Aitchison, B. Kamler, & A. Lee (Eds.), *Publishing pedagogies for the doctorate and beyond* (pp. 47–63). Routledge.

Charles, M. (2018). Corpus-assisted editing for doctoral students: More than just concordancing. *Journal of English for Academic Purposes, 36*, 15–25. https://doi.org/10.1016/j.jeap.2018.08.003

Cho, K., & MacArthur, C. (2010). Student revision with peer and expert reviewing. *Learning and Instruction, 20*, 328–338. https://doi.org/10.1016/j.learninstruc.2009.08.006

Deroey, K. L. B. (2011). *Academic English: Writing a research article: Life sciences and medicine*. Academia Press.

Fenton-Smith, B., Humphreys, P., & Walkinshaw, I. (2018). On evaluating the effectiveness of university-wide credit-bearing English language enhancement courses. *Journal of English for Academic Purposes, 31*, 72–83. https://doi.org/10.1016/j.jeap.2017.12.001

Flowerdew, L. (2015). Using corpus-based research and online academic corpora to inform writing of the discussion section of a thesis. *Journal of English for Academic Purposes, 20*, 58–68. https://doi.org/10.1016/j.jeap.2015.06.001

Gomez, S., & Collela, C. (2020). *The world of education after COVID-19: How COVID-19 has affected young universities*. YERUN: Young European Universities. www.yerun.eu/wp-content/uploads/2020/07/YERUN-COVID-VFinal-OnlineSpread.pdf

Hodges, C., Moore, S., Lockee, B., Trust, T., & Bond, A. (2020). The difference between emergency remote teaching and online learning. *Educause Review, 27*, 1–12.

Hyland, K. (2002). Specificity revisited: How far should we go now? *English for Specific Purposes, 21*(4), 385–395. https://doi.org/10.1016/S0889-4906(01)00028-X

Hyland, K. (2013). Writing in the university: Education, knowledge and reputation. *Language Teaching, 46*(1), 53–70.

OECD. (2019). *Education at a glance 2019: OECD indicators*. OECD Publishing. https://doi.org/10.1787/f8d7880d-en

Paré, A. (2010). Slow the presses: Concerns about premature publication. In C. Aitchison, B. Kamler, & A. Lee (Eds.), *Publishing pedagogies for the doctorate and beyond* (pp. 42–58). Routledge.

Thomson, C., & Allan, B. (2010). Supporting the learning and networking experiences of doctoral students. In L. H. Dir04kninck-Holmfeld, V. Hodgson, C. Jones, M. de Laat, D. McConnell, & T. Ryberg (Eds.), *Proceedings of the 7th international conference on networked learning* (pp. 421–428). Lancaster University.

Yasuda, S. (2011). Genre-based tasks in foreign language writing: Developing writers' genre awareness, linguistic knowledge, and writing competence. *Journal of Second Language Writing, 20*(2), 111–133. https://doi.org/10.1016/j.jslw.2011.03.001

Zhu, W. (2004). Faculty views on the importance of writing, the nature of academic writing, and teaching and responding to writing in the disciplines. *Journal of Second Language Writing, 13*(1), 29–48. https://doi.org/10.1016/j.jslw.2004.04.004

8

EMBRACING CHALLENGES DURING UNCERTAIN TIMES

Adaptations to a doctoral writing workshop hosted by an English language center in Chile

Gracielle K. Pereira-Rocha

Introduction

English has become the *de facto lingua franca* among academic communities worldwide (Swales & Feak, 2015). As its teaching and learning in Chile remains restricted to formal settings, English is still considered a foreign language. Meeting academics who speak English as a first or foreign language provides students in Chile with practice that improves their reasoning and spontaneous production. In light of the positive impact that publishing in English has on academia, Pontificia Universidad Católica de Chile (PUC) has established the internationalization of research as one of its main lines of action in its short-term Development Plan 2020–2025. To accomplish this goal, PUC created the English UC Language Center (EUC) in 2015. The EUC supports the learning and practice of English through the offer of language courses and academic writing workshops, among other programs and initiatives.

To fully meet the needs of PUC's academic community, especially their linguistic deficiency in academic written English, the EUC designed and currently offers a series of academic writing workshops to PUC doctoral students. The main objectives of these workshops are (1) to raise awareness about the importance of developing academic writing skills, (2) to appropriately apply linguistic conventions into the construction of texts and, (3) to devise effective writing strategies. These objectives represent efforts to even out the writing performance of Chilean researchers with that of international academics.

This chapter will focus on an activities which take place in the academic writing workshops "Writing a Research Article in the STEM Disciplines". These workshops have proven popular over the past few years with PhD students.

DOI: 10.4324/9781003283409-11

Context

The "Writing a Research Article in the STEM Disciplines" workshop

The workshops are offered every academic term at PUC. There are two intensive courses which last three weeks and two regular courses that start in March or August and end in June or December, respectively. Under normal circumstances, there are seven sessions, which take place in a computer laboratory on campus. The computer laboratory provides access to the Internet and word processing software, which facilitate the development of students' writing skills. As the workshop participants use computers throughout the sessions, a minimum level of IT literacy is expected to carry out the class activities and achieve the workshops' objectives.

The workshops follow the genre-informed approach (Tribble & Wingate, 2013), which allows students to examine texts written in English by referents in the STEM disciplines. After participants analyze the text genre, they identify the structure of the text, the relevant linguistic features, the stages of the writing process, and other elements that provide checklists to organize and develop their own writing. The students are expected to apply the aspects of the texts that are relevant to their purpose while assessing the applicability of those characteristics into their work as EFL writers. Thus, the participants connect the theoretical aspects of academic writing, and the writing process with their own academic and research interests and work in progress.

The workshop tasks provide students with the meaningful input they need to write, they encourage the application of valuable and effective strategies, and stimulate participants' reflections on aspects that need development in order to improve their English writing performance. Self-reflection assessments are included in the course, as reflection is viewed as a key component of the teaching and learning cycle (Ryan & Ryan, 2013). These elements are carried out during the prewriting and editing stages, and participants are asked to identify what they have learned about the writing process and how they can overcome their weaknesses by applying remedial strategies. Students commonly recognize technology as a useful solution to tackle their academic writing problems.

The main events that have affected the delivery of the workshops are sociopolitical unrest and the Covid-19 pandemic. The former event brought forward the integration of emergency remote teaching (ERT) at PUC and virtual platforms and software had to replace face-to-face academic activities as they were viewed as the most convenient solution to the situation.

It is important to acknowledge the distinction between the broad definition of online learning and ERT. Whereas one of the main features of online learning is related to students' self-paced processes, ERT relies on features of face-to-face teaching, such as synchronous sessions and the replication of the in-person environment in a virtual setting (Hodges et al., 2020). Given this distinction, the development of this writing workshop in a virtual context is better represented by the concept of ERT.

Chile and Pontificia Universidad Católica de Chile

Lately, Chile has faced two important uncertain scenarios that have affected how traditional educational practices are carried out in the classroom: sociopolitical unrest fomented by civilians began in October 2019 and the outbreak of the Covid-19 pandemic in March 2020.

The sociopolitical unrest continued until the end of the academic year. The civil unrest was triggered by the rise in the cost of living and transport, social inequality, and the lack of trust in state institutions (Alessandri, 2020). This led to massive protests in different locations throughout the evening and night of October 18. Numerous riots and looting occurred, which represented a serious threat to public safety. This also made it impossible to access university campuses on a regular basis since transportation services were disrupted. During these uncertain times, which were aggravated as the weeks went by, the authorities from PUC offered alternatives to the academic community in order to continue performing their regular activities and end the semester in the safest way possible (Monasterio, 2020). One of those alternatives was to hold virtual sessions for the remaining classes for all courses for which this was deemed plausible. Therefore, the university provided all PUC members with licenses for a videoconferencing software tool, so everyone could attend the remaining classes virtually, if this was the option chosen by the instructors and the students.

In the case of the academic writing workshop discussed in this chapter, some adaptations were necessary, but most students were willing to meet in person. Therefore, the remaining sessions were held face-to-face in the morning, even though the original classes were scheduled in the afternoon. Additionally, the remaining sessions were reduced from four to two classes, and each of these classes lasted longer than the regular ones. To guarantee that these academic activities were going to be carried out without major disruptions, face-to-face meetings were resumed on a different campus, since the usual allocated venue was extremely close to a district of Santiago greatly affected by the daily protests, arson, and looting (i.e., Santiago Centro commune – Universidad Católica metro station).

Five months into the sociopolitical turmoil, PUC had no other alternative except to implement virtual classes for all its courses when the cases of Covid-19 were on a steady rise in the country. As the first approach to using videoconferencing software occurred the previous year, it took PUC only one week to transition from in-person classes to ERT modality. The writing workshop was not an exception this time, as it had been delivered in the ERT mode since March 2020.

Local practices

The writing workshops described in this chapter teach students how to write a research article in the STEM disciplines. Students on this course need to use technology to undertake their assessments, regardless of the modality in which the course is taught. Therefore, the instructor and the students are expected to have a basic level of IT literacy to present the contents using audiovisual materials or develop the assignments using digital resources. There are websites and applications that participants can explore, which help them improve the quality of their written texts, especially with regard to morphology, syntax, and semantics. In addition to this, the Office of Graduate Studies at PUC was supportive of facilitating the integration of technologies into the classroom even before the start of ERT. For the last five years, they have reserved a computer laboratory where all the classes are held, and they have also provided students with premium licenses for a well-known editing and proofreading software. These circumstances have been of paramount importance to facilitate the transition from face-to-face to ERT.

Unlike courses where fieldwork or activities that require presentiality are necessary, these writing workshops can be carried out in almost the same fashion in either face-to-face or ERT. The two aspects that determine the successful completion of the workshop are the student's attendance and the final grades obtained, which must be equal to or higher than 75% and 66%, respectively.

The research

To compare and contrast the students' behavior and performance between when the workshop was delivered face-to-face with when delivered in the ERT mode, the data related to students' enrolment on the writing workshops from 2018 to 2021 was analyzed. The purpose of this comparison was to determine how the uncertain times arising from the sociopolitical unrest and the Covid-19 pandemic impacted the teaching of these workshops. Two hundred and sixty-five doctoral students took part in the research and they were divided into two groups: (a) 116 students were enrolled on the workshops when no unusual events that may have affected their attendance and/or academic performance occurred, and (b) 149 students were enrolled on the workshop while Chile was facing the effects of the sociopolitical turmoil or addressing the issues related to the pandemic.

The results show slight statistically significant differences in the levels of participants' attendance and academic performance when the workshops were taught under normal circumstances in uncertain times. While the average student attendance during the terms without unusual events was 81.95%, the average student attendance during uncertain times was 85.92%. However, the opposite trend occurred in terms of academic performance in both groups. Whereas the average academic achievement during periods without disruptions reached

89.93%, the average student academic performance during uncertain times dropped to 84.50%. Thus, it can be inferred that although the students' commitment to the workshops is not affected by the uncertainty that the two aforementioned events may have caused, the quality of their academic performance is. Additionally, as students' exposure to content is higher when the sessions are delivered remotely, the decrease in their grades is likely to be caused by other factors, such as stress, poor time management, or burnout, which are not necessarily related to the workshop teaching modality.

Lessons learnt

The experience of the implementation of ERT has provided some insights into the benefits and disadvantages of this transition. The positive and negative factors related to this change can be explained by the application of the virtual teaching modality itself or by the circumstances that characterize the uncertain times experienced lately. The factors included in this analysis are the following: class structure, assessment focus, students' participation and interaction, the sense of ubiquity, and the participants' expectations of the workshop. This section will show how PUC plans to deal with each one of these areas.

Class structure

Since the classes are held online, the Office of Graduate Studies has been asked to allocate as much time as possible to individual writing practice during the synchronous sessions. In this way, students do not spend too much time working on the assignments after classes. Before this change occurred, discussion of content and group activities was prioritized, relegating individual progress to the remaining classroom and 'out of classroom' time. As of now, 50% of the duration of a session is for individual writing practice, participants perceive they make progress with their assignments more easily and they are interested in attending more sessions. In fact, a group of students formally requested to extend the 20-hour workshop to allow more time for individual practice and feedback. Their petition was accepted, and although the students who requested this change have already successfully completed the workshop, they were invited to join the extra sessions for the following term. They worked individually and collaborated with other participants during the extra ten hours. Thus, the adaptations made to the class structure can be seen as beneficial and in line with the students' expectations.

Assessment focus

With the case of language learning, it is necessary to incorporate and emphasize the assessment of production rather than of comprehension exclusively. Students can be asked to apply the written or aural input they receive (i.e., comprehension) to develop a task that generates an original output (i.e., production) that cannot easily be reproduced. In the case of these academic writing workshops, students are strongly encouraged to develop higher order cognitive skills. For example, when participants have difficulties with some aspects of the writing practice, be it the organization of ideas, semantics, or syntax, they are asked to focus on finding resources, which will help them to solve these problems before submitting their work. This active search for solutions involves metacognitive awareness and strategy development that will help them to become more skillful writers. Students learn to discern when and how they will use specific tools. For example, although the use of translation software is not encouraged, it is still necessary to teach students how to identify situations where their usage could be appropriate. All the tools that can facilitate the learning process should be explored.

The general profile of the participants in this workshop (i.e., age, level of education, former experience with the course topic, and perception of workshop relevance to future work) may positively impact their overall performance and willingness to develop more complex assessments. PhD students know their work should be original and that this takes time to be accomplished, that they are accountable for their own learning process and should understand that all the work they do is worth their time, which is essentially what higher order cognitive skills tasks require.

Students' participation and interaction

Due to the sessions being held remotely, students could not socialize with peers during breaks. Such action facilitates communication and engagement in the class activities because students know who their peers are. Now that students do not see each other in person, some of them are not comfortable speaking and participating during the whole-class activities and discussions in the main room. Conversely, this behavior changes when they are divided into small groups and work with a few classmates only. It is possible to observe that the students who do not participate in the main room actively interact with their partners when working in the breakout rooms. To prevent this awkward interaction from happening in the main room, it is necessary to encourage students, while they work in small groups, to express their opinions and concerns in front of everyone so others can benefit from those questions and explanations. Additionally, with the videoconferencing software used at PUC, it is possible to see the students individually when they need to practice writing, a feature that reduces the distractions that occur in in-person learning (e.g., students going to the restroom, attending a phone call, or talking to a classmate). The instructor remains available at all times in ERT, and requests for help are not shared so concerns are kept private. Students seem to feel at ease when interacting on a one-on-one basis. They ask more questions and even enable the "share screen" feature when they are in the individual breakout rooms, showing their texts to the instructor without feeling exposed in front of their classmates. These actions have a positive effect on the understanding and clarification of contents and practices.

The sense of ubiquity

This is a twofold aspect that some may struggle to manage. On the one hand, remote classes help save time and money. As no one needs to commute to university to attend the sessions, the cost of transportation and time spent traveling do not exist. This allows the instructor to plan and adjust the workshops according to the participants' schedule, who usually agrees on starting and ending the virtual sessions later than the usual in-person sessions, especially in the evening. This option has stopped participants joining late or leaving earlier because they have to travel long distances. On the other hand, the sense of ubiquity has made students get involved in activities that sometimes clash. Several students need to attend meetings, academic events, or carry out non-academic activities during the time of the synchronous sessions. This also occurs in the face-to-face modality, but it has happened more frequently now that the sessions are held remotely. A possible explanation could be the common belief that everyone should always be available since they can work anywhere. Participants are aware of the implications this phenomenon entails, including their performance in the workshop. Therefore, they are encouraged to inform the instructor beforehand when they will be absent and to commit themselves to catching up with the workshop assignments before the upcoming class.

Participants' expectations of the workshop

Being enrolled in the workshop during these uncertain times in Chile has offered a different experience from the one obtained during normal circumstances. The instructor must be flexible in terms of expectations, and everyone has to deal with frustration. According to a survey carried out by the Asociación Chilena de Seguridad in April 2021, the symptoms of depression among the Chilean population increased by 46.7% compared to data obtained in November 2020 (ACHS, 2021). Facing this scenario, the instructor must be more considerate than usual, especially when students need further assistance or request an extension for an assignment. Additionally, problems with Internet connections are prone to happen while the synchronous sessions are held. This may affect the quality of the work being carried out, since it might be necessary to rearrange participants in to new groups. Sometimes there is not enough time left for students to resume the activities and share their insights or writings with their classmates. In contrast, if more time is allotted to the activities when someone has connection issues, the pace of the class is affected. All things considered, the instructor should adopt a supportive attitude that helps students thrive, regardless of the unfortunate scenarios faced. For this reason, classes can be recorded and uploaded on the corresponding Learning Management System (LMS) for students to watch especially when connectivity is affected, and they miss some moments. Additionally, students mentioned in the teaching evaluation survey that they appreciated being treated respectfully and being considered when they expressed what they are struggling with. In this case, an important aspect that goes beyond class content is valued, and it makes a difference in the experience that participants obtain from the workshop.

Global trends

The implementation of ERT reports important advantages for students. The communication between the instructor and the students has become more fluent and spontaneous. It is possible to make adaptations at the institutional level to meet the students' needs, and it is easier to interact and collaborate with academic members worldwide.

Virtual office hours

To keep up the effective communication between the instructor and the students, it would be beneficial to implement virtual office hours on a weekly basis. Instructors would be online during a specific time slot, and students would freely join the synchronous session in order to express their concerns. In places like Chile, where English is a foreign language, this opportunity would provide students with further opportunity to improve their language skills by practicing beyond the course boundaries. In addition, this experience may increase students' accountability of their learning process and reaffirm the conviction that writing requires effort and attention, especially since this is an essential activity in academia. All in all, setting times to address students' concerns conveys that instructors can be easily approached, and thus the students' perception of the workshop remains satisfying.

Online workshops

Offering online workshops can help students meet the requirement of taking optional courses – such as these workshops – more easily. The Office of Graduate Studies states that PhD students must do a research internship abroad, an activity that restricts the number of academic terms in which they can enroll on the workshops when this is offered in face-to-face modality. However, since the pandemic started, some students have attended the workshop while living in other cities or countries due to academic responsibilities or travel restrictions. In all scenarios, they have been able to move toward meeting the graduation requirements even though they are not in the city of Santiago. Thus, offering these workshops online provides students with more chances to meet this requirement at any time during their PhD journey.

Virtual networking events

The considerable increase in the number of virtual events held by academic institutions facilitates networking and communication, which fosters collaboration with other professionals in the EAP area. In this way, it is possible to contact other groups that work in academic writing and invite them to interact with the participants at their own institution. Instructors could offer talks, and students could engage in peer-review activities while communicating in English. This practice would allow students to meet new people who may have similar academic interests or may provide them with insightful perspectives to apply to their research or writing process. Everyone would benefit from this virtual interaction that would not commonly occur under normal circumstances because of the distance and the high traveling expenses. Moreover, participants in Chile would be able to show their work internationally and they would also promote the work of international fellows among the Chilean community.

Conclusion

On the basis of the premise that virtual education is here to stay, some important adaptations are necessary to increase the likelihood of a better and trustworthy online experience for all concerned. This chapter has discussed the adaptations made by the Language Center at Pontificia Universidad Católica de Chile during the Covid-19 crisis and other turbulent and challenging times, focusing on the delivery of a series of academic English writing workshops offered to PhD students. Our discussion shows that the adjustments made, although they have affected the instructor–student interactions and the class pace, were in fact beneficial. This shift to teaching and learning online has brought greater flexibility in terms of academic expectations and a sense of ubiquity. More importantly, our experience has shown that these changes have not affected the quality of the information delivered or the participants' level of commitment. Some of the main changes made were related to what assessments should focus on, and to the sustainability of virtual collaboration worldwide. Our experience has shown that it seems imperative to incorporate assessments that focus on higher order cognitive skills and assess production rather than comprehension.

Additionally, our discussion has shown that virtual networking and collaboration opportunities are not necessarily less engaging or lead to lower quality production compared to in-person activities and should therefore be encouraged. Online partnerships represent a significant change on their own, since they lower the costs of production of events, save time, and assuredly provide a positive experience to all involved in this growing global community.

The aspects mentioned in this chapter should be carefully addressed if we are to improve all that has been implemented until now. There are some adaptations that can be improved so that they can be adopted as permanent solutions to the new, virtual academic reality, even once these turbulent times are over. One of them is the implementation of assessments based on higher order cognitive skills, which would undoubtedly improve students' critical thinking when designed and customized according to the characteristics of the target audience.

Reference list

Alessandri, F. (2020). ¿El fin del Chile excepcional? *Revista Universitaria, 158*, 6–11.

Asociación Chilena de Seguridad. (2021, May 4). *Salud mental de los chilenos empeora en abril tras implementación de cuarentenas: Síntomas de depresión llegan a 46,7%.* www.achs.cl/portal/centro-de-noticias/Paginas/salud-mental-de-los-chilenos-empeora-en-abril-tras-implementacion-de-cuarentenas-sintomas-de-depresion-llegan-a-467.aspx

Hodges, C., Moore, S., Lockee, B., Trust, T., & Bond, A. (2020, March 27). The difference between emergency remote teaching and online learning. *Educause Review.* https://er.educause.edu/articles/2020/3/the-difference-between-emergency-remote-teaching-and-online-learning#fnr13

Monasterio, F. (2020, January 26). Dos tercios de las universidades chilenas aún no cierran el año académico 2019. *Pauta.* www.pauta.cl/nacional/dos-tercios -de-las-universidades-chilenas-aun-no-cierran-el-ano-2019

Ryan, M., & Ryan, M. (2013). Theorising a model for teaching and assessing reflective learning in higher education. *Higher Education Research and Development, 32*(2), 244–257. https://doi.org/10.1080/07294360.2012.661704

Swales, J. M., & Feak, C. M. (2015). *Academic writing for graduate students* (3rd ed.). The University of Michigan Press.

Tribble, C., & Wingate, U. (2013). From text to corpus: A genre-based approach to academic literary instruction. *System, 41*(2), 307–321. https://doi.org/10.1016/j.system.2013.03.001

9

TEACHING WRITING FOR PUBLICATION IN TIMES OF COVID-19

Challenges, affordances, and lessons learned from Argentina

Laura Colombo

A situated learning workshop with a dialogical approach to teaching and feedback

I have been teaching *Lectura y Escritura de Textos Académicos en Lengua Extranjera* (reading and writing academic texts in a foreign language) twice a year for almost a decade. This elective course is taken by students in their last year of *Profesorado Superior de Inglés (Higher Education, High school, and Elementary school English Language Teaching degree)*. It is offered at the *Instituto de Enseñanza Superior en Lenguas Vivas "Juan Ramón Fernández"*, the first Argentinian institution to train foreign language teachers since 1904. Before Covid-19, I met students once a week for almost three hours at the Retiro campus, a building located in the northern part of downtown Buenos Aires. In general, this is a small class (6–15 students per term) since it is offered at the end of the degree.

I designed the syllabus for the course based on situated learning theory (Lave & Wenger, 1990), as well as dialogic approaches to teaching and feedback practices (Charteris, 2015; Dysthe, 2011; Dysthe et al., 2013; Wegerif, 2013). Since academic literacy can be seen as the cumulative result of participating in a variety of social relations and discourse activities (Casanave, 2002), what characterizes this course is the fact that students choose a publication venue and work on a real writing project as detailed in previous work (see Colombo, 2017, 2018). Thus, the students gain hands-on experience on how to write an abstract, a conference paper, or a research article by actually doing it. Therefore, my expectation is for the students to develop and reflect on the professional academic writing practices that English language teachers are involved in when writing for publication. At the beginning of the term, we negotiate together the writing project they will work on during the semester. Most classes are devoted to dialogues about

DOI: 10.4324/9781003283409-12

academic texts, with a particular focus on how people produce and use these writings in specific contexts. We also devote a great deal of time to sharing writing strategies and discussing how to better manage the writing process. Delivered in a workshop format, this course focuses on writers rather than texts, and it frequently revisits these three mottos: you learn to write by writing, you learn to write well by reviewing, and you learn to write and review well by interacting with others.

Working with the writers: unveiling practices and processes through dialogues in the classroom

As previously mentioned, dialogues around texts and writing processes are at the core of this class (Colombo, 2017, 2018), taking up most of the time in the weekly face-to-face encounters. Due to the Covid-19 lockdown, face-to-face dialogues had to be replaced by e-mails, messages in a WhatsApp group, postings in Edmodo (a free learning management platform), and interactions through synchronous meetings using a free Zoom account. Therefore, interactions were mediated through synchronous and asynchronous online technologies.

The institute was not able to offer any additional financial support or paid online resources; thus, we had to rely on our personal skills and material resources. On the plus side, I was not new to online teaching platforms. In fact, I had been using Edmodo for many years to share reading and audiovisual materials, post homework, and ask students to exchange information and submit assignments. As the semester began under lockdown, contact information for students was sent by the institute on an Excel sheet. I first contacted students via e-mail to introduce myself, share the course syllabus, and provide instructions to join the Edmodo class. Additionally, I asked them to reply with a personal presentation, including details about their work, current family conditions, and access to a computer and Internet connection, all aspects that might affect their participation in class.

This first e-mail contact was essential for two reasons: first, to get to know them, and second, to determine whether they could join synchronous meetings using a video conferencing platform. As all the students were also teaching online, the necessary conditions to begin the class were met. Nevertheless, it was not possible to maintain the previous face-to-face schedule as I was faced with child-care issues due to the country's lockdown situation. Consequently, I invited the students to fill out a Doodle (free online meeting scheduling tool) to set the day and time that would be beneficial to all for our synchronous meetings. Since students had no preference for a specific platform and I was familiar with Zoom, I decided to use it for practical reasons. Meetings were shorter than in the face-to-face scenario (no longer than two hours) to avoid screen fatigue and also because we actively interacted in Edmodo and on WhatsApp.

Dialogues about the writing process

Since this class was conceived from a dialogical approach to teaching, at the beginning of the course, I doubled my efforts to open and deepen dialogic spaces (Wegerif, 2013) by encouraging discussions on the different ways of managing the writing process. In pre-pandemic times, opening spaces to different voices talking about their writing processes mainly consisted of assigning readings (e.g., Casanave & Vandrick, 2003; Lamott, 1995) and discussing them in class (for more details, see Colombo, 2018). For this iteration of the course, apart from uploading the PDF files of these readings to Edmodo, I also posted a link to a TED talk (Lamott, 2017) to encourage students to look for and suggest similar materials by replying to the post in Edmodo. This activity was meant to widen the dialogue: new voices took part in conversations about writing processes in the shape of links to Instagram profiles and blog posts. I also asked them to post a picture of their drafting process on Edmodo and write a small paragraph explaining how they usually started writing their academic papers. Although shy at first, they later become enthusiastic about these conversations.

Dialogues about different aspects of the writing process started on Edmodo, but were later discussed and deepened in the synchronous meetings. Halfway through, our class discussions connected our actions, feelings, and strategies and led to drafting a paper. I realized that since our living, working, and studying conditions had changed due to Covid-19, it was important to talk about its influence on our current writing environments. Although social presence (Richardson et al., 2017) was perceived as high during our video conference, conversations about the students' physical location, their personal circumstances, and their writing space helped to build trust and community. I found "peeking" into their workspace as they showed it on camera or in pictures very enriching. This situation made me realize that inviting students to share their immediate surroundings and their experienced realities can enrich dialogues about different ways of conceptualizing, experiencing, and reflecting on their own writing processes, especially when going through difficult circumstances. I am convinced that sharing our writing spaces was a way to defy and also come to accept the isolation and spatiality imposed by the lockdown, which impacted our literacy practices (Gourlay et al., 2021).

Dialogues about the writing-for-publication process

In addition to conversations about writing habits, strategies, and workspaces, dialogues about writing for publication practices and processes were also held in the class. One of the initial tasks was for students to choose a topic and a publication venue for their papers. Similar to dialogues about the writing process, different voices could be included about this topic since students shared their venue, bibliography searches, and findings on Edmodo.

This conversation continued in the synchronous meetings where students expressed that finding a publication venue was not an easy task since many academic events had been cancelled due to the spread of the Covid-19 virus. I noticed that this was negatively affecting them, especially when one student questioned the need to write an abstract without knowing if conferences would ever be held again. To counterbalance this "the-world-has-ended" mindset, I told them about my own experience as a scholar: even though face-to-face events had been cancelled, new opportunities arose, such as virtual European conferences, which I would not have been able to attend if they had not been held online. I illustrated this by "inviting" students into my computer. Using the share screen function in Zoom, I showed them my publication folder where I keep the information for online events. This was also a perfect opportunity to show them different types of academic writing projects: research articles to be published in research journals and abstracts and papers to be presented at conferences, among others. In other words, inviting students into my computer opened dialogues about publication practices and processes, such as the difference between a conference and a research paper, how a conference, a research paper, and an extended abstract might differ. The online nature of this particular class made it possible for me to share this type of information, which had not been the case in the previous face-to-face environment.

While discussing publication venues and different genres, I asked them to use Zoom's interactive functions to share their own information about academic events and class notes. A volunteer student copied the information from the chat and posted it on Edmodo for everyone to access. During the second term, instead of using Zoom's chat and later posting the content on Edmodo, I asked a volunteer student to create and share a word document on Google Drive. Although all of us could edit this document, I asked for a different volunteer in each class to collect detailed notes. The reason to migrate class notes from Edmodo to a shared document was because in Edmodo older posts were not easily visible. Although the platforms mentioned before had several advantages, such as free access and user-friendly interfaces, teachers planning to incorporate varied communication channels need to analyze different venues and tools, taking into account not only their pedagogical purposes but also their students' accessibility to them.

Dialogues about the teaching and learning process

Dialogues and actions around the teaching and learning process were also facilitated in different ways. Since I had experience with online teaching, I knew how challenging it was to design a course that is not teacher-centered. In this regard, delegating responsibilities to students, especially during the synchronous meetings, was very useful. For example, as mentioned earlier, I would ask for a volunteer to create and share a document in Google Drive for our collective class notes, instead of doing it myself. Then, at the beginning of each meeting,

I would ask for one or two volunteers to take notes in the aforementioned document. Another volunteer would post the tasks or homework on Edmodo to be completed before the following meeting. Delegating different classroom management tasks to students can be a means to empower them and involve them in activities that model future professional practices.

Furthermore, I would make a point of sharing the pedagogical rationale behind most of my actions as a professor, stating why I used certain tools and not others. I think opening up my pedagogical decisions encouraged enriching dialogues about teaching and learning. Since most students on this course are usually about to finish their teaching degree, many are already working as English language teachers. This double role as teacher and student provides a unique perspective, often allowing them to offer useful practical advice. For example, one student suggested that each of us could adopt a color when writing in the collective class notes so we could identify who had written it.

Another strategy that I found particularly useful to avoid teacher-centered activities and classroom communication was to suggest the creation of an additional WhatsApp group for the class where I would not be included. After making jokes about disparaging the teacher, I made it explicit that it would be a great place for them to have hallway conversations and to exchange resources and opinions with classmates. This placed peer interactions at the same level as student–teacher interactions because the more voices we could hear about how other people managed their writing project, the more we could deepen and widen the dialogues around writing, writers, and texts. Similar to the other strategies, this one shifted the focus from teacher-initiated interactions to student–student exchanges.

Too much dialogue, too little time

Setting up all the aforementioned types of dialogues was easy. However, keeping track of them took its toll on me, especially during the first term. Apart from my research duties, I teach five writing workshops at two different institutions each term. As a result, I ended up working around the clock, or so it seemed, since WhatsApp messages, e-mails, and Edmodo notifications were received throughout the day, at any hour. Lesson learned? For future online courses, I would devote some time at the beginning of each term to get my communication channels organized so as to avoid feeling overwhelmed.

To this end, I took a number of steps before the following term began. First, I set up a specific e-mail address for all teaching-related notifications to be channeled there. This meant that I invested a fair amount of time asking people to use my new e-mail address, labeling incoming e-mails, and setting up Edmodo's and WhatsApp's notification preferences. Nevertheless, this preparation time later gave me some peace of mind and allowed me to be more focused and less stressed. Second, I allocated specific time slots to my teaching duties and made an effort to respect that. I also established with my students a two-day response period to their inquiries and suggested they take this time to answer each other's inquiries when possible. Finally, dialogues about how to handle our teacher–student and student–student communication allowed us to "authorize" students to keep the conversation going without the teacher and also collectively make decisions. For example, we all agreed that the WhatsApp group would be used for urgent matters (such as not being able to join the meeting), and notifications would be muted so there was no need to establish contact hours. All in all, sharing our rationales and reaching collective agreements from the very beginning helped us to open, deepen, and widen our different types of dialogues.

Conclusion

Teaching face-to-face courses in an online environment due to an emergency situation was not an easy task. Turbulent times such as those resulting from Covid-19 can help teachers discover new tools to open, deepen, and widen dialogues (Wegerif, 2013) as was the case reported in this chapter. In addition to these new situations more and new voices are heard which can provide first-hand experience and allow us to learn from our students.

The first contact we have with students is essential not only to get to know them but also to decide how to deliver the course, ensuring that participation is not affected by technological or access issues. If students' connectivity is adequate, different platforms can be chosen to hold synchronous and asynchronous conversations. Although using different platforms can encourage students to become engaged in dialogue, teachers should be careful to avoid overtaxing themselves by getting involved in every conversation. Teaching online requires teachers to slow down their response time if they want students to participate more actively, allowing new voices to take part in class dialogues.

Another lesson learned during this pandemic is that students do not necessarily take responsibility or communicate with each other if we do not encourage or endorse this type of behavior in class. According to my experience of teaching in higher education in different countries in Latin America and in the United States, we are so accustomed to radial patterns with the professor at the center that it becomes a challenge for students to hold conversations or take responsibility for their own writing and writing processes. Student–student conversations about writing in pre-Covid times usually happened outside the classroom, but those hallway interactions disappeared. I think we can kick-start student–student conversations not only by embracing silence but also by asking them to open their own dialogic spaces.

In addition, opening and widening dialogic spaces is also essential to reach certain agreements so neither the teacher nor the students feel overwhelmed. The class as a whole can collaboratively establish clear rules about each communication channel, specific contact hours, and reasonable response times. Despite the context of the course, having collective agreements is essential. In big-size classes, these agreements can be reached by collecting information from students with a brief questionnaire in Google forms.

For me, the most important lesson learned in these difficult times is that there is no magic formula for teaching online. Every teacher should evaluate together with his/her students the advantages and challenges of using one or multiple platforms and applications and how they can be aligned with their teaching and learning needs. The hardships imposed by the Covid-19 pandemic highlighted the impact our teaching decisions can have on the class and each of our students. Collective decisions are vital, especially in challenging times and when working with future teachers. Writing this chapter helped me reflect on my own practice and come up with new ideas to implement in the future. Nevertheless, my hope is that this chapter has opened a space for dialogue with the readers.

Reference list

Casanave, C. P. (2002). *Writing games: Multicultural case studies of academic literacy practices in higher education*. Lawrence Erlbaum.

Casanave, C. P., & Vandrick, S. (Eds.). (2003). *Writing for scholarly publication: Behind the scenes in language education*. Lawrence Erlbaum Associates.

Charteris, J. (2015). Dialogic feedback as divergent assessment for learning: An ecological approach to teacher professional development. *Critical Studies in Education, 57*(3), https://doi.org/10.1080/17508487.2015.1057605

Colombo, L. (2017). Desarrollo de la escritura y la identidad profesional mediante la revisión entre pares en inglés. In S. Garófalo (Comp.), *Las lenguas en la universidad: Hacia una nueva realidad plurilingüe. Comunicaciones de la I Jornada Lengua, Cultura e Identidad* (pp. 47–56). Universidad Nacional de Quilmes. https://ediciones.unq.edu.ar/474-las-lenguas-en-la-universidad-hacia-una-nueva-realidad-plurilingue.html

Colombo, L. (2018). Teaching writing-for-publishing practices to language teacher trainees: A classroom experience. *Ideas 2da Época, 4*(4), 1–12. https://core.ac.uk/download/pdf/233948225.pdf

Dysthe, O. (2011). "What is the purpose of feedback when revision is not expected?" Case study of feedback quality and study design in a first year Master's programme. *Journal of Academic Writing, 1*(1), 135–142. https://doi.org/10.18552/joaw.v1i1.26

Dysthe, O., Bernhardt, N., & Esbjorn, L. (2013). *Enseñanza basada en el diálogo: El museo de arte como espacio de aprendizaje*. Skoletjenesten & Fagbokforlaget.

Gourlay, L., Littlejohn, A., Oliver, M., & Potter, J. (2021). Lockdown literacies and semiotic assemblages: Academic boundary work in the Covid-19 crisis. *Learning, Media and Technology, 46*(4), 377–389. https://doi.org/10.1080/17439884.2021.1900242

Lamott, A. (1995). *Bird by bird: Some instructions on writing and life*. Anchor Books.

Lamott, A. (2017, April). *12 truths I learned from life and writing* [video]. TED Conferences. https://www.ted.com/talks/anne_lamott_12_truths_i_learned_from_life_and_writing?language=en.

Lave, J., & Wenger, E. (1990). *Situated learning: Legitimate peripheral participation*. Cambridge University Press.

Richardson, J. C., Maeda, Y., Lv, J., & Caskurlu, S. (2017). Social presence in relation to students' satisfaction and learning in the online environment: A meta-analysis. *Computers in Human Behavior, 71*, 402–417. https://doi.org/10.1016/j.chb.2017.02.001

Wegerif, R. (2013). *Dialogic: Education for the internet age*. Routledge.

10

MEASURING GRADUATE STUDENTS' PERCEPTIONS OF AN ACADEMIC ENGLISH READING AND WRITING COURSE DURING TURBULENT TIMES – A CASE STUDY FROM ALBANIA

Mirela Alhasani (Dubali)

Introduction

The first Covid-19 cases in Albania were officially reported in Albania on March 9, 2020, and the Ministry of Education, Youth and Sports immediately introduced teaching and learning at home. The ensuing reliance on technology-aided teaching/learning scenarios found students, academics, and parents totally unprepared logistically and pedagogically and highlighted teachers' and learners' lack of digital competence.

This study examines a postgraduate course (*Academic Reading and Writing*) taught between September and December 2020 by the author at EPOKA University, an international private university in Albania. The research utilises a case study approach supported by a questionnaire carried out via Google forms (see the Appendix), which was sent to 92 students on the course. The questionnaire was based on a similar questionnaire entitled *How has 2020 changed academic English teaching?* conducted in October 2020 by Cambridge University (Cambridge University Press, 2020), which explored the challenges and reactions resulting from the unexpected online teaching format. By adjusting questions to the Albanian context, closed and open questions were used to obtain students' perceptions of their distant learning experience. This case study featuring the EPOKA course contributes to further improvement of the online education strategy for countries like Albania without a well-established tradition of digital education.

The results were overwhelmingly positive from both teachers and students regarding input of theoretical knowledge, students' performance on assigned tasks, and classroom management. Although students initially lacked digital competence, they soon gained greater confidence. However, they indicated problems

DOI: 10.4324/9781003283409-13

with internet access, unreliable devices, unproductive self-regulatory learning styles, and short attention spans during online lectures. Despite the unexpected switch to e-learning, students acknowledged that the online EAP course fulfilled their learning goals and skills. Nonetheless, a puzzling finding was that the participants felt that face-to-face learning cannot yet be replaced by any online teaching mode, regardless of its quality.

This chapter begins with a literature review of theoretical approaches to conventional and digital classrooms, along with empirical findings from international studies on Covid-19 teaching challenges in English for Academic Reading and Writing. Next, global and regional practices of tech-aided schooling shed light on measures, accomplishments, drawbacks, and the state of online education in Europe and beyond. The third section adds an original contribution to knowledge by analysing the perceptions of graduate students at EPOKA University regarding learning aspects, such as off-campus digital competence, the provision of functional digital devices, internet accessibility, motivation, effective learning styles, learning outcomes, and attitudes to self-confidence for future distance education. Recommendations for improving online pedagogy for EAP courses in other off-campus scenarios follow from the findings and point the way to further research on how learners can best cope with online learning.

Literature Review

Conventional teaching of an online Academic English course encompasses three pillars: teaching/learning theoretical approaches, online educational pedagogy, and tailored research about Academic English teaching. Learning in this case is defined as "A persisting change in human performance or performance potential (which) must come about because of the learner's experience and interaction with the world" (Driscoll, 2005, p. 17). Ally (2008, p. 19) describes online learning as the use of the Internet to access learning materials; to interact with the content, instructor, and other learners; and to obtain support during the learning process in order to acquire knowledge, to construct personal meaning, and to grow from the learning experience.

Online distance education (ODE) represents the use of the Internet and other technologies to produce educational content, instruction and program management (Fry, 2001). Schmidt and Werner (2007) highlight the importance of considering students' perceptions about motivation, self-regulation, and future time perspectives in designing online programs to foster their active learning in a semi-blended (virtual) environment. Students have independently been able to access technology without teachers' direct interaction, demonstrating critical thinking and systemic ordering skills (The Florida Center for Instructional Technology, 2021). This valuable finding shows that successful online teaching/learning is a complex process that includes technical adaptations and advanced analytical thinking processes beyond technical competence and acknowledges the benefits of blended learning in students' performance (Yu et al., 2021).

Digitised education has also imposed a shift from conventional learning theories of behaviourism to connectivism (Siemens, 2005). Unlike the classic taxonomy of behaviourism, cognitivism, and constructivism that focuses solely on the learning processes embedded within, connectivism addresses the impact of technology and external manipulative devices involved in the learning process (Siemens, 2005). The core feature of this theory is that learners need to be alert while coping with abundant information by discarding outdated information and learning how to effectively evaluate the importance of new information (Ally, 2008). However, despite challenges in managing online educational tools such as digital game-based activities, they have been shown to result in motivational learning styles and knowledge acquisition (Jiang et al., 2021).

Talib et al. (2021) conducted a systematic review of 40 high-impact journals to assess the impact of technology on HE during the Covid-19 period. Their study identified five research concerns: 1. Impact on education; 2. Students' experiences; 3. Proposals or experiments with a remote teaching platform; 4. Policymaking; 5. Equality between social groups during the pandemic. Their study revealed unpreparedness for the switch to tech-based working, unequal accessibility, and lack of competence to implement this type of learning.

Pokhrel and Chhetri (2021) also provided a review of Covid-19 teaching and learning insights. They discuss the practice of performing student assignments and examinations from home, raising doubts about the authenticity of their work and knowledge acquisition, suggesting different assessment mechanisms may be required for turbulent teaching times (Pokhrel & Chhetri, 2021). They also noted the incompatibility of conventional face-to-face pedagogy with online teaching. Mahyoob (2020) reveals an example of this with the dissatisfaction of EFL learners with online learning and the ensuing non-attainment of learning outcomes at the Taibah University in Saudi Arabia. Another survey concerning learning during the pandemic, which involved 2,652 secondary school students in Austria, underlined the relevance of self-regulated learning leading to the prioritisation of self-regulated learning styles in Austrian secondary education (Pelikan et al., 2021).

More recent EU members, such as Bulgaria, detected the need for intensive training of academic staff on university language programs during the pandemic with the aim of accomplishing learning outcomes equal to conventional teaching (Vesselinov, 2021). Innovative teaching techniques compatible with tech-minded learning are also prioritised in the EU's strategy for the multilingual citizen (Alhasani & Yordanova, 2020). In addition, the literature on Language for Specific Purposes (LSP) asserts that instructors of EAP courses need to adapt the linguistic input and teaching approach to the group's specific linguistic requirements after needs assessment (Stojkovic, 2020) and believes LSP/ESP and EAP courses need to anticipate future developments to enable students' attainment of academic and professional goals.

Online learning requires additional analytical approaches by both instructors and learners to achieve EAP course learning outcomes. For example, online discussion forums (ODFs) can positively affect the development of metacognitive skills, higher order thinking skills, and collaborative learning of students (Ononiwu, 2021). The motivation of online learners has been discussed to ensure quality teaching (Cambridge University, 2020), and addressing students' engagement and authentic e-assessment of absorbed knowledge have been identified as key elements of online learning (Avila et al., 2020). These authors also found that university learners saw social media as an inspirational creative teaching tool during the pandemic, while highlighting the complexity of an accurate analytical assessment of the online teaching/learning process.

Global and Local Practices

Accessibility to quality teaching via virtual classes featured widely in research during 2020–2021. The UNESCO-UNICEF-World Bank conducted a large-scale survey on Covid-19 responses in ten countries, which targeted pre-primary learners and their families (Nugroho et al., 2020). The survey revealed the necessity of addressing pedagogical concerns in the online mode. These include setting clear learning goals, space for all key development domains, and content that boosts interaction. The Global Higher Education Research Snapshot (World Economic Forum, 2020), in cooperation with the market research firm Ipsos, completed a survey of 2,200 students and academic staff. It identified five categories of attitudes relating to education during the pandemic: connection, trust, well-being, flexibility, and careers (World Economic Forum, 2020). The study revealed that 75% of the targeted students felt the need for consistent weekly communication from their home institution. In addition, 50% of the academics involved in the survey stated that the pandemic had increased trust between university leadership, students, and staff (World Economic Forum, 2020). In other words, quality online education requires coherent and cohesive coordination among all structural agents.

Virtual classrooms raise the issue of both learners' and instructors' digital competence. Tools and methods dealing with the unexpected educational lockdown and total digital reliance were immediately addressed by the European Association for Cooperation in Science and Technology (COST), which launched a series of webinars on how to manage education during Covid-19. In addition to this, the European Science Engagement Association (EUSEA) and the COST Cross-Cutting Activity on Science Communication in June 2021 organised a series of interactive seminars on lessons learned, which included practical recommendations for science communication and public management strategies (COST, 2021).

World Vision conducted an exploratory survey in Albania on families' social and economic situation during the pandemic which involved 1,199 households in 15 Albanian municipalities (World Vision Albania, 2020). Additionally, two national surveys about online learning were conducted by the Ministry of Education, Sports and Youth (MESY) and the Pre-University Education Quality Assurance Agency. The first study involved 321,911 children, parents, and teachers to measure the engagement between partners and the effectiveness of remote learning, and 43.6% of parents and 37.8% of teachers confirmed no difference in the quality of teaching (MARS & ASCAP, 2020) after the move online. The second survey with 219,590 participants measured the effectiveness of the teaching process and logistics. Results showed that learners and parents overwhelmingly relied on their smartphones to follow online learning: 95.7% of pupils, 96.8% of parents, and 95.8% of teachers (MARS & ASCAP, 2020). It ascertained the need to combine the adaptation of learning and development objectives by both families and educational institutions for attaining quality interconnectivity (World Vision Albania, 2020).

Regarding university teaching, a study from the State University of Tirana measured students' perception of the influence of Covid-19 through a survey of 627 college students from the natural, medical, and life sciences domains (Xhelili et al., 2021). Students did not consider online learning to be a viable alternative to a physical classroom due to their lack of learners' technology knowledge and lack of self-organisation by instructors. This recent study does not include any analysis about the teaching processes of English for Academic Reading and Writing, and there is no specific literature on EAP courses taught during the Covid-19 pandemic in Albania. EAP courses deserve their own focus due to their important role in equipping those studying at a post-graduate level with necessary research skills. This chapter and its original research aim to address this gap and to demonstrate how EAP courses can be better implemented online.

EPOKA University Survey: Discussion and Follow-up Suggestions

The Google form survey (see the Appendix) was based on a questionnaire by Cambridge University seeking to support EAP instructors during the Covid-19 pandemic (Cambridge University Press, 2020). The original questions were adapted and given to 92 participants (77 master's students and 15 doctoral students from the EAP graduate class) with the aim of assessing learners' perceptions of the challenges and benefits of an English reading/writing course held during the fall semester of the academic year 2020–2021 at EPOKA University in Tirana.

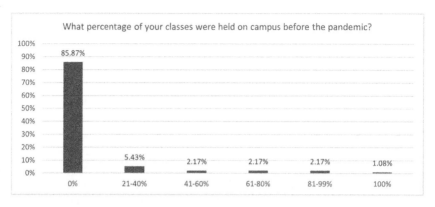

FIGURE10.1   Percentage of classes held on campus before the pandemic.

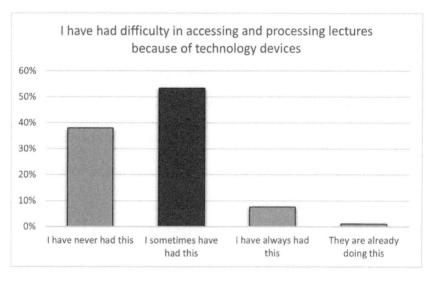

FIGURE 10.2   Percentage of students having difficulty in accessing and processing lectures because of technology devices.

Questions were divided into two thematic groups. The first 13 questions sought feedback from learners about the use of technology, accessibility of the Internet, digital skills level, and the effectiveness of online teaching according to language course learning outcomes. The other ten questions tackled EAP learning/teaching, feedback about linguistic input and output during the online course, motivation, human interaction, learning challenges, and achievements for each language dimension (reading, writing, speaking, listening). Two open questions provided the opportunity for evaluative comments and constructive suggestions.

Figure 10.1 illustrates the starting point of how the clear majority of respondents (85.87%) claimed no previous experience of online learning at university.

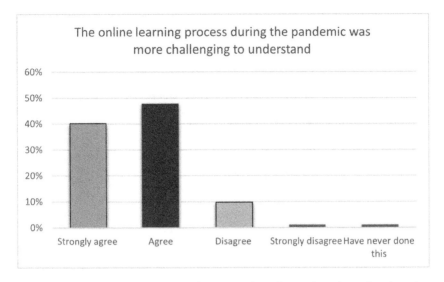

FIGURE 10.3   Students' views on challenges with understanding the online learning process.

Figure 10.2 shows how this lack of experience was then compounded through difficulties related to technology. The lack of solid digital mastery negatively appeared to affect the understanding of class materials with 60.9% of participants claiming to have had difficulty "sometimes" and "always" in processing lectures because of their technological devices.

This lack of experience with the online format and technology difficulties led to challenges with the whole learning process that was introduced in response to the pandemic. 40.22% of the respondents strongly agreed that "the learning process held online during the pandemic was more challenging to understand", and 47.83% just agreed, as shown in Figure 10.3.

Figures 10.4 and 10.5 show how poorly the students rated the effectiveness of online teaching in comparison to face to face, and this was particularly true in areas such as the facilitation of peer interaction and course engagement.

When asked to consider opportunities for a blended approach, combining online and in-person elements, a more nuanced picture emerges. For example, the acquisition of critical thinking scored slightly better for the blended option than for face-to-face alone (51.1% in favour). Developing critical thinkers, capable of judging and interpreting scientific literature, is a key aim of the course, and the willingness to favour a combined approach here points towards some hope for a blended teaching scenario in the future (Figure 10.6).

The open questions offered further insights into the themes which emerged from the survey questions, not least the unreliable internet access at home and

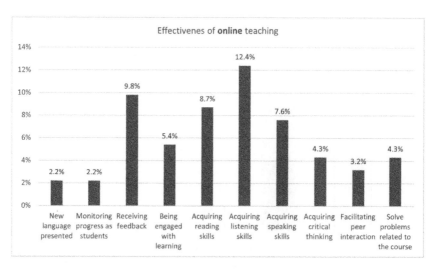

FIGURE 10.4   Percentage of students who believed **online** teaching was more effective for developing selected academic and language skills.

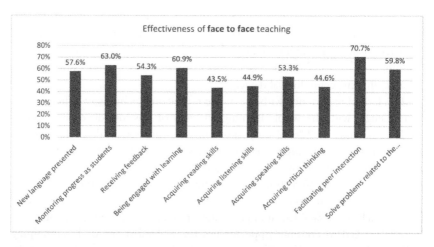

FIGURE 10.5   Percentage of students who believed **face-to-face** teaching was more effective for developing selected academic and language skills.

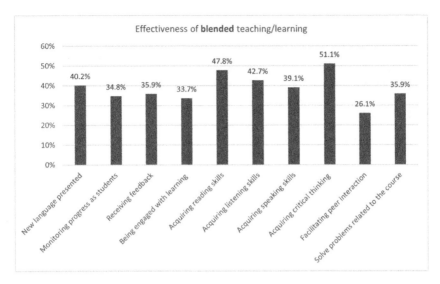

FIGURE 10.6   Percentage of students who believed that blended face-to-face and online teaching was more effective for developing selected academic and language skills.

old devices causing difficulties for learners. Another frequent comment made by students was the lack of motivation and focus throughout the online lecture process. Moreover, they confessed a lack of interest in actively participating since they believed interaction should be generated by the instructors. Some found it hard to submit assignments within the deadlines due to procrastination and lack of self-discipline towards setting agendas to attain learning goals. Despite such challenges, students considered the online courses as an accomplishment for both teachers and students, although they generally rejected more extensive e-education in the future.

Considering the aforementioned feedback, EAP instruction may benefit from encouraging metacognitive abilities to enable self-regulatory learning. Teachers need to integrate the principles of the learning taxonomy (behaviourism, cognitivism, social constructivism) with connectivism (Siemens, 2005). To achieve this aim, further training is required to adapt to learners' needs in the digital environment. A computer does not guarantee quality teaching, rather it is the instructional strategy applied by the teacher that enables effectiveness. Hence, instructors must reflect on the appropriate learning style to be applied in an online classroom. Moreover, EAP instructors should apply cognitive-oriented syllabi to analyse the level of understanding of the class materials, thus facilitating knowledge acquisition and understanding of online learning. Apart from class materials, multi-layered design for personalised learning styles, lack of motivation, and self-discipline proved to be problematic for the survey participants. Lack of learners' motivation calls for a review of strategies by the instructors. Their online teaching activities and task-based exercises should generate systematic preparation, commitment, and enthusiasm for active interaction in virtual classrooms.

Conclusion

This original research aimed to gain insights into the limitations, barriers, and benefits of online university teaching which arose as an unavoidable necessity during the Covid-19 pandemic in Albania. Some surveys on the needs of learners were conducted at secondary level in some municipalities and at the State University of Tirana, but these did not extend to a national level or include private institutions as this research now does. This study comprises a modest, yet original, contribution to the literature on the effectiveness of the online university teaching of EAP. It ascertained that, overall, the 92 respondents were satisfied. However, despite improvements in digital competence, students do not feel ready for total reliance on online teaching and learning.

The overall feedback from students was positive considering the unpreparedness and suddenness the Covid-19 responses required. However, the students in this study were predominantly against wholly online provision largely due to unsustainable internet connections and inadequate smart devices. The open questions and comments pointed to the Albanian government prioritising a reliable digital environment for learners. Such challenges require further elaborative research at a national level for other academic courses. It is the responsibility of academics to provide an effective online teaching environment that anticipates a scenario of fully online teaching rather than the compromise of a blended learning approach. The positive assessments along with critiques and suggestions offered by the survey participants of this investigation point to designs for digital teaching environments that can meet university learners' needs. Academic English teaching processes in turbulent times entail greater efforts by educational authorities and deeper reflections from both teachers and students about the newly emerging digital skills. This study and others that may follow can build both conceptual frameworks and a feasible national educational platform of successful EAP knowledge acquisition in future turbulent times. The Covid-19 pandemic quickly had a negative impact on our lives, but technology allowed education to continue and it can again be used as a vital counterbalance against similar situations in the future.

Reference list

Alhasani, M. D., & Yordanova, M. (2020). Measuring achievement of the formula 'mother tongue+two': A need to improve foreign language proficiency in Europe? In D. Vesselinov & M. Yordanova (Eds.), *Linguodidactic perspectives* (pp. 559–568). Sofia University Press.

Ally, M. (2008). Foundations of educational theory for online learning. In T. Anderson (Ed.), *The theory and practice of online learning* (pp. 19–52). Athabasca University Press.

Avila, E. C., Gracia, A. M., & Genio, J. (2020). Motivation and learning strategies of education students in online learning during pandemic. *Psychology and Education, 57*(9), 1608–1614.

Cambridge University. (2020, October). *Academic English conference* [Video]. YouTube. www.youtube.com/playlist?list=PL-oYKB0D9-E08N3cRkaLtMSFKkLIaufPe

Cambridge University Press. (2020). *How has 2020 changed academic English teaching?* English with Cambridge. www.cambridge.org/al/files/3216/1315/0308/LP_EDITED_EAP_Teacher_Survey_Results_Infographic_Final.pdf

COST. (2021) *EUSEA-COST hot pot on 'public engagement beyond COVID- where do we go from here?'*. www.cost.eu/events/eusea-cost-hot-pot-on-public-engagement-beyond-covid-where-do-we-go-from-here/

Driscoll, M. P. (2005). *Psychology of learning for instruction* (3rd ed.). Pearson.

Fry, K. (2001). E-learning markets and providers: Some issues and prospects. *Education + Training, 43*(4/5), 233–239. https://doi.org/10.1108/EUM0000000005484

Jiang, Y., Yingying, C., Jiasheng, L., & Yiqing, W. (2021). The effect of the online and offline blended teaching mode on English as a foreign language learners' listening performance in a Chinese context. *Frontiers in Psychology*. https://doi.org/10.3389/fpsyg.2021.742742

Mahyoob, M. (2020). Challenges of e-learning during the COVID-19 pandemic experienced by EFL learners. *Arab World English Journal, 11*(4), 351–362. https://dx.doi.org/10.24093/awej/vol11no4.23

MARS & ASCAP. (2020). *Sontazhi i Mesimit online 1*. Tirane: MARS & ASCAP. https://arsimi.gov.al/sondazhi-i-mesimit-online/

Nugroho, D., Lin, H.-C., Borisova, I., Nieto, A., & Ntekim, M. (2020). *COVID-19: Trends, promising practices and gaps in remote learning for pre-primary education*. UNICEF Office of Research- Innocenti Working Papers 1166.

Ononiwu, C. (2021). Role of online discussion forums in enhancing users' cognitive skills. *The Journal of Teaching English for Specific and Academic Purposes, 9*(3), 307–320. https://doi.org/10.22190/JTESAP2103307O

Pelikan, E. R., Luftenegger, M., Holer, J., Korlat, S., Spiel, C., & Schober, B. (2021, March 4). Learning during COVID-19: The role of self-regulated learning, motivation, and procrastination for perceived competence. *ZFE*, 1–7. http://doi.org/10/10007/s11618-021-01002-x

Pokhrel, S., & Chhetri, R. (2021). A literature review on impact of COVID-19 pandemic on teaching and learning. *Higher Education for the Future, 8*(1), 133–141. https://doi.org/10.1177%2F2347631120983481

Schmidt, J., & Werner, H. C. (2007). Designing online instruction for success: Future oriented motivation and self-regulation. *Electronic Journal of e-Learning, 5*(1), 69–78.

Siemens, G. (2005). Connectivism: A learning theory for the digital age. *International Journal of Instructional Technology and Distance Learning, 2*(1). www.itdl.org

Stojkovic, N. (2020, June 4). Narrow-angled ESP as a proponent of neoliberal capitalism and its inherent empowering/disempowering dichotomy. *ILCEA (Online), 40*, 3. http://doi.org/10.4000/ilcea.10549

Talib, M. A., Bettayeb, A. M., & Omer, R. I. (2021, March). Analytical study on the impact of technology in higher education during the age of COVID-19; Systematic literature review. *Education and Information Technologies*, 3–10. https://doi.org/10.1007/s10639-021-10507-1

The Florida Center for Instructional Technology. (2021). https://fcit.usf.edu/matrix/what-do-we-mean-by-independent-access/

Vesselinov, D. (2021). Editorial. *Chuzhdoezikovo Obuchenie – Foreign Language Teaching, 48*(1), 7–8. https://azbuki.bg/wp-content/uploads/2021/02/Foreign_Language_1_21_Kum-chitatelite.pdf

World Economic Forum. (2020, November). *The evolution of global education and 5 trends emerging amidst COVID-19.* www.weforum.org/agnda/2020/11/evolution-higher-education-covid19-coronavirus

World Vision Albania. (2020). *Impact assessment of the COVID-19 outbreak on wellbeing of children and families in Albania.* www.wvi.org/publications/report/albania/impact-assessment-covid-19-outbreak-wellbeing-children-and-families

Xhelili, P., Ibrahimi, E., Ruci, E., & Sheme, K. (2021). Adaptation and perception of online learning during COVID-19 pandemic by Albanian University students. *International Journal on Studies in Education, 3*(2), 103.

Yu, Z., Rong, H., Shen, L., Jiayan, Z., Yimin, C., Meijing, C., & Yazhu, L. (2021, May). Effects of blended versus offline case-centred learning on the academic performance and critical thinking ability of undergraduate nursing students: A cluster randomised controlled trial. *Nurse Education in Practice, 53.* https://doi.org/10.1016/j.nepr.2021.103080

Appendix

I've invited you to fill out a form:

Teaching and Learning Academic English during Covid-19 pandemic in Albania – master course Epoka University

Teaching and Learning Academic English during Covid-19 pandemic in Albania – master course Epoka University

Dr. Mirela Alhasani (Dubali) – EAP lecturer for ENG 401 Master course⋆

1. **Before 2020, what percentage of your classes was taught online?**

   o   ○ 0%
   o   ○ 21–40%
   o   ○ 41–60%
   o   ○ 61–80%
   o   ○ 81–99%
   o   ○ 100%

2. **Between February 2020 and April 2021 what percentage of your classes were online?**

   o   ○ 0%
   o   ○ 1–20%
   o   ○ 21–40%
   o   ○ 41–60%
   o   ○ 61–80%
   o   ○ 81–99%
   o   ○ 100%

3. **The learning process held online during pandemic was more challenging to understand.★**

   o ○ a. I strongly disagree.
   o ○ b. I disagree.
   o ○ c. I agree.
   o ○ d. I strongly agree.

4. **I adapted easily to online learning.★**

   o ○ a. I strongly disagree.
   o ○ b. I disagree.
   o ○ c. I agree.
   o ○ d. I strongly agree.

5. **I have had difficulty in accessing and processing lectures because of technology devices.**

   o ○ a. I have never had this.
   o ○ b. I always have had this.
   o ○ c. I sometimes have had this.

6. **Have you been tested regularly with online-based assignments?**

   o ○ a. I have never done this.
   o ○ b. I have recently started doing this due to Covid-19.
   o ○ c. I was already doing this.

7. **How confident did you feel about using technology at home before the pandemic? 1- not at all confident;10-extremely confident.**

   o ○ a. 1
   o ○ b.2
   o ○ c.3
   o ○ d.4
   o ○ e.5
   o ○ f.6
   o ○ g.7
   o ○ h.8
   o ○ i.9
   o ○ j.10

8. **How confident do you feel about using technology now? 1–10**

   o ○ a.1
   o ○ b.2
   o ○ c.3

o   ○ d.4
o   ○ e.5
o   ○ f.6
o   ○ g.7
o   ○ h.8
o   ○ i.9
o   ○ j.10

9. **How does the preparation time needed for online classes compare to physical classes? On average you needed:**

   o   ○ a. Less time
   o   ○ b. The same amount of time
   o   ○ c. More amount of time

10. **What is the most effective way of presenting new language ?**

    o   ○ a. Online
    o   ○ b. Face to face
    o   ○ c. Both

11. **What is the most effective way of monitoring your progress as students?**

    o   ○ a. Online
    o   ○ b. Face to face
    o   ○ c. Both

12. **What is the most effective way of receiving feedback?**

    o   ○ a. Online
    o   ○ b. Face to face
    o   ○ c. Both

13. **What is the most effective way of keeping yourself engaged with learning?**

    o   ○ A. Online
    o   ○ b. Face to face
    o   ○ c. Both

14. **What is the most effective way of acquiring academic reading skills?**

    o   ○ a. online
    o   ○ b. face to
    o   ○ c. both

15. **What is the most effective way of acquiring academic listening skills?**

    o   ○ a. Online
    o   ○ b. Face to face
    o   ○ c. Both

16. **What is the most effective way of acquiring academic speaking skills?**

    o   ○ a. Online
    o   ○ b. Face to face
    o   ○ c. Both

17. **What is the most effective way of acquiring other academic skills such as critical thinking?**

    o   ○ a. Online
    o   ○ b. Face to face
    o   ○ c. Both

18. **What is the most effective way of facilitating peer interaction?**

    o   ○ a. Online
    o   ○ b. Face to face
    o   ○ c. Both

19. **What is the most effective way of solving problems related to the course?**

    o   ○ a. Online
    o   ○ b. Face to face
    o   ○ c. Both

20. **What were your main challenges when attending lessons online?**

21. **How have you adapted to online lessons? (1 = not well at all; 10=extremely well)**

    o   ○ a. 1
    o   ○ b.2
    o   ○ c.3
    o   ○ d.4
    o   ○ e.5
    o   ○ f.6
    o   ○ g.7

o ⭘ h.8
o ⭘ i.9
o ⭘ j.10

22. **Which aspect of academic English class have you found challenging to do online?**

23. **How do you feel your progress towards reaching your language objectives has changed as a result of having classes online?**

o ⭘ a. Their progress is a lot faster.
o ⭘ b. Their progress is a little faster.
o ⭘ c. Their progress is about the same.
o ⭘ d. Their progress is a little slower.
o ⭘ e. Their progress is a lot slower.

24. **Is there any other comment/recommendation you would like to add to this survey related to Covid-19 pandemic learning experience?**

11

TRANSITION TO ONLINE LEARNING IN UZBEKISTAN

Case of teaching academic English at Westminster International University in Tashkent

Diana Akhmedjanova and Feruza Akhmedova

Introduction

Distance education refers to educational practices delivered via various technological devices, and over the past few decades, it has gradually been introduced into higher education (HE). The Covid-19 pandemic led to the accleration of the global adoption of digital technologies to alleviate disruptions in educational practices (World Bank, 2020). As a result, educational institutions in many countries faced challenges such as limited access to technologies, a lack of expertise among practitioners in educational technology, and digital literacy skills (Barber, 2021). While the educational system of Uzbekistan was not ready to fully switch to the online mode in spring 2020, the government of Uzbekistan was quick to respond to the Covid-19 pandemic. For example, the National Television and Radio Company of Uzbekistan (the national broadcaster) had been recording and broadcasting lessons for schoolchildren during the spring/autumn of 2020 and teachers had been collecting students' assignments through social media channels such as *Telegram*. Many HE institutions in Uzbekistan adopted Learning Management Systems (LMSs) such as *Moodle* to distribute materials and collect student assignments. Some teachers used video conferencing software such as *Zoom* to offer synchronous lessons. Those decisions allowed for a continuation of educational provision; however, very little evidence exists on how various disciplines have been taught online.

This chapter focuses on Westminster International University in Tashkent (WIUT) and its implementation of new technologies and methods to deliver online education on the Academic English (AE) module during the pandemic.

DOI: 10.4324/9781003283409-14

WIUT is an international university, offering undergraduate and postgraduate degrees in such fields as business, economics, finance, law, marketing, and information systems. The student population is around 5,000 students, predominantly from Uzbekistan and a small number of international students from South Korea, Japan, Afghanistan, Egypt, and China.

In autumn 2020, WIUT, alongside other HE institutions, resorted to distance learning and closed their campuses to students. By September 28, 2020, WIUT had adopted the necessary technology to deliver high-quality education using: (1) a modified LMS: *WIUT Learning Board* and (2) video conferencing software: *BigBlueButton* (BBB), which is embedded within WIUT Learning Board to facilitate synchronous online classes. Another decision was the automatic recording of each teaching session delivered via BBB.

For the first eight weeks of the autumn 2020 semester, all classes were delivered online. While students were participating in classes from their homes, staff were required to teach from campus at their request to access more reliable internet connections and other necessary resources. As for resuming face-to-face classes, WIUT offered this opportunity to postgraduate students (level 7) on November 16, 2020. The decision to bring postgraduate students back first was due to their lower numbers ($N = 295$), in comparison to the number of undergraduate students ($N = 4,364$).

Once the postgraduate classes were underway, WIUT's administrators decided to bring back foundation students, taking the Certificate of International Foundation Studies (CIFS; level 3), in order to give them an opportunity to experience university life. CIFS students ($N = 1,330$) started their face-to-face studies on November 30, 2020. The decision to bring CIFS students to campus was driven by: (1) many of them not having stable internet connectivity to access resources online, and (2) opportunities to develop the sense of community with peers and teachers.

The remainder of the chapter focuses on the AE module offered to the CIFS students. The CIFS is the first stage in HE at WIUT, and successful completion of this level provides students with opportunities to continue their studies at the honours level in their respective fields. The next section provides a brief review of the literature that informed the pedagogical decisions in the AE module.

Literature Review

This review focuses on the recent research of English for Academic Purposes (EAP) and the use of technology in EAP. It also presents the Technological Pedagogical Content Knowledge (TPACK; Koehler & Mishra, 2009) framework technology integration, which facilitated our reflection on the AE module at WIUT.

English for Academic Purposes

EAP is a branch of English for Specific Purposes (ESP), and it focuses on the use of English in academic contexts; however, unlike ESP, EAP does not necessarily focus on English in various disciplines (Charles, 2013; Charles & Pecorari, 2016; Guardado & Light, 2020). EAP research has mainly focused on corpora, genre, and social practice (Charles, 2013; Charles & Pecorari, 2016; Riazi et al., 2020). Corpora studies have allowed researchers to describe academic registers, and then target pedagogical practices and materials for students to master these registers. Genre studies have focused on the use of diverse linguistic features within various social contexts. Both corpora and genre approaches target the evaluation of written texts (Charles & Pecorari, 2016); however, further developments in rhetoric have moved the focus to social contexts. Thus, social approaches to EAP have examined it within sociocultural contexts and how students construct their knowledge within these contexts and develop academic literacies (Charles, 2013).

Riazi et al. (2020) provided support for this claim by reviewing 416 empirical articles published in the Journal of English for Academic Purposes from 2002 to 2019 and examined (1) contexts and participants, (2) research foci and theoretical orientations, (3) research methodology and sources, and (4) pedagogical implications. The genre theoretical framework turned out to be the predominant theoretical orientation (26.4%) in the articles published in the journal up to 2019. Genre theories were followed by cognitive (22.6%), discourse (15.9%), and social (11.1%) theories. Irrespective of the theoretical frameworks used to evaluate the field of EAP, Charles and Pecorari (2016) advocated the use of a combination of all these approaches for both research and pedagogical decisions.

Recent developments in educational technology have resulted in the adoption of various technological decisions in EAP courses. For example, having reviewed the literature on the application of various technological tools in EAP, Dashtestani and Stojkovic (2016) found that EAP courses rely on the use of LMSs, corpus, and wikis which were associated with the positive learning outcomes and effective teaching practices. Similar positive sentiments were identified in a study of teachers, students, and administrators across 40 universities and colleges across the United States and Canada (Lawrence et al., 2020). The surveyed and interviewed participants believed that inclusion of technology in EAP courses could lead to increased levels of student engagement, development of autonomous learning, new teaching methodologies, and 21st-century skills. Nevertheless, Lawrence et al. (2020, p. 102) also identified that all stakeholders emphasized the need to develop "sound theoretically informed techno-pedagogy" to deliver successful technology-enhanced EAP classes. In an attempt to address this criticism, this chapter provides a reflection on the EAP practices in the AE module through the TPACK framework discussed later.

Technological, Pedagogical and Content Knowledge (TPACK)

The TPACK approach operates within three domains – technology, pedagogy, and content – should be seamlessly integrated to promote technology-enhanced teaching (Koehler & Mishra, 2009). Content knowledge refers to teachers' knowledge of the domain they teach. Pedagogical knowledge refers to the knowledge of the teaching and learning processes. The intersection of the Pedagogical and Content knowledge results in the adoption of the methods and techniques used to deliver content within a certain domain. Technology knowledge goes beyond digital literacy and refers to a developed knowledge of technology and how it can be incremental or detrimental in teaching within domains. Technological and Content knowledge are intertwined because developments in technology lead to developments in the disciplines. As a result, it can be instrumental in delivering instruction. Teachers should have a strong knowledge of the subject matter and the technologies that are instrumental in moving this discipline forward. The intersection of technological and pedagogical knowledge reflects how teaching and learning can transform with the use of particular technologies.

TPACK posits that all three components of technology, pedagogy, and content are intertwined and interact with each other to deliver successful technology-infused teaching and learning. The use of technology should be constructive – teachers should know which technology promotes or impedes learning. A recent modification to the TPACK framework brings to the forefront XK, or contextual knowledge, which refers to "organizational and situational constraints that teachers work within" (Mishra, 2019, p. 77). According to Koehler et al. (2014), TPACK is content or discipline specific; therefore, technological, contextual and pedagogical content and knowledge will vary. While there is extensive research examining the application of TPACK in various disciplines, available research on examining EAP using TPACK in contexts where English is used as a medium of instruction is scarce.

The attempts to locate research studies examining the use of technology in EAP classes during the pandemic were unsuccessful. To date, the available literature focuses on teaching General English rather than EAP during the pandemic. The current research on General English mostly reports on the challenges of online teaching/learning (Atmojo & Nugroho, 2020; Bashitialshaaer et al., 2021; Hakim, 2020); the tools and methods the teachers used to support the students (Cheung, 2021; Pérez et al., 2020; Yi & Jang, 2020); and effects of online learning on students' performance during the Covid-19 pandemic (Hakim, 2020; Rahayu & Wirza, 2020; Rinekso & Muslim, 2020; Yi & Jang, 2020). Therefore, the remainder of the chapter examines the AE module through the lens of TPACK in an attempt to fill this gap.

Academic English at WIUT

The focus of this chapter is on the AE module at WIUT, which is taught twice a week to CIFS students for the duration of 12 weeks for two consecutive semesters. The main goal of the module is to develop students' academic reading, writing, and listening skills, and includes grammar and vocabulary-building activities. This chapter describes the experiences of teaching AE in the first (autumn) semester of the 2020–2021 academic year. Upon completing the first semester, students are required to submit coursework in the form of a portfolio that includes: (1) a summary of the listening material, (2) a summary and response essay on a reading and (3) a reflection on their experiences in AE. Twenty-one lecturers were divided into four teams, and each team developed seminars on one of the assigned topics: Environment, Health, Work, and Education.

Pedagogy

Prior to the pandemic, the AE lecturers relied on Communicative Language Teaching (CLT) pedagogy to deliver instruction (Richards & Rodgers, 2014). That is, the emphasis was on the development of students' competences across three skills: academic writing, listening, and reading. The instructional practices employed in AE classes at WIUT were learner-centred, giving students multiple opportunities to practice target AE skills. In addition, the AE module incorporated such EAP pedagogical decisions as teaching students to write in different genres, incorporating appropriate linguistic and discourse structures. There was an emphasis on formative assessment techniques since teachers provided feedback on students' written drafts; students were encouraged to revise and edit their drafts before including them in the final portfolio for summative assessment. However, these pedagogical practices had to be altered due to teaching online.

Technology

In the autumn semester of 2020, lecturers adapted the AE learning materials for the synchronous delivery via BBB to enhance student engagement. For example, teachers incorporated tasks that required them to use tools within BBB such as taking polls, sharing notes, public chat, or sharing the screen to encourage student participation. Those BBB tools also allowed formative feedback from lecturers and peers. Teachers also incorporated a range of video materials related to the module. Both teachers and students could also use *WIUT Learning Board* – an LMS for both in- and out-of-class tasks. Availability of those tools had changed teaching practices in AE with the use of technology.

TPACK in AE

Teaching AE online was the first online teaching experience for the majority of AE lecturers. As a result, WIUT administration was interested in faculty's experiences with online teaching and distributed a survey in November 2020. Seventy-three faculty members responded to the survey, and 23 lecturers taught at the Department of Global Education who offered the AE module. Sixteen of these lecturers claimed they used a combination of synchronous and asynchronous modes of online teaching.

The AE classes were delivered in the synchronous format, and lecturers primarily used the BBB software. In a survey, lecturers claimed they used the following features in BBB: public chat ($n = 22$), breakout rooms ($n = 20$), uploaded presentation ($n = 21$), shared external video and shared notes ($n = 19$), started a poll ($n = 17$), and saved usernames ($n=12$). However, the *WIUT Learning Board* – a university-wide LMS, was underused: lessons ($n = 22$), pages ($n = 19$), files ($n = 16$). Even though lecturers claimed they used discussion boards ($n = 17$), students did not actively participate in them. Very few lecturers used quizzes ($n = 7$), assignments ($n = 5$), or peer-review functions within the *WIUT Learning Board*. In this way, the *WIUT Learning Board* was mostly used as a repository for teachers to upload materials and video recordings of the lessons, as well as assess students' final portfolios.

In addition to BBB ($n = 22$) and the *WIUT Learning Board* ($n = 21$), lecturers in AE resorted to using additional tools such as *Google documents* ($n = 18$), *H5P* ($n = 10$), *Kahoot* ($n = 7$), *Quizizz, Quizlet,* and *Padlet*. These tools were used for a variety of purposes. For instance, *Google documents* served as a tool for students to work on and submit their drafts; they created a single *Google document* for the whole semester and compiled all of their writings in it. The use of *Google documents* enabled students to track their progress in writing because teachers provided detailed feedback on each entry. Also, it was convenient for teachers to observe how students reacted to feedback and how they used it to improve their drafts.

Another useful tool was *Padlet*, which is an interactive space for students to practise writing and share their ideas. Specifically, *Padlet* was used for students to practice the reflection – the third entry in the coursework. Students shared their reflections on the *Padlet* wall, read their peers' writing, considered if they met all of the criteria, and rated them by clicking on the stars that appeared underneath. This exercise served as a modest attempt to encourage students to provide feedback to each other on the quality of their writing. AE lecturers noticed that students were more eager to rate each other's writing rather than exchange oral feedback.

As is evident from the survey reported earlier, teachers tried to use a variety of technological affordances within BBB and the *WIUT Learning Board* to enrich the online version of AE. However, many surveyed lecturers reported experiencing technology and teaching-related challenges with online teaching. Lecturers claimed to struggle with such things as poor internet connection ($n = 18$), access to the *WIUT Learning Board* ($n = 7$), and use of tools within BBB ($n = 10$). Lecturers also reported motivating students to participate ($n = 17$), increasing workload and stress ($n = 17$), managing time ($n = 10$), and assessing students' progress and learning ($n = 9$) to be the main challenges while teaching online. However, when asked if they would consider teaching online after the pandemic, the majority of them responded affirmatively ($n = 14$).

In terms of student engagement, during the AE classes, students would typically lose either internet connection or electricity, which resulted in poor participation and attendance. Most of the time, students did not turn on their cameras and, in some cases, they could not use audio during discussions because the internet connection was unstable. Hence, while watching videos during the class, due to electricity issues and, in some instances poor English language skills, some students lagged behind in understanding the video materials and made other students wait to continue the class. As a result, only a handful of students regularly participated during online classes, while others were online but could not or chose not to participate. Those challenges created a host of issues for how AE classes were taught since they limited the use of certain technological affordances of BBB, such as the use of breakout rooms, sharing the screen when students were trying to report back on their group work, or watching videos as a whole class. In some instances, it led to teachers lecturing for a good portion of the AE class, rather than using skill-building tasks.

Nevertheless, AE lecturers also benefited from online teaching in substantial ways. Even though many of the lecturers struggled with the technology and lacked digital literacy skills, this experience encouraged them to seek opportunities to improve these skills. For instance, during the autumn 2020 semester, AE lecturers met every week to discuss the seminars for the upcoming week. During those meetings, colleagues had a chance to share their lesson plans, seek feedback on the tasks and assignments, and share with each other novel ways in which to facilitate students' practice of AE online. Those meetings helped to boost teachers' confidence in using online teaching software for the first time; they also helped to improve the quality of the online seminars.

A further benefit of teaching AE online was teachers' eagerness to continue using certain pedagogical decisions even in face-to-face classes. For example, while modest attempts were made to introduce online assessments prior to the Covid-19 pandemic, they were not as successful. During the pandemic, both lecturers and students had to opt for online assessment, which was met with hesitation at first. However, the availability of such tools as *Turnitin* to check for plagiarism, use of online rubrics, and easy access to scores and feedback for both lecturers and students made online assessments in AE a less stressful experience.

Discussion

The purpose of this chapter was to reflect on teaching the AE module online through the lens of the TPACK framework (Koehler & Mishra, 2009; Mishra, 2019). Overall, the content of the AE curriculum still focused on such EAP evidence-based practices as teaching students to write in different genres by applying appropriate discourse and linguistic features during the online semester in autumn 2020. However, the pedagogical methods shifted from the CLT to teacher-centred approaches in online environments. This might be due to the students' limited access to reliable technology and stable internet connections. As a result, teachers could not use such features of video conferencing, such as breakout rooms, screen sharing, and watching videos. Hence, a lack of students' engagement in switching on their cameras and microphones during the synchronous sessions did not facilitate learner-centred instruction.

Distance education in the AE module gave teachers an opportunity to enhance their digital literacy skills, learn and use new technologies, adapt and co-develop online lessons in teams, as well as expand their pedagogical repertoires. Nevertheless, teachers failed to use the technological affordances of the *WIUT Learning Board* to facilitate students' engagement asynchronously. The *WIUT Learning Board* was used as a repository in order to share class materials and assess students' final work. Meanwhile, teachers could have used such features as discussion forums, quizzes, and peer review to give students with unstable internet connections an opportunity to participate asynchronously. This reflection suggests that AE lecturers at WIUT are novices in their TPACK of teaching AE online.

In order for AE teachers in WIUT and across Uzbekistan to become confident experts in TPACK and improve distance education, the following suggestions should be considered. Regarding infrastructure, access to reliable and fast internet connection should be provided across Uzbekistan. Also, WIUT and other universities across Uzbekistan should have technology available for students to borrow when they have to study online since not all students have the means to own these tools.

The AE curriculum at WIUT primarily focuses on the writing, reading, and listening modalities, which do not give students an opportunity to practice their speaking skills. This observation resonates with EAP research, which highlights the predominant focus on the written texts rather than other modalities (Riazi et al., 2020). Charles (2013) also notes that a large proportion of available research focuses on academic writing, which is only one of "the main means of assessment in the academy" (p. 147). Given the challenges with unstable internet connections, students had even fewer opportunities to practice their academic English speaking skills. As a result, lecturers in the AE module need to consider developing alternative opportunities to fill in this gap, such as letting students do videos or voiced-over presentations.

In terms of pedagogical decisions, online performance assessments were a great success in the AE module at WIUT. However, peer review was an unused technique in the module when it was offered online. Students were required to summarize readings and videos as well as write essays and reflections. However, they did not have an opportunity to provide feedback on each other since teachers were hesitant to use the discussion boards within the *WIUT Learning Board*. A careful attempt of using *Padlet* to provide peer feedback on students' reflections was successful in class. However, the task was superficial since it asked students to rate each other's work, but not provide feedback using a set of criteria so students did not benefit from this activity to a greater extent.

While WIUT administration organized a one-day training for faculty before online classes started, this was not enough. Many faculty members had a distorted view that online teaching of English was similar to face-to-face classes; the only difference was the means of delivery. Many faculty members had changed their views after their first experiences teaching online. Nevertheless, only six faculty members teaching AE participated in the ten-week digital teaching course offered in the spring 2021 semester. Therefore, the main goal of WIUT, as well as other universities in Uzbekistan, is to facilitate professional development on digital pedagogy and materials design for online education in AE among other disciplines. These workshops should cover pedagogical, technological, and lesson planning aspects of distance education. These workshops should be followed up with online peer observations of colleagues, who could give feedback on strengths and areas in need of improvement of their online teaching processes (i.e., confidence in using the platform; students' engagement; appropriateness of tasks and materials for online delivery). Another important suggestion comes through trial and error with online AE classes. It is important for both teachers and students to show their faces to have better communication and maintain alertness throughout the class meaning all students and AE teachers should be required to turn their cameras and microphones on during online classes.

Students also need support in learning AE online. To facilitate this, AE teachers should set virtual office hours and announce them at the beginning of the semester. If needed, teachers could prepare extra consolidating tasks for struggling students. Instructors often found that AE students with lower language proficiency struggled more than those with higher level language skills. For this reason, it is imperative teachers organize additional tasks for such students depending on their needs. Moreover, it is advisable for lectures to be recorded and shared through the *WIUT Learning Board* for students to access.

In future, the department of Global Education at WIUT should consider offering online sections of AE courses. These online sections should provide both synchronous and asynchronous tasks for students to practice AE skills, utilizing discussion forums and quiz functions of the *WIUT Learning Board*. Also, the scope of AE should include the development of speaking skills, which can be facilitated with the use of multimodal presentations employing voice-over technology.

In addition, all AE lecturers teaching online sections should undergo rigorous online teaching professional development, which should incorporate materials and assessment design along with pedagogical methods using technology.

Conclusion

The Covid-19 pandemic accelerated the process of digitalization in HE in Uzbekistan as evident in the AE module at WIUT. However, little is known about the experiences of other EAP teachers in Uzbekistan, in both face-to-face and online settings. To bring the aforementioned initiatives to life, researchers in Uzbekistan should conduct a country-wide study researching experiences of teaching EAP courses in both private and public universities. This information would facilitate the development of a roadmap for teaching EAP online across the republic. Meanwhile, the department of Global Education at WIUT should develop and test curricula targeting the online teaching of EAP.

Reference list

Atmojo, A. E. P., & Nugroho, A. (2020). EFL classes must go online! Teaching activities and challenges during COVID-19 pandemic in Indonesia. *Register Journal*, *13*(1), 49–76.

Barber, M. (2021). *Gravity assist: Propelling higher education towards a brighter future – Digital teaching and learning review*. The Office for Students.

Bashitialshaaer, R., Alhendawi, M., & Lassoued, Z. (2021). Obstacle comparisons to achieving distance learning and applying electronic exams during COVID-19 pandemic. *Symmetry*, *13*(1), 99.

Charles, M. (2013). English for academic purposes. In B. Paltrifge & S. Starfield (Eds.), *The handbook of English for specific purposes* (pp. 137–153). Wiley.

Charles, M., & Pecorari, D. (2016). *Introducing English for academic purposes*. Routledge.

Cheung, A. (2021). Language teaching during a pandemic: A case study of Zoom use by a secondary ESL teacher in Hong Kong. *RELC Journal*, 003368822098178. https://doi.org/10.1177/0033688220981784

Dashtestani, R., & Stojkovic, N. (2016). The use of technology in English for Specific Purposes (ESP) instruction: A literature review. *Journal of Teaching English for Specific and Academic Purposes*, *3*(3), 435–456.

Guardado, M., & Light, J. (2020). *Curriculum development in English for academic purposes: A guide to practice*. Springer Nature.

Hakim, B. (2020). Technology integrated online classrooms and the challenges faced by the EFL teachers in Saudi Arabia during the COVID-19 pandemic. *International Journal of Applied Linguistics and English Literature*, *9*(5), 33–39.

Koehler, M. J., & Mishra, P. (2009). What is technological pedagogical content knowledge (TPACK)? *Contemporary Issues in Technology and Teacher Education*, *9*(1), 60–70.

Koehler, M. J., Mishra, P., Kereluik, K., Shin, T. S., & Graham, C. R. (2014). The technological pedagogical content knowledge framework. In J. M. Spector, M. D. Merrill, K. Elen, & M. J. Bishop (Eds.), *Handbook of research on educational communications and technology* (pp. 101–111). Springer. https://link.springer.com/chapter/10.1007/978-1-4614-3185-5_9

Lawrence, G., Ahmed, F., Cole, C., & Johnston, K. P. (2020). Not more technology but more effective technology: Examining the state of technology integration in EAP programmes. *RELC Journal, 51*(1), 101–116.

Mishra, P. (2019). Considering contextual knowledge: The TPACK diagram gets an upgrade. *Journal of Digital Learning in Teacher Education, 35*(2), 76–78. https://doi.org/10.1080/21532974.2019.1588611

Pérez, M. J. S., Jordán, R. M. C., & Granda, G. K. A. (2020). Creating learning paths through Symbaloo to facilitate formative assessment for EFL learners. *Journal of Science and Research: Revista Ciencia e Investigación, 5*(1), 545–561.

Rahayu, R. P., & Wirza, Y. (2020). Teachers' perception of online learning during pandemic Covid-19. *Jurnal Penelitian Pendidikan, 20*(3).

Riazi, A. M., Ghanbar, H., & Fazel, I. (2020). The contexts, theoretical and methodological orientation of EAP research: Evidence from empirical articles published in the Journal of English for Academic Purposes. *Journal of English for Academic Purposes, 48,* 1–17. https://doi.org/10.1016/j.jeap.2020.100925

Richards, J. C., & Rodgers, T. S. (2014). *Approaches and methods in language teaching.* Cambridge University Press.

Rinekso, A. B., & Muslim, A. B. (2020). Synchronous online discussion: Teaching English in higher education amidst the covid-19 pandemic. *JEES (Journal of English Educators Society), 5*(2), 155–162. https://doi.org/10.21070/jees.v5i2.646

World Bank Group Education. (2020). *The COVID-19 pandemic: Shocks to education and policy responses.* World Bank. www.worldbank.org/en/topic/education/publication/the-covid19-pandemic-shocks-to-education-and-policy-responses

Yi, Y., & Jang, J. (2020). Envisioning possibilities amid the COVID-19 pandemic: Implications from English language teaching in South Korea. *TESOL Journal, 11*(3). https://doi.org/10.1002/tesj.543.

PART III

Collaboration and online learning communities

James Fenton

Academic English (AE) in Higher Education (HE) is a collaborative endeavour. That applies to the regional and national mandates driving expectations, down to the planning and delivery each university provides, through to the interaction and group work in classrooms. Anyone within this framework may sometimes work alone, but any resulting impact is reliant on the input and recognition of others. Amongst the many adjustments and adaptations necessitated by the Covid-19 pandemic, ways also had to be found to maintain the constructive relationships that AE administration, instruction, and learning depend on. The chapters in this part reveal how this was made possible, despite the difficult circumstances, and point to numerous ways that constructive collaboration can continue to take place in the future.

The wide-ranging role of collaboration in AE across multiple levels is reflected in the chapters from this part. Starting far removed from the classroom, Nigel Caplan (Delaware, USA) highlights how collaboration was needed to address attitudes and expectations within his department – "changing the defaults". This required collaboration at an institutional level, while all the time looking to reconcile new strategies with the national and international requirements (e.g., visas), which are a familiar aspect of AE courses in HE. Collaborating with colleagues from institutions across Europe (Linda Steyne, Slovakia; Agnes Simon and Jan Beneš, Czechia; Angeniet Kam, the Netherlands; and Eszter Timár, Hungary), Steyne et al.'s chapter outlines how they redesigned an academic writing course for university instructors and PhD candidates. With a similar focus, Elisabeth Rodas (Ecuador) shares how peer-feedback groups were adapted to support academics' writing and research across disciplines and institutions. Moving towards the classroom, Joe Lennon, Petra Trávníková, Alena Hradilová, and Libor Štěpánek (Czechia) reveal how opportunities around, rather than just within the

DOI: 10.4324/9781003283409-15

classroom, were created by enhancing virtual spaces for dynamic communication on English for Academic Purposes (EAP) courses. Now in the (online) classroom, David Ishii (New Zealand) examines engagement and social presence through a lens of humanising the experience for all those involved.

The humanising that David Ishii explores, as recognition of others' needs that prefaces and is manifested through collaboration, permeates all the chapters in this part. Caplan first raises collaboration as a means of realising the changes arising from the pandemic. The "defaults" that had become entrenched needed to be reset, but his chapter reveals how that was only possible through successful collaboration within the AE department and also across the university. Many of the ostensible challenges discussed were related to realigning pedagogy to fit the new online format during the pandemic, and this was achieved by recognising the abilities and concerns of everyone involved while including other departments in supporting their adaptations.

Both of the chapters from Steyn et al. and Rodas explore course design, with collaboration a vital part of the process and also an explicit aim for all those participating. Rodas's original research highlights what this means in practice. Her examples include building trust between participants and creating clear rules that everyone can share in, while emphasising how both are predicated on an understanding and appreciation of others' needs while serving an important role in enabling effective collaboration. With five instructors from universities across Europe, collaboration was unavoidable to some extent for Steyn et al. and had to be integrated into their course from the outset. What their chapter so effectively reveals, however, is the ways their team teaching moved beyond just efficiently working together and towards effectively utilising their strengths (and weaknesses) to provide a clear exemplar which led to increased collaborative opportunities for everyone involved.

Lennon et al. also share opportunities for collaboration and how they were made possible through the technology that needed to be increasingly relied on. Importantly, the chapter shows how it is not the technology itself that provides the opportunities or the collaboration. Rather, what made it possible was their novel use of online tools and how they tailored them to the requirements of the courses and needs of their students. This insight returns us to Ishii, who provides multiple ways to utilise technology to maintain the social presence he sees as essential for effective learning and collaboration in online classrooms. Again, it is his utilisation of the technology in online classrooms that recognises each individual through targeted personalised subject matter that achieves the goal of absorbing them into the collaborative endeavour.

Both those chapters, like all those in this part, recount how technology supported the communal nature of AE while revealing how the pandemic led to a reshaping of interconnected "communities" of collaborators. In Steyn et al.'s and Rodas's chapters, this evolved across different universities around the globe; for Caplan, it happened at multiple levels within the university; and Lennon et al.'s and Ishii's chapters reflect how they created opportunities for students to build their own new communities, both within and alongside more traditional classrooms. We yet again see how the challenging times may have restrained and altered practice but also take inspiration from how innovative practitioners can find successful responses.

The chapters that follow provide a range of such novel responses to learn from now and in similar times of crisis in the future. Considerations for institutions, course design, team teaching, and methods for engaging students are just a few of the areas where lessons have been provided for building the successful relationships that AE relies on. Also revealed in this section is the central role that collaboration continues to play in the successful organisation, delivery, and learning of AE. The pandemic did not change that, but it did mean that universities, practitioners, and students had to find new ways to progress together in their shared aims. The chapters in this section provide illuminating insights and proven ways for how this can be achieved.

12

CHANGING THE DEFAULT

From emergency to sustainable online teaching in a U.S. Intensive English Program

Nigel A. Caplan

Context

Intensive English Programs (IEPs) play a vital if not always fully visible role in international higher education in the United States. Although there is considerable variation among programs, the majority fulfil two important functions: providing English language training to short-term visitors and serving as a conduit to degree programs at their own and other institutions. Typically, prospective undergraduate and graduate students who do not meet their university's English language requirement on standardized or internal proficiency tests will study in an IEP full-time or as part of a pathways program. In the United States, students in a pathways program take English as a Second Language (ESL) courses alongside "content" classes that count toward their degree requirements. In a language training program, they take only ESL courses, which do not usually confer degree credit. Upon successful completion of their academic language training, they will either matriculate or apply to a university. Of particular note for the current context, before the Covid-19 pandemic, international students present in the United States on visas designated for language study were prohibited from taking any online classes. Therefore, most IEPs had little or no experience with online teaching. And then campuses across the country shut down.

Prior to March 2020, in-person teaching was, therefore, not just the default mode in IEPs: it was the only form of teaching for which the majority of instructors were trained and students were prepared. The sudden change in the default mode of instruction from room to Zoom was disorienting for everyone, quite aside from the fear and uncertainty brought about by the pandemic itself. The sequence of events was different in every state, but in Delaware, there was a single 24-hour period in March during which the first coronavirus case was

DOI: 10.4324/9781003283409-16

confirmed in the state, the University of Delaware canceled in-person classes for the remainder of the semester, and the governor declared a state of emergency. Within another two days, schools were closed, and "non-essential personnel" at the university (including all faculties) were told to work online. One week later, with a stay-at-home order in place, our IEP resumed a normal schedule a week ahead of the rest of the university, with all classes running fully synchronously on Zoom. One year later we were still teaching almost all our classes online but with new insights, techniques, technologies, and approaches. This chapter recounts our journey from emergency remote teaching of academic English to sustainable online learning (Hodges et al., 2020) and suggests ways in which the lessons learned can light the rocky road ahead.

Default Positions in Online and EAP Teaching

Default positions and decisions are those taken automatically, without consideration of other choices or options. As such, they are normalized as best practices, prevailing wisdom, or simply the intractable way things are. Gunzenhauser (2003) argues that default philosophies in education "[result] from a lack of reflective, engaged dialogue by educators and school communities about their goals and practices" (p. 52). Such dialogue may be absent due to a lack of awareness of other possibilities, a lack of motivation to pursue change, or – as in the case of online IEP classes – local and national policies. Just as computer software is programmed with default settings that aim to please most of the users most of the time, each field of education comes with its own defaults, that is, dominant practices and expectations that render other choices "more difficult to articulate and implement" (Gunzenhauser, 2003, p. 55) and are thus only questioned in times of crisis.

The response to the coronavirus pandemic was exactly such a crisis for IEPs since it made visible a number of largely unchallenged assumptions about academic second-language learning. However, the unique demands and well-developed methodologies of ESL and English for Academic Purposes (EAP) programs themselves caused us to question some of the default positions taken in online teaching and educational technology. Consequently, the unprecedented switch to online teaching and learning brought two sets of defaults into dialogue and sometimes conflict, the resolution of which would require engaged dialogue among faculty, instructional designers, and administrators. The pre-pandemic defaults in our and other IEPs included:

- The classroom is inherently the best place for academic language acquisition to occur: language programs under US visa regulations must provide a minimum number of classroom hours (18 per week); indeed the entire premise of a degree-preparation program – at least until recently – has been predicated upon in-person attendance.

- Instructed second language acquisition is necessarily synchronous, since it requires a balance of comprehensible input, interaction, opportunities for negotiation of form and meaning, language production, and timely feedback (Ellis & Shintani, 2013). Students' physical presence is thus presumed to be a condition for attention and ultimately language learning.

Meanwhile, some of the defaults that we initially encountered in the online teaching world were:

- Asynchronous learning is or should be the default mode of online education: since online teaching developed from distance learning, the dominant modality has typically been asynchronous, with synchronous instruction associated with in-person not online classes (Mick & Middlebrook, 2015). Educational technologists on social media in the early days of the pandemic were vocal in warning against synchronous teaching because of the demands on Internet bandwidth as well as valid concerns about accessibility, privacy, time differences, and exhaustion (e.g., Kim, 2020).
- The purpose of a learning management system (LMS), the centerpiece of most online courses, is to organize content into modules, for example, one module a week: the typical approach to the LMS is to rely on the "easy affordances of the online world" by creating course websites whose purpose is to "deliver" learning through curated and organized materials (Richards & Valentine, 2020).
- Students should be encouraged to find their own path through online content because the most important advantage of online classes is the convenience of participating in their own time (Richards & Valentine, 2020).

In educational technology, default options "are default *values* and therefore particularly open to critique" (Bayne, 2008, p. 400). To be clear, some default positions for ESL and online teaching remain valid in many contexts, but just as advanced computer users learn to tweak the settings in order to make the technology work better for them, my colleagues and I learned through trial, error, help, study, and reflection where both sets of defaults fell short in the particular setting of teaching ESL/EAP classes online. These discoveries will probably not be confined to the crisis management of the covid campus but will stay with us as we move into hybrid and in-person teaching.

Beyond the Synchronous/Asynchronous Dichotomy

Synchronous teaching occurs when the instructor and students are all in the same physical or virtual place at the same time. Synchronous teaching is such a fixed default in IEPs that it really could just be called teaching. Under pre-covid (and presumably eventually once more under post-covid) visa laws, students had to attend a minimum of 18 hours a week in the classroom, which is one reason IEPs deserve the name "intensive". While there are developed pedagogies for "flipped classrooms" in ESL (Brinks Lockwood, 2018), they still rely on intensive synchronous classroom time. This preference for in-person learning is not just a legal mandate, but it is also the approach suggested by the broad consensus of ESL research and methodologies. Language learners need comprehensible input, extensive opportunities for interaction with negotiation of form and/or meaning, immediate as well as delayed corrective feedback and recasting, and the chance to produce output, particularly modified through interaction or indicating uptake of instruction (Ellis & Shintani, 2013). Hence the typical structure of an IEP with daily lessons and an emphasis on in-person attendance has justifiably become the default for instructed second-language acquisition, especially for academic purposes. As Hinkel (2004) somewhat wryly notes, the reason students cannot pick up academic language from everyday interaction is that it is not present there. Thus, the classroom environment has been seen as the only place where students will be exposed to academic genres.

Meanwhile, many online educators grew concerned as their colleagues latched onto Zoom, Teams, Google Meet, and other video platforms at the start of the pandemic with little training in online pedagogy. Zoom in particular became synonymous with emergency remote teaching leading to scathing editorials about the presumed inferior quality of "Zoom University" (e.g., Kim, 2020; Lauria, 2020) and even court cases demanding tuition refunds. From the perspective of online instructional design, live video is a risky and undesirable default for learning: it demands very high bandwidth, reliable Internet connections, and relatively powerful devices, all of which entail costs and raise accessibility issues. Synchronous teaching also mitigates against some of the benefits of (asynchronous) online classes: the ability to learn on one's own schedule, accommodations for students with disabilities, and the flexibility to manage education alongside other responsibilities (Flaherty, 2020). In one widely read and shared article, a prominent professor and author complained that on Zoom "the communicative signs that embodied humans rely on are thinned, flattened, made more effortful or entirely impossible" (Blum, 2020). Since these communicative signs are not only essential to language teaching but also often learning outcomes of academic language courses, synchronous teaching might appear impossible and even counterproductive. Set against all these benefits of asynchronous learning, though, were the needs and perceptions of ESL faculty who had never questioned the default of classroom teaching and were concerned that students would not pay attention and learn language if they were not under constant observation.

Our compromise required us to reset several defaults. At times, the determination to use Zoom seemed to indicate a quixotic desire to simply replicate the classroom online (Kim, 2020). Yet now students could turn off their cameras, mute their microphones, and all but vanish. This new reality called into question a default assumption of in-person instruction, namely, that physical presence means students are paying attention. The only solution was to return to the fundamentals of language teaching – input, interaction, and output – and also reimagine what engagement could mean in the online ESL classroom. Each instructor made different choices in response to the language level of their course and both their own and their students' comfort with technology. Through reading, discussion, and support from instructional designers, these solutions included:

- Blending predominantly synchronous courses with asynchronous components, up to a maximum of 40% of class time;
- Ensuring that asynchronous modules alternated between opportunities for input (readings, audio, videos, Quizlet vocabulary sets) and output (quizzes, discussion boards, low-stakes assignments) for both practice and accountability;
- Creating opportunities for asynchronous interaction so that asynchronous learning could be social and interactive as well as individualized, self-paced, and monologic; for example, using Padlet (a flexible platform for generating shared content), Flipgrid (a video recording and feedback app), discussion boards (both text and audio/video), and Perusall (an interactive reading tool);
- In synchronous classes, using technologies such as Zoom's in-meeting chat, Google Docs, Padlet, Kahoot, Quizlet Live, NearPod, and Poll Everywhere to provide multiple means for students to interact, negotiate, produce language, receive feedback, and engage with target language;
- Deploying breakout rooms with clear roles and outcomes, for example completing an online handout or creating a slide within a shared presentation, so that all students can engage (and be observed engaging) with the language.

Changing the default was not a simple or smooth transition. It required the support of the university's Academic Technology Services, as well as an internal task force chaired by a faculty member (the author) given release time to support online teaching and learning. Some students and faculty longed to return to the classroom and their prior defaults, but many saw advantages in the "new normal" that could be retained.

Learning or Management Systems?

One of the biggest challenges with moving online was the increased reliance on the university's supported LMS, Canvas. More than any other tool, the LMS seems to propose a default use that tends more toward management than learning (Castañeda & Selwyn, 2018). A simple illustrative example of this is the home page that students first see when they open each course from their LMS dashboard. Canvas offers several options, but the default in our instantiation of the LMS is a list of modules. The rationale behind these options appears to be the assumption that online courses are either asynchronous, thus divided into modules that correspond to major topics in the course, or synchronous with one module per week. Indeed, the optional course-site template provided by the university automatically populates Canvas with 16 modules, one for each week of the semester.

The modular view makes certain assumptions about teaching and learning. As Bayne (2008) explains, the LMS interface "creates – and occludes – particular 'ways of seeing' information space, and both opens and closes off particular ways of being and acting online" (p. 396). Modules are essentially lists of resources that students work through in a linear fashion: there is a "next" button at the end of each page, quiz, discussion board, or assignment. There is an inherent rigidity to the module structure, even though the contents of modules are highly flexible. Modules manage asynchronous courses quite effectively by guiding students through a learning path that has been predetermined by the instructor or course designer. A prominent button allows the instructor to "view progress" and determine whether students have "completed" the modules. The implied default – "a value system and an ontology" (Bayne, 2008, p. 397) – is that learning occurs in a top-down "hierarchy", which is at odds with the information structure of the Internet itself with its hyperlinks and rabbit holes of clicking.

The hierarchical structure is maintained in a curious feature of Canvas: when building a new course with modules, the interface defaults to inviting the designer to "Drop files here to add to module" as if the best practice is simply to upload documents, handouts, images, and slides, turning modules into little more than weekly repositories of materials. It is of course perfectly possible to ignore this suggestion and instead build modules that are sophisticated and interactive collections of videos, readings, discussion boards, and quizzes. However, the default pushes toward a course design that is at odds with the interactive and recursive nature of language learning.

Navigating an LMS takes some practice and can be daunting for students learning English and digital literacy at the same time. When open in the default module view, Canvas presents four different means of navigation; from left to right, they are: a global menu to move between course sites, the LMS in-box, and calendar; the course-specific menu with access to the syllabus, assignments, grades, and sections of the site; the list of modules and their content; and a final set of buttons (view course stream, calendar, and notifications) above a to-do list and recently graded assignments. Quite aside from the vocabulary (course stream? modules? media gallery?), the sheer volume of information on the screen can be overwhelming to an English learner who may never have encountered an LMS before. Indeed, students' responses to some of our most elaborate and detailed course sites was confusion. As McMillan Cottom (2019) notes, "it doesn't matter whether or not a tool can do something; it matters whether or not students can make sense of what the tool is doing".

The goal of an LMS should not really be to manage learning but to facilitate or organize it. In the case of language courses delivered in synchronous or blended modes, the LMS needs to be very easily navigable, present a consistent interface among courses, and provide students with the information they need quickly and easily. Furthermore, since our IEP runs on short schedules with very little time between sessions, we needed a way to easily share materials without reinventing the digital wheel. What emerged from trial, error, and a lot of advice from the university's instructional design team was the importance of viewing the LMS from two different perspectives: the teacher's and the student's. From the teacher's perspective, the LMS is an organizational tool; from the student's perspective, it is a means of navigation.

The system we settled on attempts to serve both purposes. We constructed a Canvas template, a new default created in response to local needs, comprising:

- A static homepage with information organized according to frequency of use: that is, information which students need most often should be highest on the page. Our current home page includes course title and description; links to each week's launchpad page (see below); instructor's information (name, contact information, Zoom link); class schedule and time-zone convertor; textbook information and links to ancillary sites; help bar with links to events, activities, and institute resources.
- Launchpad pages for each week: Since modules were overwhelming, we switched to providing a page for each week with links, documents, and homework clearly labeled in daily tabs. Class recordings from the Zoom meetings are linked here after each lesson. This means students have all the resources they need within one or two clicks of the homepage. Furthermore, teachers can easily edit the pages to reflect the reality of IEP teaching: moving activities between days, and quickly updating the course and the site to meet students' needs and unexpected shifts in the schedule. Essentially, the launchpad page is the LMS equivalent of writing the daily agenda and homework on the whiteboard at the start of class, except students can view the page at any time, for example, to catch up after an absence or technical difficulty (a way of life in the age of emergency and sustained online teaching). Launchpad pages also contain tabs for asynchronous work in blended courses; since the links point to content that is organized in modules, students can still proceed linearly and/or use the launchpad page as a checklist. My colleagues Jackie Whitney, Wakako Pennington, and Monica Farling were instrumental in developing the launchpad pages and this entire approach to Canvas site design.
- Modules with the underlying content and resources: The modules section of the LMS is teacher-facing not student-facing (in fact, it can be hidden from students). This allows teachers to keep handouts, teacher notes, answer keys, and unpublished assessments organized.
- Announcements sent as e-mails: Teachers were initially asked to send an announcement with the links and homework for each class. However, since classes meet daily, the quantity of emails generated became frustrating for students. While this method – a default of many online courses – is still valid

for classes that meet less frequently, for example, a graduate course with one seminar a week, it turned out to be inappropriate and overwhelming for the IEP. Since all the information is now quickly available on the homepage and weekly launchpad, announcements are now used more sparingly for actual announcements, not regular class business.

- Shared coursepacks that can be imported into "shell" sites each session: Unlike many university courses, our IEP regularly runs multiple sections of a course that share the same materials, and teachers may be assigned to different courses every session with limited preparation time. We were fortunate that our IEP administration was able to offer course release time throughout the first year of the pandemic to allow instructors and course designers to create "coursepacks", that is complete LMS sites with all the resources future teachers would need. Coursepacks include course guides for teachers who are new to the class. These coursepacks are uploaded to a password-protected area of Canvas Commons, which allows colleagues to import course materials. Maintaining and updating these coursepacks are challenges that we are still addressing, but there is broad consensus that this method is an efficient and sustainable way of ensuring consistency and collaboration among colleagues even as we return to in-person teaching.

- A branded homepage and templates for discussion boards, quizzes, assignments, and launchpad pages: The template has gone through several iterations but quickly emerged as a way not only to standardize the look and feel of the courses (so that students would not have to learn new methods of interacting with the LMS for each class every eight weeks) but also to promote good practices in (online) ESL teaching. For example, the template for a writing assignment has blocks for teachers or designers to fill in the purpose of the task, the learning outcomes addressed, the directions for the task, the target language students should try to use, the schedule for drafts, a rubric, and help links (e.g., how to submit a file).

Ultimately, the LMS has to be molded to the shape of the class and not the other way around. Bayne (2008) challenges designers to ask:

> What social and pedagogical practices does the [Virtual Learning Environment] interface reflect, inform and inscribe? What meanings does it produce? What version of pedagogy does it 'make visible', and what alternatives does it blind us to?
>
> *(p. 397)*

The "version of pedagogy" made visible in the coursepack is derived from the principles of instructed second-language acquisition as well as a concern for an interface that is clear and consistent. At the same time, it attempts to reflect and inscribe the understanding that language can be taught and learned in online and hybrid environments in addition to the traditional classroom. Castañeda and Selwyn (2018) are rightly concerned that "regardless of the pedagogic intent of university educators, the software they use shapes what can and cannot be done" (p. 6). A linear approach that neatly divides a course into separate units is a poor fit for an academic language class in which skills are developed and recycled as students interact with each other, with the instructor, with assignments, and with texts in various media. At the same time, using an LMS rigorously, as online teaching demands, can also help EAP instructors make the structure, expectations, and outcomes of the course more visible, benefits that will carry forward to the brick-and-mortar classroom.

Conclusion

One way to view the social impacts of the Covid-19 pandemic is to say that it accelerated trends that were previously just gathering momentum, including the "slow, two-decade march toward more digital business models" in higher education (Gallagher & Palmer, 2020). Indeed, none of the tools that seemed novel to many teachers in March 2020 was in fact new: even Zoom, which became synonymous with online teaching during the pandemic, was already nine years old and had been the market leader in video conferencing software since 2017 (Dooley, 2020). A 2016 marketing flyer claimed that "over 5,600 educational institutions, including 88% of Top US Universities, use Zoom" (Zoom Video Communications, 2016); the University of Delaware was one of those early adopters.

Now, though, Zoom as well as Canvas and their competitors are as familiar in higher education as blackboard chalk and overhead projectors once were. Castañeda and Selwyn in a prescient 2018 article warn that "this requires an ongoing suspicion and skepticism (rather than cynicism) toward seemingly 'ubiquitous' technologies that are all too easy to take for granted as they recede into the background of everyday life" (p. 8). In other words, as much as technology may have rescued IEPs during a period in which programs' very existence was under threat, it will continue to be essential to question the new defaults that have emerged to ensure that they continue to meet students', faculty's, and institutions' needs. Default options "bear a burden of assumption relating to how the software should be used and how meaning is to be constructed (Bayne, 2008)". As new norms and expectations emerge, they too must be challenged and the values they inscribe questioned, particularly as they relate to the commodification of higher education, the global role of English and English-medium institutions, and faculty workloads and teaching conditions.

The longest lasting lesson of the pandemic for academic language instruction in IEPs is probably not going to be techniques for managing interaction in synchronous online lessons, nor organizing information more clearly in an LMS.

Instead, it will be the process that the shift to online learning required in order for IEPs to remain vibrant and viable: the engagement in dialogue and reflection on pedagogy, student engagement, and educational defaults for which there is too often no time or energy.

Reference list

Bayne, S. (2008). Higher education as a visual practice: Seeing through the virtual learning environment. *Teaching in Higher Education, 13*(4), 395–410. https://doi.org/10.1080/13562510802169665

Blum, S. D. (2020, April 22). A professor explores why Zoom classes deplete her energy. *Inside Higher Education.* www.insidehighered.com/advice/2020/04/22/professor-explores-why-zoom-classes-deplete-her-energy-opinion

Brinks Lockwood, R. (2018). *Flipping the classroom: What every ESL teacher should know.* University of Michigan Press.

Castañeda, L., & Selwyn, N. (2018). More than tools? Making sense of the ongoing digitizations of higher education. *International Journal of Educational Technology in Higher Education, 15*(22). https://doi.org/10.1186/s41239-018-0109-y

Dooley, R. (2020, September 30). How Zoom conquered video conferencing. *Forbes.* www.forbes.com/sites/rogerdooley/2020/09/30/how-zoom-conquered-video-conferencing/

Ellis, R., & Shintani, N. (2013). *Exploring language pedagogy through second language acquisition research.* Routledge.

Flaherty, C. (2020, April 29). Zoom boom. *Inside Higher Education.* www.insidehighered.com/news/2020/04/29/synchronous-instruction-hot-right-now-it-sustainable

Gallagher, S., & Palmer, J. (2020, September 29). The pandemic pushed universities online. The change was long overdue. *Harvard Business Review.* https://hbr.org/2020/09/the-pandemic-pushed-universities-online-the-change-was-long-overdue

Gunzenhauser, M. G. (2003). High-stakes testing and the default philosophy of education. *Theory into Practice, 42*(1), 51–58. https://doi.org/10.1207/s15430421tip4201_7

Hinkel, E. (2004). *Teaching academic ESL writing: Practical techniques in vocabulary and grammar.* Lawrence Erlbaum.

Hodges, C., Moore, S., Lockee, B., & Bond, A. (2020, March 27). The difference between emergency remote teaching and online learning. *Educause Review.* https://er.educause.edu/articles/2020/3/the-difference-between-emergency-remote-teaching-and-online-learning

Kim, J. (2020, November 8). Higher ed needs to go on a zoom diet. *Inside Higher Education.* www.insidehighered.com/blogs/learning-innovation/higher-ed-needs-go-zoom-diet

Lauria, S. (2020, September 19). Zoom University is cheating students out of a proper education. *The Statesman.* www.sbstatesman.com/2020/09/19/zoom-university-is-cheating-students-out-of-a-proper-education/

McMillan Cottom, T. (2019, August 26). *Rethinking the context of edtech.* https://er.educause.edu/articles/2019/8/rethinking-the-context-of-edtech

Mick, C. S., & Middlebrook, G. (2015). Asynchronous and synchronous modalities. In B. L. Hewett, K. E. DePew, E. Guler, & R. Z. Warner (Eds.), *Foundational practices of online writing instruction* (pp. 129–148). The WAC Clearinghouse and Parlor Press. https://doi.org/10.37514/PER-B.2015.0650.2.03

Richards, R., & Valentine, S. J. (2020, March 13). A letter to educators teaching online for the first time. *EdSurge*. www.edsurge.com/news/2020-03-13-a-letter-to-educators-teaching-online-for-the-first-time

Zoom Video Communications. (2016). *Create your classroom in the cloud*. http://wp.auburn.edu/biggio/wp-content/uploads/2017/07/zoom_education_data_sheet.pdf

13

TEAM UP

Lessons from moving an academic writing course for University teachers in Slovakia and Czechia online

Linda Steyne, Agnes Simon, Angeniet Kam, Eszter Timár, and Jan Beneš

Introduction

Though the negative impact of the unwelcome transition from face-to-face to online education precipitated by the Covid-19 pandemic has been widely discussed (e.g., Shin & Hickey, 2020; Ferri et al., 2020; Petillion & McNeil, 2020), some outcomes have been positive. This applies to the newly designed intensive face-to-face academic writing course we created for full-time academics of social sciences and humanities at two Central European universities. These academics face publication requirements no less demanding than their Western contemporaries, all the while writing in a foreign language with no writing support. Our group of five instructors from diverse backgrounds in academic writing at various European universities set out to address these needs and designed a pioneering academic writing course for faculty members. Before having the chance to implement it, however, the Covid-19 pandemic forced us to transform it to online delivery. In this chapter, we show how such a transformation can positively influence teaching and learning processes. We first introduce the context which led to the creation of the original face-to face – as yet, undelivered – course, and then describe course objectives, principles, and design. Subsequently, we explain our transition to forced online distance education (FODE), and finally reflect on how that transformation and, in particular, team teaching influenced the experience for us as teachers and our participants as learners. We conclude with recommendations for how teachers of academic writing – especially those co-teaching – could benefit from our experience, whether teaching face-to-face or online.

DOI: 10.4324/9781003283409-17

Academic writing in Central and Eastern Europe

The limited number of studies that analyse academic writing practices at Central and Eastern European (CEE) universities focus on students rather than staff. Scholars prioritize exploring the needs, writing quality, and writing culture of students of English philology and teaching English as a foreign language (TEFL) degree programmes (e.g., Hublová, 2017; Foltýnek & Rybička, 2013; Bérešová, 2015; Jančaríková et al., 2020), as these programmes tend to include the few academic writing courses that exist (Harbord, 2010). The perceptions and English language publication experience of faculty members are largely neglected (cf. Curry & Lillis, 2004), as is the explicit teaching of academic writing.

Yet, the careers and livelihoods of faculty members depend on English academic writing skills. As elsewhere, full-time academic staff at CEE universities are increasingly required to publish their research in international, peer-reviewed English-language journals. However, these institutions rarely support faculty members in their academic writing needs, with many papers ending up in low-impact national or regional journals.

The situations at the two universities where our course was offered are cases in point. At Comenius University in Bratislava (UNIBA), Slovakia, the only academic writing courses for students, taught primarily by adjuncts, are offered by the Department of Foreign Languages at the request of other departments, while the Department of British and American Studies offers one undergraduate elective. No writing course is available for doctoral candidates or faculty members nor is there a writing centre or institutional support for either students or faculty members. At the same time, contract renewal is tied to yearly targets: assistant professors should produce two publications, while associate and full professors are expected to produce three low-impact or two high-impact publications (Comenius University in Bratislava, 2020a). And yet, in 2019, only one-third of all publications, whether articles or books, by faculty members were published internationally (Comenius University in Bratislava, 2020b).

The situation at Masaryk University (MUNI), Czech Republic, is slightly better. University-wide academic writing courses are offered as introductory, intensive workshops about once a year. Other elective courses are sometimes offered by individual faculties or the Pedagogical Competence Development Centre (CERPEK), and consultation services – primarily for Czech academic writing – are provided by faculty libraries. In 2020, a small online writing lab was established in the Language Centre. Unlike UNIBA, job security at MUNI does not depend on a minimum number of publications. Instead, faculty members are motivated to publish peer-reviewed impact articles in English by performance bonuses and by the Czech Ministry of Education's recently adopted methodology for evaluating publication output (Flégl et al., 2015).

Course objectives and design principles

The intensive *Academic Writing for Publication* course for faculty was proposed as part of the Erasmus+ project *Improving academic teaching and internationalisation through enhanced competences of university teachers* (IMPACT) to address some of the challenges discussed earlier. The IMPACT project's commitment to improving the experience of home and international students by developing faculty competencies predetermined certain aspects of the course design. First, the course targeted 40 academics (in two iterations) at the faculties of arts at UNIBA and MUNI. Second, since the course was proposed to enhance publication in English-language journals, only faculty members and doctoral students with sufficient English language skills were eligible. Third, the project brought together an international group of academic writing experts from four European partner universities – UNIBA, MUNI, Central European University (Hungary), and Delft University of Technology (the Netherlands) – to design and deliver a five-day, face-to-face academic writing course, first in January 2021 (UNIBA), then January 2022 (MUNI).

Thus, while the primary objective was to equip participants with the knowledge and skills needed to successfully submit papers to peer-reviewed English-language journals, our course also devoted about one-third of class time to incorporating academic writing into participants' own courses. Additionally, in the CEE higher education context, where frontal lecturing remains the predominant teaching method, we sought to promote student-centred active-learning techniques. This was achieved by combining mini lectures with critical reading and thinking exercises, group and pair work, peer learning, and emphasizing the process of writing during instruction. We encouraged participants to adopt a similar approach when integrating elements of academic writing into their own teaching.

As the target publication was a journal article, we built the syllabus around its typical organization and characteristics. We expected participants to start the course with preliminary drafts of articles and finish with completed drafts, near ready for submission. Therefore, both morning sessions concentrated on developing participants' general academic writing skills while advancing their manuscripts. Finally, to reduce the stress of writing in English, all feedback was formative, with certificates of completion awarded on the basis of attendance, participation, and completion of writing tasks.

Regional variations were also taken into consideration. Thus, day 1 provided a general introduction to academic writing with attention to cultural differences, as Czech and Slovak scholars may be unaware that expectations differ when writing in English (Jančaríková et al., 2020). Participants were also familiarized with the requirements of the journal manuscript genre. Day 2 focused on the journal introduction, highlighting the importance of clearly stated research questions and a thesis statement. On day 3, the focus was on manuscript organization, including features of paragraphing, coherence, and cohesion. Day 4 was devoted to the effective and fair use of sources, including the integration of relevant literature alongside referencing and citations. Referencing was of particular importance due to less awareness of referencing expectations compared to Western academia (Foltýnek & Rybička, 2013). Day 5 saw participants learning about conclusions and abstracts, as well as navigation of the journal submission and editing process through a live discussion with the editor of an international, English-language, peer-reviewed journal.

The original course

On the basis of the principles and decisions for course content outlined earlier, we developed session plans and instructional materials between November 2019 and September 2020. Efficiency, a limited travel budget, and previous best practices during similar projects, prompted the assigning of each thematic teaching day to a different instructor who would be on site only for that day. Having agreed on three 90-minute sessions for the five consecutive days, we each had considerable independence in designing our three sessions. To ensure consistency in content and approach, we reviewed each other's session plans and implemented modifications to avoid repetition and omissions. After the final session each afternoon, a writing lab was planned for interested participants to collaboratively work on their manuscripts and receive feedback from that day's instructor.

By May 2020, the only preparation remaining was the creation of instructional materials and details of the writing lab. We were confident that the worst of the pandemic was behind us, and universities would return to face-to-face instruction in the 2020/2021 academic year. The experience of a relatively pandemic-free summer in Europe, as well as communications between the partner universities and the project manager, encouraged us to believe the *Academic Writing for Publication* course could take place in person the following January. As the autumn semester approached in mid-September, however, it became increasingly clear that we would be teaching online.

The challenges and opportunities of FODE

Our experience transforming a face-to-face academic writing course to online delivery differs distinctly from online education during the Covid-19 pandemic. First, while many of the chapters in this book belong within the framework of emergency remote teaching (ERT) (Hodges et al., 2020), our experience fits more closely with the concept of FODE (Dolenc et al., 2021, p. 19). ERT's emphasis on providing "temporary access to instruction and instructional supports" is in contrast to our objective of developing a sustainable course with "a robust educational ecosystem" (Hodges et al., 2020), regardless of the medium of delivery. This is reinforced by the course's two iterations: the experiences of the first iteration would inform improvements to the second; and offering it twice would lead to greater awareness and support from the faculty and university leadership.

Furthermore, the timeframe of our transition from one medium of instruction to another was much longer than the immediate switch associated with ERT (Hodges et al., 2020). Instead of a few days, we had nearly three months. Thus, we experienced the essence of FODE, that is, "a combination of content and pedagogy in an online environment with the mostly unwanted pressure to go online" (Dolenc et al., 2021, p. 2) but without time pressure.

While like others we were "forced online" irrespective of our "abilities and the condition of [participants' and our own] equipment" (Hodges et al., 2020), we were fortunate to have already had experience in either traditional online education or ERT. Because our experiences varied greatly, we could offer a wider range of expertise than an individual instructor facing similar decisions. Moreover, creating a web-enabled, face-to-face course benefited the emphasis on writing (Means et al., 2014, pp. 6–8) by allowing storage of easily accessible digital versions of all in- and outside-class writing tasks on the MUNI Information System (IS), an online course management system.

Unlike most who transitioned to ERT, the motivation of our target participant – faculty and doctoral students – was less likely to lead to additional challenges. In contrast to many ERT classes, our course would exclude the "less prepared and less-mature learners [who] have reduced success in fully online courses" (Means et al., 2014, p. 181). Our participants enrolled voluntarily, were aware of the difficulties of online delivery, and remained committed to attending regardless of the mode of delivery, and therefore resembled highly motivated online adult learners of pre-pandemic times (Cercone, 2008).

The primary challenge for us, apart from the online teaching realities of reduced attention spans and possibly less material being covered, is not commonly associated with online education: co-teaching. As five instructors, we needed closer and fuller cooperation regarding what to teach, how to teach, and when to teach in order to work within the limitations of online delivery. In addition to considering the interests of the course participants, we also had to be sensitive to each other's teaching styles and technological skills and could only proceed with adapting course content when these issues had been resolved.

Course adjustments

As mentioned previously, the challenges and negative aspects of ERT have been widely studied and it is the "undesirable side effects" that Dolenc et al. (2021) also emphasize in FODE. One of these is the assumption that while instructors can manipulate the new environment to work for themselves, students have no choice but to adapt or quit. We set out to move *Academic Writing for Publication* online with the conviction that our responsibility was to create an environment that benefits both the teacher and the learner. Thus, we aimed to create an "online community of learners" (Means et al., 2014, p. 28) while taking into account the "instructional design dimensions" (ibid. p. 26) of online education. These nine dimensions – modality, pacing, student–instructor ratio, pedagogy, instructor role online, student role online, online communication synchrony, role of online assessment, and source of feedback (ibid. pp. 26–28) – were adapted to the context of Covid-19 lockdown, during which when both instructors and participants were confined to their homes. The challenges of this new environment were undeniable, but they also created new opportunities.

Modality

With Covid-19 restrictions in place, "all instruction and assessment [had to be] carried out using online, Internet-based delivery" (Means et al., 2014, p. 7). For the live lessons, rather than using the universities' preferred Teams, we chose Zoom as we found it more user-friendly and practical since it makes no distinction between participants from within and outside the hosting institution. For digital material storage and exchange, we relied more heavily on the MUNI IS and uploaded all learning materials – reading, links, videos, PowerPoint slides, task descriptions, assessment rubrics, and formative feedback – to this virtual learning environment. Receiving all participant submissions in the MUNI IS also enabled all instructors to follow participants' progress.

Pacing and online communication synchrony

As with the original course, the online version was largely class-paced and synchronous, with some self-paced and asynchronous elements. Nevertheless, we decided to adjust the online course schedule to better match both the medium of instruction and the participants' working – and learning – conditions. Our experience with ERT convinced us that a five-day, content-heavy, online writing course would result in "Zoom fatigue" (Bailenson, 2021), hindering both our teaching and participants' learning. In addition, participants attending sessions while sitting at home would almost certainly face other distractions from work and family.

To mitigate these issues, we first trimmed the two morning sessions from 90 to 75 minutes, shortening the course day. Second, we moved to teaching every other day, extending the course from five to ten days. An extra half day was added on the 11th day for a Q&A session and reflections on the benefits of the course. Third, due to its impracticality online, we abandoned the idea of a writing lab, instead encouraging participants to work on their manuscript on their own. Fourth, we exploited technological opportunities inherent in online delivery and placed pre-recorded preparatory videos and recordings of the daily sessions on the MUNI IS. Introducing these asynchronous elements meant participants could prepare at their own pace and catch up if they missed a session.

The greatest communication challenge was the loss of informal discussions among participants and instructors, for instance, during coffee breaks. These allow for community building and offer invaluable learning opportunities, factors which are harder to facilitate in an online setting. Under the circumstances, we could only offer limited alternatives. In class, we implemented more collaborative activities and ensured that everyone had the chance to meet and work with everyone else during small group exercises. We offered our time during coffee and lunch breaks to discuss questions and added the informal Q&A session to the last day.

The role of online assessment and source of feedback

Our commitment to a student-centred active-learning environment and overall pedagogical approach changed little in the move online. Following Means et al.'s (2014, p. 27) four styles of learning, both the original and online courses were expository (via short presentations), practice (via short writing activities and revising), exploratory (via analysis of benchmark articles for standard norms), and collaborative (via pair and group work as well as peer feedback). It was the balance and manifestation of these learning styles that were altered. For instance, we placed some preparatory materials and tasks online, prioritizing a flipped classroom approach. This provided more time for collaborative activities and Q&A sessions. We also discarded time-consuming and organization-heavy activities. To ensure a common vocabulary, we created a glossary of academic writing accessible to both instructors and participants.

Formative assessment was central, whether oral or written, from peers and instructors. Its principal purpose was to "provide [. . . participant] and teacher with information about learning" (Means et al., 2014, p. 12) to help participants improve. Without the writing lab, however, participants lost the opportunity to receive immediate feedback while revising their manuscripts. We offset this in three ways. First, we used shorter, in-class tasks that addressed essential features of academic writing which participants could apply towards more extensive revision. Second, we offered feedback outside the course framework to those who submitted their papers. Finally, we prioritized oral peer feedback over instructor feedback in many of the collaborative tasks, especially in the afternoon sessions when participants sought to create academic writing activities for their courses. Peer feedback was followed up by either short plenary debriefings or written feedback from the instructors via the MUNI IS.

Student-instructor ratio and the roles of the instructor(s) and participants

In moving online, the role of the participants changed little. As previously discussed, Means et al.'s (2014, p. 27) four styles of learning varied little between our face-to-face and online course, and thus students fulfilled all four roles from "listening or reading; to working on problems or answering questions; to exploring a set of resources . . .; to working with peers in a collaborative project" (Means et al., 2014, p. 12).

What changed dramatically were the student-instructor ratio and the instructor's role. The original ratio of participant to instructor was 20:1. Online, that changed to 4:1, as we all became a constant presence in every session. This transformed our roles: When not the primary instructor, we became teaching assistants, an expert panel, and, for one day each, a facilitator for a teammate's day, taking attendance, fielding questions and comments in chat, creating breakout rooms, sharing links, and solving technical issues. Thus, these changes in the instructors' role cannot be characterized by how active or passive they were as Means et al. (2014, pp. 11–12) suggest, but rather by how the group of instructors for the planned face-to face course transformed into a team of instructors online.

Discussion: team teaching as the benefit of FODE

In our case, team teaching is the most positive outcome of the online transition for both instructors and participants. Team members' compatibility and expertise, alongside the classroom environment, can create a positive experience for students (Anderson & Speck, 1998). "When a team of individuals share the belief that through their unified efforts they can overcome challenges and produce intended results, [they] *are* more effective" (Donohoo et al., 2018, p. 41). Such a belief in collective teacher efficacy (CTE) improves the team's effectiveness substantially and thus greatly increases student achievement (Eells, 2011). Our individual commitment to providing the most beneficial learning experience for participants, our shared belief that writing skills can and must be trained, and our "clear . . . vision of the class" (Anderson & Speck, 1998, p. 677) made that compatibility possible. Thus, we worked harmoniously from the start, but FODE was crucial to our transformation from group to team.

This transformation is most notable where we differed – in background, expertise, experience, and skills. Our previously unscheduled, and eventually frequent, online meetings were instrumental: we got to know each other, not only professionally but also personally, as we shared our daily (pandemic-related) experiences. More importantly, we gained a better understanding of each other's strengths and challenges, and so could respond where we felt most comfortable, for example, reporting on an area of the literature, organizing the MUNI IS, working on the glossary, training Zoom skills, or screening the benchmark articles submitted by students. Through conscious effort, our differences became complementary, and the changes to our roles contributed to this. The realization that our collaboration, including the presence of all instructors, was supportive and collegial rather than intrusive and intimidating was what ultimately solidified our work as a team of teachers, rather than just a group of instructors.

The close collaboration of team members had a twofold benefit for participants. The first, curriculum flexibility, was the result of being able to see what was covered, what content the participants already knew, and what they struggled with. Thus, we could adjust future sessions and activities accordingly, ensuring that we maximized learning through meeting course objectives while responding to immediate participant needs. The second, a collaborative classroom environment, was the result of high levels of collegiality among team members, and this also encourages student participation (Anderson & Speck, 1998, p. 673). The continued presence of all five instructors not only allowed us to share multiple perspectives from a variety of institutions but also served as a model of mutual respect. Participants followed our lead, constructively supporting one another and dispelling our initial concerns about how CEE participants at various stages in their careers would treat those "beneath" them on the academic ladder during collaborative tasks and peer feedback. This made for a positive learning environment, facilitating additional opportunities for learning such as when two participants held a tutorial on reference managers for interested peers during a lunch break.

Future implications and recommendations

The online design and delivery of *Academic Writing for Publication* not only provide us with invaluable insights for future iterations of the course, but also allow us to offer recommendations to colleagues. Transitioning to online delivery has helped us clarify what content is essential, what may work better as preparatory material, and how to increase the coherence and logic of the course. Pedagogically, both the increased use of the flipped classroom model and peer feedback brought positive outcomes. Above all, teaching online has highlighted the benefits of teaching as a team, rather than simply as a group of instructors, and it may serve as a model of instruction for similar short-term intensive online courses and beyond, no matter the context.

We cannot emphasize enough the need for academic writing courses for faculty members. Seeing course participants' limited knowledge and skills in academic writing at the beginning of the course and their appetite for knowledge have strengthened our conviction that English language academic writing courses and institutional support for CEE faculty are crucial in assisting individual social scientists in their career advancement and in facilitating global recognition of CEE scholarly output. We witnessed mid- and late-career faculty become familiar with the basic principles of research questions, thesis statements, topic sentences, appropriate paraphrasing, and the various elements of effective writing for the first time in their careers. Participants demonstrated noticeable improvement in their receptive understanding of good practices in academic writing as they analysed benchmark articles and gave peer feedback. Therefore, we encourage academic writing instructors at universities in regions which lack a tradition for academic writing support for faculty to educate colleagues about academic writing and raise awareness by offering such intensive short courses.

Nevertheless, because these types of courses alone are insufficient for participants who lack foundational writing skills to noticeably improve, we recommend including a writing lab and extending the course over one semester. We found the loss of the lab hindered the advancement of participants' manuscripts. Although some consultations did take place with a few participants via e-mail, this lacked the benefit immediate feedback can bring. Therefore, in the case of an intensive short course, we propose consultations after the third session of each course day. With a semester-long course, consultations can be scheduled on a different day, appropriate to the needs of the instructors and participants. Team teaching could make the writing lab more manageable and effective, both face-to-face, and online by dividing participants among instructors and allowing them to form mentoring relationships. While the writing lab establishes time and space exclusively for writing, it takes longer for writing skills to be honed and texts to mature. This process of extensive redrafting requires reflection that cannot be rushed. Additionally, time is also needed for the course instructors (or participants) to provide in-depth feedback on multiple revisions. We believe that a semester-long course, meeting one full day every other week, with three, at least 90-minute, sessions each of those days would be most effective to that end.

Finally, sustainable improvement in the quality of CEE university students' academic writing is likely to begin through the teaching of their instructors. As with UNIBA and MUNI, the general lack of such courses and a writing centre makes a top-down institutional initiative unlikely. However, while the benefits of academic writing instruction become more widely recognized – and until the need for academic writing courses for students gains support beyond foreign language, English philology, and TEFL departments, and writing centres are seen as essential – teaching faculty can integrate tasks that implement academic writing skills into the courses within their discipline. In doing so, they can increase the impact of their courses exponentially by equipping hundreds of students with writing skills they are required to know and use but currently do not have the opportunity to develop.

Acknowledgements

This study resulted from the international cooperation project *Improving academic teaching and internationalisation through enhanced competences of university teachers* (IMPACT) that has been funded through an external grant under the KA2 – Cooperation for innovation and the exchange of good practices and

KA203 – Strategic Partnerships for higher education schemes of the Erasmus+ grant (Grant No. 2019–1-SK01-KA203–060671). This project is co-funded by the European Union.

Reference list

Anderson, R. S., & Speck, B. W. (1998). "Oh what a difference a team makes": Why team teaching makes a difference. *Teaching and Teacher Education, 14*(7), 671–686. https://doi.org/10.1016/S0742-051X(98)00021-3

Bailenson, J. N. (2021). Nonverbal overload: A theoretical argument for the causes of zoom fatigue. *Technology, Mind, and Behavior, 2*(1). https://doi.org/10.1037/tmb0000030

Bérešová, J. (2015). An e-learning course in EAP – Enhancing academic study skills, language and culture. *Procedia – Social and Behavioral Sciences, 174*, 3619–3624. https://doi.org/10.1016/j.sbspro.2015.01.1080

Cercone, K. (2008). Characteristics of adult learners with implications for online learning design. *AACE Journal, 16*(2), 137–159.

Comenius University in Bratislava. (2020a). *Vnútorný predpis č. 1/2020: SMERNICA DEKANA FAKULTY o minimálnych požiadavkách na individuálny výkon vysokoškolského učiteľa a výskumného pracovníka na Univerzite Komenského v Bratislave Filozofickej fakulte*. Filozofická Fakulta, Univerzita Komenského v Bratislave. https://fphil.uniba.sk/fileadmin/fif/o_fakulte/dokumenty_vnutorne_predpisy/vnutorne_predpisy/vp_1_2020.pdf.

Comenius University in Bratislava. (2020b). *Výročná správa o činnosti a hospodárení fakulty za rok 2019*. Filozofická Fakulta, Univerzita Komenského v Bratislave. https://fphil.uniba.sk/fileadmin/fif/o_fakulte/dokumenty_vnutorne_predpisy/dokumenty/Vyrocna_sprava_FiFUK_2019.pdf.

Curry, M. J., & Lillis, T. (2004). Multilingual scholars and the imperative to publish in English: Negotiating interests, demands, and rewards. *TESOL Quarterly, 38*(4), 663–688. https://doi.org/10.2307/3588284

Dolenc, K., Šorgo, A., & Virtič, M. P. (2021). The difference in views of educators and students on Forced Online Distance Education can lead to unintentional side effects. *Education and Information Technologies, 4*, 1–27. https://doi.org/10.1037/tmb0000030

Donohoo, J., Hattie, J., & Eells, R. (2018). The power of collective efficacy. *Educational Leadership, 75*(6), 40–44.

Eells, R. (2011). *Meta-analysis of the relationship between collective efficacy and student achievement* [unpublished Doctoral dissertation, Loyola University of Chicago]. https://ecommons.luc.edu/luc_diss/133/.

Ferri, F., Grifoni, P., & Guzzo, T. (2020). Online learning and emergency remote teaching: Opportunities and challenges in emergency situations. *Societies, 10*(4), 86. https://doi.org/10.3390/soc10040086

Flégl, M., Krejčí, I., & Brožová, H. (2015). Impact of score recalculation of publication evaluation on the Czech higher education institutions. *Acta Universitatis Agriculturae et Silviculturae Mendelianae Brunensis, 64*, 28. http://dx.doi.org/10.11118/actaun201664010245

Foltýnek, T., & Rybička, J. (2013). Training of academic writing: Improving competitiveness of Czech universities. *Acta Universitatis Agriculturae et Silviculturae Mendelianae Brunensis, 61*(7), 2111–2115. http://dx.doi.org/10.11118/actaun201361072111

Harbord, J. (2010). Writing in Central and Eastern Europe: Stakeholders and direction in initiating change. *Across the Disciplines*, 7(1), 1–14. https://doi.org/10.37514/ATD-J.2010.7.1.03

Hodges, C., Moore, S., Lockee, B., Trust, T., & Bond, A. (2020, March 27). The difference between emergency remote teaching and online learning. *EDUCAUSE Review.* https://er.educause.edu/articles/2020/3/the-difference-between-emergency-remote-teaching-and-online-learning.

Hublová, G. (2017). Reiteration relations in EFL student academic writing and the effects of online learning. *Discourse and Interaction*, 10(1), 71–89.

Jančaríková, R., Povolná, R., Dontcheva-Navratilova, O., Hanušová, S., & Němec, M. (2020). An academic needs analysis of Czech university graduate students. *Discourse and Interaction*, 13(1), 42–66.

Means, B., Bakia, M., & Murphy, R. (2014). *Learning online: What research tells us about whether, when and how.* Routledge.

Petillion, R. J., & McNeil, W. S. (2020). Student experiences of emergency remote teaching: Impacts of instructor practice on student learning, engagement, and well-being. *Journal of Chemical Education*, 97(9), 2486–2493. https://doi.org/10.1021/acs.jchemed.0c00733

Shin, M., & Hickey, K. (2020). Needs a little TLC: Examining college students' emergency remote teaching and learning experiences during COVID-19. *Journal of Further and Higher Education*, 45(7), 973–986. https://doi.org/10.1080/0309877X.2020.1847261

14

SUSTAINING WRITING-FOR-PUBLICATION PRACTICES DURING COVID-19

Online writing groups at an Ecuadorian University

Elisabeth L. Rodas

Introduction

Both experienced and early career academics face pressure to write and publish their research since their publication record influences their access to promotions and future research grants, while at the same time, universities place great value on said publications (Habibie & Hyland, 2019; Nygaard, 2015). However, due to the lack of explicit training in writing (Starke-Meyerring, 2014), many scholars are unprepared to assume this research role, thus becoming frustrated when faced with the challenges of academic writing (Sword et al., 2018). In different contexts, workshops, tutorials, and writing groups (WGs) are offered to face this challenge with varying regularity (McGrail et al., 2006). This is also the case at many universities in Latin America, where most support given to academics relies on sporadic workshops or tutorials presented mostly in the framework of graduate programs (Chois-Lenis et al., 2020; Colombo, 2013; Navarro, 2017). Few WGs in this region provide more sustained accompaniment to the development of scholars' publication output (e.g., Márquez Guzman & Gómez-Zermeño, 2018; Rodas et al., 2021b).

WGs are understood as spaces where "two or more people come together to work on their writing in a sustained way, over repeated gatherings, for doing, discussing or sharing their writing for agreed purposes" (Aitchison & Guerin, 2014, p. 7). In this context, WGs are meant to provide support for the development of academic scientific writing as a social activity. Through the support of the university's writing center, I began implementing faculty WGs in 2017. Their main purpose was to provide support and peer feedback on academics' writing-for-publication projects. However, as Covid-19 spread across the globe in 2020, any type of face-to-face support came to a standstill.

DOI: 10.4324/9781003283409-18

In order to adjust to this unprecedented situation, the education system at all levels around the world was forced to turn to an online environment. This sudden change was extended to areas of academic support offered not only to students (e.g., Haas et al., 2020) but also to researchers, as was the case of the in-person WGs I had implemented. The WGs' flexible nature made it possible for this initiative to be sustained at the university through digital technology, allowing the contact mode and meeting place to change due to the special circumstances we faced.

The purpose of this chapter is to consider the aspects that positively influenced the implementation and continuation of three online WGs at an Ecuadorian public university brought about by the state of confinement due to the 2020 pandemic. This is undertaken based on my experience as a coordinator with both contact modes and through the analysis of semi-structured interviews with the 11 online WG members. All participants were asked and accepted to be interviewed, since each one was in a position to provide relevant information and varied perspectives about their participation (Creswell, 2007).

Through recurring readings (Seidman, 2006) of the 11 interview transcriptions and my own observations, three important themes seem relevant to the sustainability of these online WGs, which could have implications for future implementations: the structure and consistency provided by established functioning rules, the coordinator's role enhanced by shared experiences and trust, and the role of digital technology to facilitate asynchronous and synchronous peer feedback and its influence on group meetings.

In the first section of the chapter, I present the background information regarding the set-up of these online WGs through personal experience and a literature review. After, the three themes mentioned are analyzed to understand their influence on the online WGs. Finally, the chapter concludes with strategies that can be implemented in similar contexts and situations in the future.

Setting up the online WGs

The change to online WGs took into consideration my previous experience of implementing in-person WGs as well as aspects highlighted by other virtual WGs organized before the 2020 pandemic. One such consideration was to establish a clear purpose for the group at its inception (e.g., Dawson et al., 2013; Johnson & Lock, 2020). In this case, the three online groups herein came about due to the relationship between a research team coordinator (RTC) at the university and me as the facilitator of a faculty WG in which the RTC had previously participated. The RTC's objective was to advance the team's writing-for-publication projects through WGs. Thus, the online WGs' purpose was clear from the start: to provide support and peer feedback to advance texts for publication, coinciding with the purpose of my previous in-person WGs (Rodas et al., 2021b).

Another important consideration was to determine organizational structure. The implementation of these online WGs included a leadership role, which could have a direct influence on their development (e.g., Kozar & Lum, 2015; Johnson & Lock, 2020). In this case, the RTC asked me to organize these groups not only to provide leadership and structure (e.g., Haas et al., 2020; Lock et al., 2019) but also to give feedback on writing and English as a second language based on my background in this area and because most of the texts were written in this language. The RTC also participated in all three WGs to provide expert feedback, thus fulfilling part of her leadership role as research coordinator.

The final aspect to take into account was what role technology would play in the WGs' functioning and development. With the proliferation of digital tools to remotely promote collaborative activities (e.g., Healey & Matthews, 2017; Hicks et al., 2013), it is important to choose the combination of digital elements to maintain and encourage interaction among WG members. For example, a previous study of online WGs (Kozar & Lum, 2015) indicated that participants were more satisfied with groups that also had a synchronous element, which gave them the opportunity to ask for clarifications of comments or give additional suggestions. This coincided with my own experience with in-person WGs, where participants most appreciated interaction with each other (Rodas et al., 2021a). Thus, it was important to include both asynchronous and synchronous elements to maintain the WGs' dynamics. The asynchronous element would continue to be the written feedback provided through the use of Google Docs, which we had been using already with in-person WGs. On the other hand, the main change consisted of incorporating Zoom-based synchronous virtual conferences to replace the in-person meetings previously held at the university's writing center. E-mail communication continued to play a key role to help with reminders and changes to meeting dates if necessary, as it had been pre-pandemic.

These considerations regarding purpose, leadership, and technology's role in the implementation of the online WGs were fundamental as they paved the way for easier implementation and development where all participants understood what was involved.

Positive aspects that influenced the online WGs' implementation and sustainability

Structure and consistency through WG functioning rules

The in-person faculty WGs implemented in 2017 began with clear functioning rules for their development. Among others, these rules included the establishment of a clear WG purpose (i.e., the advancement of texts for publication), which has shown to influence their sustainability (e.g., Johnson & Lock, 2020; Wardale et al., 2015) and a two-step feedback process to facilitate the provision of readers' perspectives on each member's texts (Rodas & Colombo, 2021). The personally tried-and-proven feedback process specifically played an important role in easing the change to an online format as it already incorporated digital tools. It works as follows: first, a member shares in advance a text using Google Docs, a platform chosen for its collaborative functions and easy access for all university staff, in a shared folder created for this purpose. Other members then read the text and provide their reactions and suggestions through the "Suggesting" function. During the in-person meetings, written feedback on content and structure is reviewed, giving both the author and reviewers the possibility to expand, question, or add new comments as the session progresses.

During a preliminary interaction held through Zoom with the RTC and the members of her team who voluntarily decided to participate in the online WGs, I explained the WG's purpose and its functioning rules, including the two-step feedback process. Since participants had experience using Google Docs, it was not necessary to spend too much time on how it would work for the WG, a definite plus. This first encounter through Zoom also gave us the opportunity to experience this format together and clarify any doubts about how it would work to share documents during WG meetings.

Part of the functioning rules also included collectively agreeing on a schedule for members to present their texts. This was meant to help participants maintain consistency in their writing endeavors by agreeing on a specific date to submit their work on a rotating basis, one text per week. Agreed-upon dates prompted WG members to consciously make room in their agendas not only to advance their own writing based on when they had offered to present a text, but also to reserve time to review their peers' drafts. Scheduling meetings together, then, is an important component of the WGs as it fosters an environment of equal give and take, what has been termed as *reciprocal gift giving* (Guerin, 2014).

All in all, the structure and consistency prompted by the facilitator through the functioning rules seem to have helped to organize the tasks performed within and for the WG while working online, reinforcing the idea that the collaborative environment experience in the face-to-face WGs could also be achieved in an online space.

The coordinator's role enhanced by shared experiences and trust

Another factor which positively impacted the implementation of the online WGs during Covid-19 was the establishment of a leadership role (Haas, 2014). This had an impact in three specific areas. Firstly, as has been the experience with other WGs (e.g., Plummer et al., 2019; Aitchison, 2009), setting the tone of the meetings and also developing trust among the members is a key aspect of the facilitator's role, which also impacts the WG's sustainability (e.g., Lock et al., 2019; Fallon & Whitney, 2016). Due to a pre-established relationship through an in-person faculty WG, an element of trust already existed between the RTC, three of her team members, and me as WG facilitator, which paved the way for easier collaboration in a digital format.

Unintentionally, the three team members had been assigned to each of the new online groups; thus, their already easy camaraderie with the other research team members and also with me had a positive impact, allowing a smoother development of trust and supportive climate within the WGs (Alsharo et al., 2017), which was strengthened as the weekly meetings progressed. However, even though there was an element of trust already established among some of us at the beginning, a drawback of the online WGs seemed to be the lack of direct, in-person interaction. One of the members suggested that, in future implementations, participants should have at least one face-to-face session at the start and then every other month to become better acquainted, even if the rest of the meetings were online. In fact, he stated

> [T]here were some [research team] members who had had no interaction with [the coordinator], so they are not close to her, for example, as we are [those that had been in previous in-person WG], and [they] might experience some mistrust.
>
> For this member, then, being able to spend time together face-to-face would alleviate this initial awkwardness.

Second, my role as an outside facilitator, disconnected from their research team and activities, added an element of accountability to these online WG sessions (e.g., Allen, 2019; O'Dwyer et al., 2017) by providing structure and focused interaction during the meetings (Haas et al., 2020). The RTC had unsuccessfully tried to implement no-leader WGs the semester before the pandemic took place. As several of the participants pointed out in the interviews, their collaboration in different research projects and the close relationships already developed through continued contact had made it easy to justify canceling WG meetings to give their other research activities precedence. In this case, their established collaboration and trust was playing against their writing objectives. As a result, the matter of writing their research findings was set aside. Thus, the presence of an outsider was felt as positive. For example, one member indicated that they had

> tried without one for a time, but having a coordinator checking that we connect, who sends the [Zoom] link is very good. One has that idea that there is that person waiting, that all the [scheduling and preparation] work has been done, so one has to connect.
>
> For another member "an outside coordinator is the glue that maintains the group, so it works".

Finally, as mentioned earlier, apart from facilitating the groups, I also gave feedback regarding academic writing and the English language when relevant, which was a plus for these groups. The pressure to write in a foreign language was keenly felt by all WG participants and confirmed by the RTC, who pointed out that they rarely wrote in Spanish. As one participant stated, "whether you want to or not, if you want to send your article to a high impact journal, they are generally in English". Thus, due to the members' varying degree of language proficiency, several participants commented on the benefit of having an English language expert in the WGs to help them improve their academic prose and to review frequent grammatical and vocabulary issues having to do with this foreign language.

For these online WGs, the presence of a facilitator represented a positive aspect. As can be seen, building trust was a key element. Even though there was some previous face-to-face interaction between the coordinator and some of the members, this did not preclude the possibility of facilitators building trust and commitment only from online contact through active communication and supportive leadership (Garo-Abarca et al., 2021). In this context, providing general guidance and support when needed during online sessions and also constantly communicating through e-mail with WG members could help sustain future online WGs.

Digital technology and its influence on members' interactions

The continued support offered to these research writers during the 2020 pandemic was possible thanks to digital technology. Even before it was necessary to change our contact mode from in-person to online WGs, technology had already been part of this initiative from its inception. As mentioned earlier, the first step in the peer feedback process was to provide asynchronous written comments through Google Docs that would be later discussed during Zoom meetings. This video conference platform helped us to safely breach the limitations placed by the pandemic through its sensorially enriched context and to work together on a text through its shared screen option. E-mail was also used to remind members of future meetings and to confirm when a text had been uploaded and was ready to be reviewed.

Another technological benefit that became more relevant for these online WG members than for previous in-person participants was accessing the audio files of each session, which I recorded for research purposes with their consent. While previous face-to-face WG participants had rarely resorted to these audios, several of the online WG participants used them to focus more closely on their peers' in-meeting feedback. As one member put it: "what I do to work on the article is listen to the meeting again, which is recorded". In this case, Zoom was useful since meetings were recorded automatically and saved to my computer. Later, I uploaded the files to each group's shared Google Drive folder.

Perhaps more importantly, our meetings' virtual mode was seen as a time saver. Although we were forced overnight to engage with each other through an online environment, when I asked participants if they would prefer to continue working online or meet face to face when social distancing ended, all of them stated a preference for online sessions because they helped members to save time. Since the in-person meetings had usually been held at the university's central campus, this implied that they would have to mobilize back and forth, cutting into their already heavy schedules. Furthermore, various members indicated that it was very easy to connect to our sessions and, as soon as we were finished, to continue working on other projects or have other activities also online. This saved a great deal of time.

However, changing from in-person to online WGs did present some drawbacks. It is true that online WGs eliminate the travel factor (e.g., O'Dwyer et al., 2017), but it cuts into a protected space and time. One main reason for holding in-person WGs at the university's writing center had been to help participants disengage from other activities and avoid disruptions as much as possible (Murray, 2013; Rodas et al., 2021b). Because of Covid-19, our work environments unavoidably shifted and merged with our homes, meaning that any type of boundary between our work space and private lives was erased. Thus, during Zoom meetings WG participants were oftentimes interrupted and distracted by family members, be it human or animal. Our attention could also be diverted by our cellphones (e.g., beeping noises from open apps), which during in-person meetings most members made a point of putting away while we all gathered around a conference table and focused on the texts.

Apart from losing this protected space, as the online WGs progressed, I also noticed longer pauses involving more reading of the screen and less speaking interaction. During online sessions, authors silently read comments made by their peers while we looked at the shared screen. This prompted me to consciously point out whose comment it was and ask that member to read it aloud. It was important not to lose what all interviewed participants had also agreed, which was one of the main benefits of the online WGs: discussing written feedback during synchronous meetings. For example, when asked if the asynchronous written comments would be enough, one member explained:

It would not be the same. There is a benefit in being able to review together. As the author of the article, you have a better idea, which is very different from only looking at the written comments than when you review them together.

Thus, a drawback of the online WG was the focus on the shared screen where all our eyes rested, minimizing the interaction among the people involved in the activity. This was sometimes compounded by unstable internet connections, which forced some members to turn off their cameras. As such, it is important to be aware of this situation and consciously bring back the focus to the people who make this type of academic support worthwhile.

Lessons learned for future implementations

The Covid-19 pandemic undoubtedly presented many challenges for everyone involved in the educational system. However, it also offered opportunities for growth and innovation. For me as a WG coordinator, the shift to an online WG contact mode provided first-hand experience of a different way to support seasoned as well as early career academics in their writing-for-publication projects. Additionally, the experiences of these online WG participants provided some insights into how this type of initiative can support researchers in their writing during challenging times and beyond.

In the first place, as it has been the case for other WGs (e.g., Dawson et al., 2013; Johnson & Lock, 2020; Plummer et al., 2019), a common purpose and functioning rules help members to have a clear path to move forward with their WG activities. Allocating time for writing in their busy agendas through involvement in online or in-person WGs pushes this activity to the forefront of researchers' endeavors. Second, an outside facilitator seems to have added an element of accountability and structure that had not been present when these research team members tried to have leader-less WGs. However, the role of an outside facilitator needs to be considered in future implementations as it might not be feasible or desirable to rely on someone else to continually organize WGs. In the long term, it would be better to have an outside facilitator only as a start-up leader (Haas, 2014) to guide members in their first meetings and eventually turn over facilitation to them. This would make WGs more sustainable across time as members take greater responsibility for their development.

Additionally, the element of trust already established between the members was a positive contributing factor in the implementation of our online WGs, as has been the case elsewhere (e.g., Alsharo et al., 2017; Lock et al., 2019). Building trust within online WGs could be fostered by having some in-person sessions, if possible, to give members opportunities to know each other in a more natural setting than a virtual conference platform can offer. Additionally, this type of WG could be organized, as was the case here, with members in the same position and experiencing similar demands, poteintially making those involved appear to be more trustworthy in online environments (Jamali et al., 2014).

As this experience shows, online WGs have the potential to eliminate certain constraints that might prevent academics from joining them. First, time, travel, and geography become irrelevant (O'Dwyer et al., 2017) since academics can join from anywhere (e.g., home or office) cutting travel time out of their busy schedules. The trade-off, however, is the loss of a protected space where members can experience fewer interruptions (Murray, 2013). Apart from eliminating borders, digital tools and environments continue to proliferate and offer new and advanced ways to collaborate with others in different locations. For these participants, familiarity with Google Docs and Zoom made their online interactions easier and more productive, even though it was necessary to focus on our interactions with each other and not only on the shared screen. Additionally, it is worth mentioning that the software licenses provided by the university allowed us to stay connected during this difficult time. However, not everyone enjoys easy access to the ever-growing digital technologies, many of which are not free; academics in different contexts might be limited due to financial reasons.

The lessons gained from these online WGs implemented during harsh times can serve as a guide for future iterations and make this type of support available to everyone wishing to participate in them. In other words, having a clear purpose, establishing functioning rules, building trust, and choosing digital technologies easily accessible to WG members should be taken into consideration by future facilitators in different contexts. These considerations could ease the creation of an environment that fosters collegial interactions and helps improve the writing practices of scholars at different stages of their academic career.

I hope that this chapter contributes to the existing literature on WGs and how digital tools can play a role in fostering continued support for academics. On the basis of the insights gained from this experience, online WGs can serve as spaces where researchers develop their writing-for-publication literacy practices beyond the confines of time, location, and special circumstances.

Reference list

Aitchison, C. (2009). Writing groups for doctoral education. *Studies in Higher Education*, *34*(8), 905–916. https://doi.org/10.1080/03075070902785580

Aitchison, C., & Guerin, C. (2014). *Writing groups for doctoral education and beyond: Innovations in practice and theory*. Routledge.

Allen, T. J. (2019). Facilitating graduate student and faculty member writing groups: Experiences from a university in Japan. *Higher Education Research and Development*, *38*(3), 435–449. https://doi.org/10.1080/07294360.2019.1574721

Alsharo, M., Gregg, D., & Ramirez, R. (2017). Virtual team effectiveness: The role of knowledge sharing and trust. *Information & Management*, *54*(4), 479–490. https://doi.org/10.1016/j.im.2016.10.005

Chois-Lenis, P. M., Guerrero-Jiménez, H. I., & Brambila-Limón, R. (2020). An analytical view of writing in graduate school: A review of documented practices in Latin America. *Íkala*, *25*(2), 535–556. https://doi.org/10.17533/udea.ikala.v25n02a09

Colombo, L. (2013). Una experiencia pedagógica con grupos de escritura en el posgrado [A pedagogical experience with postgraduate writing groups]. *Aula Universitaria*, *15*, 61–68. http://bibliotecavirtual.unl.edu.ar/publicaciones/index.php/AulaUniversitaria/article/view/4368/6643

Creswell, J. W. (2007). *Qualitative inquiry and research design: Choosing among five approaches* (2nd ed.). Sage Publications.

Dawson, C. M., Liu Robinson, E., Hanson, K., Vanriper, J., & Ponzio, C. (2013). Creating a breathing space: An online teachers' writing group. *English Journal*, *102*(3), 93–99. www.jstor.org/stable/23365380

Fallon, L. C., & Whitney, A. E. (2016). "It's a two-way street": Giving feedback in a teacher writing group. *Teaching/Writing: The Journal of Writing Teacher Education*, *5*(1), Article 4. https://scholarworks.wmich.edu/wte/vol5/iss1/4

Garo-Abarca, V., Palos-Sanchez, P., & Aguayo-Camacho, M. (2021). Virtual teams in times of pandemic: Factors that influence performance. *Frontiers in Psychology, 12.* https://doi.org/10.3389/fpsyg.2021.624637

Guerin, C. (2014). The gift of writing groups: Critique, community and confidence. In C. Aitchison & C. Guerin (Eds.), *Writing groups for doctoral education and beyond* (pp. 138–141). Routledge.

Haas, S. (2014). Pick-n-Mix: A typology of writers' groups. In C. Aitchison & C. Guerin (Eds.), *Writing groups for doctoral education and beyond: Innovations in practice and theory* (pp. 30–47). Routledge.

Haas, S., De Soete, A., & Ulstein, G. (2020). Zooming through Covid: Fostering safe communities of critical reflection via online writers' group interaction. *Double Helix, 8,* 1–10. https://wac.colostate.edu/docs/double-helix/v8/haas.pdf

Habibie, P., & Hyland, K. (2019). Introduction: The risks and rewards of scholarly publishing. In P. Habibie & K. Hyland (Eds.), *Novice writers and scholarly publication: Authors, mentors, gatekeepers* (pp. 1–10). Palgrave Macmillan. https://doi.org/10.1007/978-3-319-95333-5

Healey, M., & Matthews, K. (2017). Learning together through international collaborative writing groups. *Teaching & Learning Inquiry, 5*(1). doi.org/10.20343/teachlearninqu.5.1.2

Hicks, T., Busch-Grabmeyer, E., Hyler, J., & Smoker, A. (2013). Write, respond, repeat: A model for teachers' professional writing groups in a digital age. In K. E. Pytash, R. E. Ferdig, & T. V. Rasinski (Eds.), *Preparing teachers to teach writing using technology* (pp. 149–161). ETC Press.

Jamali, H. R., Russell, B., Nicholas, D., & Watkinson, A. (2014). Do online communities support research collaboration? *Aslib Journal of Information Management, 66*(6), 603–622. http://dx.doi.org/10.1108/AJIM-08-2013-0072

Johnson, C., & Lock, J. (2020, November 3–7). *Virtual writing groups: Collegial support in developing academic writing capacity* [Paper presentation]. Proceedings of the 2019 ICDE World Conference on Online Learning, Dublin City University, Dublin, Ireland. http://dx.doi.org/10.5281/zenodo.3804014

Kozar, O., & Lum, J. F. (2015). Online doctoral writing groups: Do facilitators or communication modes make a difference? *Quality in Higher Education,* 1–14. https://doi.org/10.1080/13538322.2015.1032003

Lock, J., Kjorlien, Y., Tweedie, G., Dressler, R., Eaton, S. E., & Spring, E. (2019). Advancing the writing of academics: Stories from the writing group. In N. Simmons & A. Singh (Eds.), *Critical collaborative communities* (pp. 55–65). Koninklijke Brill NV. https://doi.org/10.1163/9789004410985_005

Márquez Guzmán, S., & Gómez-Zermeño, M. G. (2018). Grupo virtual de escritura académica. Una e-innovación para impulsar la publicación científica. *Revista Mexicana de Investigación Educativa, 23*(76), 203–227. www.scielo.org.mx/scielo.php?script=sci_abstract&pid=S1405-66662018000100203&lng=es&nrm=iso

McGrail, M., Rickard, C., & Jones, R. (2006). Publish or perish: A systematic review of interventions to increase academic publication rates. *Higher Education Research & Development, 25*(1), 19–35. https://doi.org/10.1080/07294360500453053

Murray, R. (2013). 'It's not a hobby': Reconceptualizing the place of writing in academic work. *Higher Education, 66,* 79–91. https://doi.org/10.1007/s10734-012-9591-7

Navarro, F. (2017). Estudios latinoamericanos de la escritura en educación superior y contextos profesionales: Hacia la configuración de un campo disciplinar propio [Latin

American studies of writing in higher education and professional contexts: Towards the configurations of our own disciplinary field]. *Lenguas Modernas, 50,* 8–14. https://lenguasmodernas.uchile.cl/index.php/LM/article/view/49247/51714

Nygaard, L. (2015). Publishing and perishing: An academic literacies framework for investigating research productivity. *Studies in Higher Education, 42*(3), 519–532. doi.org/10.1080/03075079.2015.1058351

O'Dwyer, S. T., McDonough, S. L., Jefferson, R., Goff, J. A., & Redman-MacLaren, M. (2017). Writing groups in the digital age: A case study analysis of shut up & write Tuesdays. In A. Esposito (Ed.), *Research 2.0 and the impact of digital technologies on scholarly inquiry* (pp. 249–269). IGI Global. http://doi.org/10.4018/978-1-5225-0830-4.ch013

Plummer, L., Pavalko, E., Alexander, J., & McLeod, J. (2019). Faculty writing groups: A tool for providing support, community, and accountability at mid-career. In A. Welch, J. Bolin, & D. Reardon (Eds.), *Mid-career faculty: Trends, barriers, and possibilities* (pp. 126–142). Brill Sense. https://doi.org/10.1163/9789004408180_008

Rodas, E. L., & Colombo, L. (2021). Self-managed peer writing groups for the development of EFL literacy practices. *Teaching English as a Second Language Electronic Journal (TESL-EJ), 24*(4). https://tesl-ej.org/wordpress/issues/volume24/ej96/ej96a7

Rodas, E. L., Colombo, L., Calle, M. D., & Cordero, G. (2021a). Escribir para publicar: Una experiencia con grupos de escritura de investigadores universitarios [Write to publish: An experience with faculty writing groups]. *Maskana, 12*(1), 5–15. https://doi.org/10.18537/mskn.12.01.01

Rodas, E. L., Colombo, L., Calle, M. D., & Cordero, G. (2021b). Looking at faculty writing groups from within: Some insights for their sustainability and future implementations. *International Journal of Academic Development.* https://doi.org/10.1080/1360144X.2021.1976189

Seidman, I. (2006). *Interviewing as qualitative research: A guide for researchers in education and social sciences* (3rd ed.). Teachers College Press.

Starke-Meyerring, D. (2014). Writing groups as critical spaces for engaging normalized institutional cultures of writing in doctoral education. In C. Aitchison & C. Guerin (Eds.), *Writing groups for doctoral education and beyond: Innovations in practice and theory* (pp. 65–81). Routledge.

Sword, H., Trofimova, E., & Ballard, M. (2018). Frustrated academic writers. *Higher Education Research and Development, 37*(4), 852–867. https://doi.org/10.1080/07294360.2018.1441811

Wardale, D., Hendrickson, T., Jefferson, T., Klass, D., Lord, L., & Marinelli, M. (2015). Creating an oasis: Some insights into the practice and theory of a successful academic writing group. *Higher Education Research and Development, 34*(6), 1297–1310. https://doi.org/10.1080/07294360.2015.1024621

15

LOCKING DOWN AND OPENING OUT

Creating new virtual spaces for writers and presenters during the pandemic

Joe Lennon, Petra Trávníková, Alena Hradilová, and Libor Štěpánek

Introduction

The Czech government declared a state of emergency due to the coronavirus pandemic on March 12, 2020, and urged educators to immediately end contact lessons and reorganise teaching and assessment. Masaryk University, like all Czech higher education institutions, rushed to set up additional technical support and training for teachers. Materials and activities had to be quickly redesigned to facilitate quality remote learning.

At Masaryk University Language Centre/Centrum jazykového vzdělávání (CJV MU), the largest language centre in the Czech Republic (serving 10,000 students each term), efforts to maintain teaching at a high level under these exceptional circumstances led to the development of novel approaches, which opened up more space for students and teachers to communicate and learn from each other. This chapter presents three success stories from our pandemic-forced transition to remote teaching: the redesign of a presentation skills course to increase asynchronous and autonomous student collaboration; the discovery of the potential of experiential learning via videoconferencing; and an exploration of "windows on the world" for developing critical analysis skills in an academic writing course. We end the chapter with a few principles and strategies for building on these positive outcomes and adapting them to post-pandemic teaching.

Previous studies

Before the Covid-19 crisis, computer-mediated learning (also referred to as e-learning, online learning, or distance learning) had become an indelible part of ELT research (see, e.g., Hiltz, 1986; Arcavi & Hadas, 2000; Anderson, 2004;

DOI: 10.4324/9781003283409-19

Moore et al., 2010). After the quick spread of the coronavirus, and the sudden need for social distancing, universities and schools were forced to switch to fully remote teaching, testing this previous research in an extreme and unprecedented way. The sudden changes were quickly reflected in the scholarly literature. In 2021, for example, several studies were published which compared pre-Covid online teaching to emergency remote teaching (Hodges et al., 2020; Moser et al., 2020; Radić et al., 2021). These studies all concluded that previous experience with teaching online, while certainly helpful, was not able to provide teachers with everything they needed to face the novel challenges the pandemic posed. As we looked to apply our own previous experiences to the new reality, we took comfort and practical advice from these researchers who described having to considerably adapt established online teaching methods to the new situation.

We found a great deal of inspiration in studies coming from higher education contexts, describing how particular universities around the world dealt with the situation. Ross and DiSalvo (2020), for example, explain how the Harvard Language Centre provided support mechanisms and changed communication strategies to bring the scattered academic community back together. Nuere and de Miguel (2020) show how two universities in Spain adapted to the new conditions, emphasising that their goal was to achieve the same learning outcomes but with different means. Kawasaki et al. (2021) examine the efficiency of online courses at a medical faculty in Japan, with special attention given to students' motivation. In another inspiring study, Hapsari (2021) shows how students' anxieties over emergency distance learning in an Indonesian language class were minimised by increasing student collaboration and autonomy. There are also studies highlighting the changed role of the teacher; for example, Schaffner et al. (2021) or Rapanta et al. (2020), who stress that efficient online teaching will be seen as one of the key components of teachers' overall competencies in the post-Covid era. The methods and principles for managing emergency remote teaching, which were noted in all these studies, were invaluable for us as we re-designed our courses. In line with Rapanta et al., we came to realise that switching to online teaching was a great opportunity for our self-development as teachers, and that it would offer us many opportunities to reassess and restructure our everyday teaching practices.

Online support at Masaryk University Language Centre

Before the pandemic required us to move our teaching fully online, the Language Centre had laid some foundations in ICT skills and remote education which we could build on in the emergency. CVJ MU teachers had become accustomed to designing ICT enhanced and blended learning courses (Štěpánek & Arriaga, 2018; Hradilová & Vincent, 2018). Moreover, CJV MU had been highly active in promoting videoconferencing in language teaching. Our first video conferencing courses were set up in 2005, and these were followed by an EU project exploring the potential of videoconferencing. In the years preceding the pandemic, we developed extensive expertise in this area (Štěpánek et al., 2018), which was helpful when quickly reformatting the videoconferencing aspect of the English for Law course (further details follow later).

Pre-pandemic, 96% of the courses at CJV MU (in January 2020) were face-to-face, but most courses already had some online support through the Masaryk University Information System (IS MU). IS MU provides a space for teachers to post instructional materials, syllabi, and assessment criteria. It also facilitates activities that mirror and supplement classroom instruction (such as interactive quizzes), and it features discussion forums where students and teachers can post recorded or written feedback. Teaching materials on IS MU can be used independently and/or asynchronously from any location. Thus, before the pandemic, we were meeting some basic principles of a well-designed online course as recommended in the 2018 Quality Matters rubric (Quality Matters, 2018).

Even though teachers at CJV MU had some competence in online and blended instruction, and a bank of materials and resources to draw from, our courses at the start of the pandemic mostly fell into the category of what Hodges et al. (2020) call "emergency remote teaching" rather than true "online learning". Crucial aspects of successful online course design were still missing. For example, we had to move completely to new online teaching interfaces (mostly Zoom or Microsoft Teams) and establish new modes of learner interaction to foster community building and imitate face-to-face classroom interaction (Meskill & Anthony, 2015). We had to do further research on online teaching and learning, design new assessment methods, and convert more materials into attractive and interactive digital forms. Both the university and CJV MU held a series of workshops for teachers to develop their remote teaching skills. Even with this institutional support, teachers had to find new ways of collaborating with their students to meet learning goals. In the following section we will share three successful outcomes from this process of improvisation and discovery.

Implementation

1. New spaces for sharing ideas in a presentation skills course

One of the courses presenting a considerable challenge for remote teaching was an EAP presentation skills course for master's students of Social Sciences. The course focuses on public speaking skills, and the class dynamic relies heavily on audience participation and student interaction. Throughout the semester, the students give several mini-presentations, some individually and some in tandem with their classmates. These oral tasks are the main part of their portfolio assessment, and their final grade is calculated on the basis of their individual performances. The presentations could not be delivered face to face as they usually are, and this led to some new worries and difficulties that had to be overcome. In the pre-crisis environment, students' self-reflection journals repeatedly emphasised that a positive atmosphere in the classroom and supportive relationships with others were essential for improving their public speaking skills. Kaur & Ali (2018) report that in this type of class, lack of confidence and fear of speaking in front of others are often cited as the main challenges. Considering the added anxieties aroused by the abrupt switch to remote teaching, it was clear that for the course to be successful, a great deal of attention would have to be paid to allaying these fears and establishing rapport online. After the class moved fully online, students expressed doubts in their pre-course expectations about whether it was even possible to practice presenting online. They worried about the inevitable problems with technology, the lack of visible body language, the impossibility of keeping eye contact with others, and the inability to gauge audience reactions. They were also concerned about the lack of practice in pairs or small groups. Before students started presenting, we discussed the advantages and disadvantages of giving presentations online and how to overcome the obstacles posed by the technology. But it was clear that the format of the course would need to be changed so that the students' confidence could be built up through repeated practice in presenting online.

After the switch to remote teaching, students were asked to give presentations synchronously online (from 1 to 10 minutes long), to record one mini-presentation at home, and to upload a three-minute recording to the IS discussion forum. Having uploaded their recording, they were asked in the following week to write detailed feedback on three of their classmates' mini-presentations and then post the feedback beneath the recordings in the discussion thread. This activity proved very effective in numerous ways. First, the students put a lot of effort into the recordings. In their self-reflection journals, many of them expressed surprise at not only how time-consuming but also how beneficial this experience was, as it made them aware of the many aspects of giving presentations. The peer feedback was also productive. Students were more sincere in their reflections and were not afraid to give recommendations and suggestions for improvement (as they often had been in live presentations). Since the whole feedback process was done asynchronously, they could watch the recordings several times (and many of them did) to capture the minutest details. They often realised and admitted they were making the same mistakes as their classmates. Finally, as peer feedback was posted on a discussion board, there were some follow-up discussions in which the presenters responded constructively to the feedback they were given.

As the term proceeded, the atmosphere in the online class became friendlier and more relaxed. The Zoom breakout rooms proved extremely useful when preparing for tandem presentations. In traditional classes, this can get quite difficult, because when students are preparing synchronously in a crowded classroom, they often disturb each other. When they have to prepare and practice their presentations before the class, arranging more than one face-to-face meeting may be difficult. The virtual breakout rooms made it easier. They now had a space of their own without a teacher monitoring them where they could discuss anything, both during class and before or after class. Before students entered the breakout rooms, they agreed with the teacher on whether they wanted the teacher to visit the room, or whether the teacher should drop in only when asked. This made a big difference for some of the shyer students, who felt more comfortable working on their tandem presentations knowing the teacher was at hand if needed, but not immediately present in the room.

The activities described earlier helped create a strong social aspect in the online classes; students felt they could share their feelings, experiences, and even problems with others, which was reflected in both their journals and final course feedback. As one student wrote: "Breakout rooms were very useful and I loved all the exercises and activities. . . I think our online classes have been great not only thanks to amazing teacher, but also thanks to students". Another student said: "I must say that sometimes the remote teaching suited me better than contact teaching. . . I tended to speak more tha[n] during contact teaching because I was not so shy". In line with Tuomainen (2016, p. 34), we realised that students "value the classroom teaching context . . . which can be vital in engaging students in a sense of community" even in a remote teaching mode.

Reflecting on our experiences after the course, we realised that many of the changes adopted in the emergency setting were worth integrating into classes, even in "normal" times. In the post-pandemic version of the course, to take advantage of all the benefits we observed, students will be asked to do one or two of their mini-presentations and give peer feedback on them asynchronously online. In addition, two to three sessions will be taught synchronously online, in which students will work in breakout rooms to collaborate on tandem presentations and rehearse individually. They will also be encouraged to use the platform outside of class to work on joint projects.

2. Community building in videoconferencing with English for Law students

The Covid crisis demanded creativity and experimentation, and this led to some breakthroughs with experiential learning in a communication skills course for law students from Masaryk University and the University of Helsinki. The traditional course always had a video conferencing component, but our two videoconferencing groups were in classrooms on their campuses, and one group met the other group on a big screen in each classroom. Pre-pandemic, we had never tried synchronous web conferencing using desktop computers fitted with cameras. Students always had parts of the sessions in their monolingual groups to prepare in teams for the international communication, which was later facilitated by the VC technology. Their international communication in the course was mostly synchronous, structured, and thus limited. To talk to their foreign classmates without a teacher present, the students needed to meet outside the sessions (Hradilová & Vincent, 2018). The Covid-19 crisis brought an end to this practice. A more natural classroom environment was exchanged for what we anticipated would be an anonymous collection of individuals on cameras, or just voices. However, the experiential content of the course, delivered partly via tasks in breakout rooms, led to more active community building.

When adjusting the course to the new circumstances, we had to consider the number of students who had signed up (30 rather than the usual 20), and their reluctance to turn their cameras on or speak publicly without being specifically addressed (their relative anonymity). We needed to develop a new, manageable authentic task. We wanted the course to remain experiential to allow the students to experience academic communication skills naturally, observe their peers actively, and discuss and reflect with each other on their observations and experience, even though they could not meet physically. We decided to run an online student conference with the presenting teams being of mixed nationality. We decided that the conference should be organised by the students to make the experience as immediate as possible.

Groups of three international students were invited to give papers on comparative legal issues. The students wrote and peer-reviewed their abstracts and produced a final book of abstracts (presented in Google Jamboard). To practice the differences between academic writing and speaking, they reworded the abstracts to provide oral invitations to the presentations, and they received formative peer and teacher feedback on the content and delivery. Finally, they agreed on the conference programme and presented their papers at concurrent conference sessions, organised in breakout rooms using Zoom. The presentations were followed by self-reflection and more peer feedback, as well as summative feedback from the teacher. A complete experiential Learning Cycle was thus achieved (Kolb et al., 2001).

Along with the international aspect of the course, which can be easily kept in our future syllabi, in their course evaluations, students identified the new community-building component, that is being able to talk in international groups synchronously and without the teachers' presence, as essential to the learning outcomes. They said their fluency, soft skills, and general communication skills improved considerably, not only from the public presentations, but also from working in teams in breakout rooms. They valued their time together in the safe environment of the rooms. When asked if they would be interested in a similar course that would run in the traditional way as described earlier, they admitted that being physically together would be beneficial. Still, they were worried they would lose their talking time in the rooms. The international community-building aspect is likely to affect the future course design. Students have always been encouraged to meet outside the sessions asynchronously, but according to our course feedback, this did not happen due to the students' time constraints. As breakout rooms allow for various formal and informal authentic concurrent activities, we plan to keep them for the post-pandemic experiential synchronous teaching.

3. Windows on the world in academic writing

As a response (and a resistance) to the sensory privations brought on by the pandemic, we developed a series of short observation and writing exercises using multimedia websites for an advanced academic writing course for Social Science students. Besides offering a reprieve from the audio-visual monotony of Zoom classes (which are often just a screen full of talking heads), these exercises opened up new spaces for the students to theorise and practice close observation and descriptive writing, which in turn improved their critical writing.

One of the course assignments is a short critical review. Students choose a subject to describe and evaluate in the review (most choose a film, TV show, or song). The main purpose of the assignment is to improve students' textual analysis and argumentation skills. They are told that their claims about the value and impact of their review subject should be backed up with evidence – evocative details which show the reader what it was like to experience the subject as the author did, and which give the reader some verifiable data – some idea of what they, too, might experience if they encountered the subject. The first drafts of the students' reviews tend to show a similar pattern; most students have no trouble expressing passionate opinions about their subject ("the acting was great" or "the music was powerful"), but they often include little or no evidence for their opinions – descriptive details about the formal properties of their subject.

The *WindowSwap* website offered a new way for students to practice the observation and descriptive skills they needed to write more convincing reviews. *WindowSwap* allows you to view a randomly chosen video filmed from a window somewhere in the world. Some windows show busy urban streets, while others show peaceful, sun-dappled gardens. Opening and sharing *WindowSwap* in a Zoom classroom is pleasantly startling. There's an immersive, meditative quality to most of the videos, as the viewer's senses are stirred by an exotic landscape and ambient noises of wind and weather.

At the beginning of the lesson, a random *WindowSwap* window was opened and shared, and students were asked to write for about 6–7 minutes, describing what they saw and heard in as much detail as possible. They were told to avoid evaluative statements ("The weather is nice"), and instead use only sensory descriptions ("The sky is light blue near the horizon, and it gets darker as it goes up"; "two white, fluffy clouds are floating above the trees"). When the writing time ended, the students were paired in breakout rooms. They were asked to compare their writing and reflect on the differences, with these discussion prompts: "Did you notice different things in the window? Did you notice the same things but in a different order? Did you give different levels of detail?" When they returned to the group Zoom meeting, they were asked to share any interesting comparisons/contrasts they noticed or any difficulties they had. We finished the discussion with the observation that although they were all looking at the same thing, and all using objective language to describe it, their descriptions were still very different. They were asked to consider the implications of that for academic writers and readers – for example, how the ordering of information in a text can affect its interpretation. For homework, the students were asked to perform a similar writing task with the subject of their review – to pinpoint a moment during their experience of their subject (a scene of a film, a guitar solo), and to write a short paragraph describing that moment in vivid sensory imagery, avoiding (for the moment) evaluative language. In the following lessons, as they worked on drafts of the review, we discussed how they could incorporate these descriptions into the rest of the review text, adding evaluative language and further context about the subject to shape their overall argument.

The *WindowSwap* exercise, and the focus on observation and description which it inspired, had a noticeable impact. The first drafts of the students' review texts were much more vivid and engaging than those written in previous semesters, as they showed more convincing evidence for the students' evaluative claims. The reviews of films tended to describe more explicitly what could be seen on screen or how the camera was moving; the music reviews included more names of specific instruments and additional colourful comparisons of sounds to other sensory imagery. In general, the reviews showed more attention to the reviewer's bodily experience of the subject. Several students even incorporated the homework paragraph modelled after the *WindowSwap* exercise into their first draft as a captivating opening "hook" for their review. The time spent on this exercise itself also proved memorable to students, even though it was relatively short and came early in the course. In the end-of-course feedback, when asked "Which assignment(s) were the most useful/interesting?" several students named the *WindowSwap* task. A few of them highlighted the exercise (along with other exercises mentioned below) as a moment of welcome variety, with one student commenting, "I found interesting and useful those small writing tasks in class . . . in those moments we really had a chance to write, and write spontaneously".

The success of the *WindowSwap* exercise inspired a series of similar in-class writing exercises based on sensory experiences. Two other websites that generated productive exercises (and compelling writing from the students) were the *Field Recordings* website (n.d.), self-billed as "A podcast where audio-makers stand silently in fields", and the *New York Times* article "Welcome to our Museum of Smells" (2020). The *Field Recordings* site was used in almost exactly the same way as *WindowSwap*; the students listened to a few minutes of the recording and described the sounds they heard. This led to a discussion of various strategies for "translating" sounds into words (onomatopoeia, simile, etc.) The Museum of Smells inspired a two-part task using the entries on the website as a model. The students were asked to describe in a few sentences the smell they would include in their own Museum, and then in a few additional sentences give their reason for including it. These exercises, like the *WindowSwap* one, were followed with tasks in which the students used language (and ideas) generated in the exercises as building blocks for more sophisticated arguments in their longer texts.

Although these exercises were developed in response to an emergency, we will use them again in future online and face-to-face courses. They can give a greater sense of depth to the Zoom window (and to the classroom), through which the students and the teacher can feel closer connections to places and sensations which seem out of reach (especially during a pandemic lockdown). They can also help students make stronger connections between their physical, embodied experiences and the process of writing more precisely and evocatively. If the pandemic's sensory deprivations have made many of us appreciate more deeply those moments when we are exposed to new and startling sensations, then multimedia activities like these can help language teachers create such moments during class meetings, taking advantage of "what people might learn, do, or make with their experiences of heightened vitality" (Ceraso, 2014, p. 106).

Future strategies and applications

The Covid-19 crisis forced us to make changes to the format of established courses, to adapt existing technology to new purposes, and to develop activities which we hoped would bring surprise and comfort to what were often dark and stressful days. At first, these moves were reactions to what we perceived as obstacles to "normal" teaching, and we thought of them as inconveniences. However, as the examples given earlier show, some of the changes we made created spaces for even more effective language practice and mediation. Learning from our pandemic experiences, we plan to adopt these principles and strategies for our future courses:

- Offering more online and hybrid courses (where the study program accreditations allow for it), since many students preferred these modes of learning
- Using online platforms such as breakout rooms in otherwise face-to-face courses (for example, training students to use breakout rooms asynchronously to prepare for group presentations)
- Devoting the synchronous time of language courses to communication and community building, while shifting activities aimed at practising receptive skills to the asynchronous mode
- Rather than having students give all their presentations face-to-face, asking them to record some of their presentations at home and post them in the discussion board where they can give and receive feedback online
- Promoting internationalisation by putting physically distant classes together in online sessions and bringing more guests from abroad into our sessions

- Using audio-visual materials and multimedia to open space in the lessons for students to engage more physically with the process of developing academic language skills
- Continuing to look for ways that online tools and activities can sustain, and even enhance, physical and social connections in the inevitably hybrid- and blended-learning landscape of post-Covid higher education.

Reference list

Anderson, T. (2004). Teaching in an online learning context. In T. Anderson & F. Elloumi (Eds.), *Theory and practice of online learning* (pp. 273–294). Athabasca University Press.

Arcavi, A., & Hadas, N. (2000). Computer mediated learning: An example of an approach. *International Journal of Computers for Mathematical Learning, 5*(1), 25–45. www.learntechlib.org/p/89017/

Ceraso, S. (2014). (Re)Educating the senses: Multimodal listening, bodily learning, and the composition of sonic experiences. *College English, 77*(2), 102–123. www.jstor.org/stable/24238169

Field Recordings. (n.d.). https://fieldrecordings.xyz/

Google Jamboard. (n.d.). https://workspace.google.com/products/jamboard/

Hapsari, C. (2021). Distance learning in the time of Covid-19: Exploring students' anxiety. *ELT Forum: Journal of English Language Teaching, 10*(1), 40–49.

Hiltz, S. (1986). The "virtual classroom": Using computer-mediated communication for university teaching. *Journal of Communication, 36*(2), 95–104. https://doi.org/10.1111/j.1460-2466.1986.tb01427.x

Hodges, C., Moore, S., Lockee, B., & Bond, A. (2020). The difference between emergency remote teaching and online learning. *Educause Review, 27,* 1–12.

Hradilová, A., & Vincent, K. (2018). Daring to videoconference: Ideas for teachers. In L. Štěpánek, K. Sedláčková, & N. Byrne (Eds.), *Videoconferencing in university language education* (pp. 127–141). Masarykova univerzita.

Kaur, K., & Ali, A. M. (2018). Exploring the genre of academic presentations: A critical review. *International Journal of Applied Linguistics and English Literature, 7*(1), 152–162.

Kawasaki, H., Yamasaki, S., Masuoka, Y., Iwasa, M., Fukita, S., & Matsuyama, R. (2021). Remote teaching due to Covid-19: An exploration of its effectiveness and issues. *International Journal of Environmental Research and Public Health, 18,* 2672. https://doi.org/10.3390/ijerph18052672

Kolb, D. A., Boyatzis, R. E., & Mainemelis, C. (2001). Experiential learning theory: Previous research and new directions. In R. J. Sternberg & L. Zhang (Eds.), *Perspectives on thinking, learning, and cognitive styles* (pp. 227–247). Routledge.

Meskill, C., & Anthony, N. (2015). *Teaching language online.* Multilingual Matters.

Moore, J. L., Dickson-Deane, C., & Galyen, K. (2010). E-Learning, online learning, and distance learning environments: Are they the same? *The Internet and Higher Education, 14*(2), 129–135. https://doi.org/10.1016/j.iheduc.2010.10.001

Moser, K. M., Wei, T., & Brenner, D. (2021). Remote teaching during Covid-19: Implications from a national survey of language educators. *System, 97,* 102431. https://doi.org/10.1016/j.system.2020.102431

Nuere, S., & de Miguel, L. (2020). The digital/technological connection with Covid-19: An unprecedented challenge in university teaching. *Tech Know Learn, 26,* 931–943. https://doi.org/10.1007/s10758-020-09454-6

Quality Matters. (2018). *QM rubrics & standards.* www.qualitymatters.org/qa-resources/rubric-standards

Radić, N., Atabekova, A., Freddi, M., & Schmied, J. (Eds.). (2021). *The world universities' response to COVID-19: Remote online language teaching.* Research-publishing.net.

Rapanta, C., Botturi, L., Goodyear, P., Guàrdia, L., & Koole, M. (2020). Online university teaching during and after the Covid-19 crisis: Refocusing teacher presence and learning activity. *Postdigital Science and Education, 2,* 923–945.

Ross, A. F., & DiSalvo, M. L. (2020). Negotiating displacement, regaining community: The Harvard Language Center's response to the Covid-19 crisis. *Foreign Language Annals, 53,* 371–379.

Schaffner, S., Radić, N., Stefanutti, I., Zamborova, K., & Tobias, R. (2021, June 30). CercleS online talks: *On the outcomes of the survey impact of the COVID-19 pandemic on language teaching in HE.* www.youtube.com/watch?v=MYI_1_qg7Yk

Štěpánek, L., & Arriaga, C. (2018). Video summaries of academic texts. In C. Hua Xiang (Ed.), *Cases on audio-visual media in language education* (pp. 328–349). IGI Global.

Štěpánek, L., Sedláčková, K., & Byrne, N. (2018). *Videoconferencing in university language education.* Masarykova Univerzita.

Tuomainen, S. (2016). A blended learning approach to academic writing and presentation skills. *International Journal on Language, Literature and Culture in Education, 3*(2), 33–55. http://dx.doi.org/10.1515/llce-2016-0009

Welcome to our museum of smells. (2020, November 18). *The New York Times.* www.nytimes.com/2020/11/18/at-home/welcome-to-our-museum-of-smells.html

WindowSwap. (n.d.). www.window-swap.com/

16

CULTIVATING SOCIAL PRESENCES IN AN UNDERGRADUATE WRITING COURSE

David Ishii

Introduction

Covid-19 has rapidly transitioned English for academic purposes (EAP) instruction from physical to virtual classrooms. While this has enabled institutions to provide remote instruction, it has also introduced new challenges in engaging learners online. For both instructors and students, being present in a physical classroom is different from sitting in front of a camera. The social norms of classroom interaction that include questions and answers, open discussion, and other conversational exchanges may not necessarily transfer over to an online learning environment. One of the challenges is that students may not perceive the need to contribute and, instead, disengage from their online classes. Anagnostopoulos et al. (2005) commented that "students can easily choose not to respond to teacher questions and postings" (p. 1703). The decision to opt out may not be related to issues of motivation or passivity but could be attributed to pandemic- or isolation-related factors. Responding to this challenge, instructors are faced with the issue of how to co-develop a social presence in their online classrooms. In a simple sense, social presence refers to being present and aware of others. This chapter aims to explain what social presence is and how social presence impacts learning. The pandemic has significantly affected teaching and learning. In these challenging circumstances and times ahead, cultivating a social presence may be an important step towards improving levels of engagement in our online classrooms.

Interaction and engagement

Research in applied linguistics has examined interaction from both cognitive (e.g., Gass, 1997; Long, 1996) and social perspectives (e.g., Firth & Wagner, 1997;

DOI: 10.4324/9781003283409-20

Storch, 2002) and has furthered academic discussion regarding what and how language learning occurs (Block, 2003; Sfard, 1998). These studies highlight the influential role of language in interaction and illustrate how language learning is both a social and cognitive process. Other researchers have foregrounded issues of power, agency, identity, and community and their influence on the kinds of inter-actions that take place in language learning environments (Norton Pierce, 1995; Pavlenko & Blackledge, 2004). It is not surprising that earlier interaction studies focused on analyses of language discourse; however, as later studies illustrated, interaction encompasses more than just language in use.

Although the terms interaction and engagement may appear synonymous, researchers within the field of education have generally focused on defining what engagement is and how it is best achieved. A considerable body of research (e.g., Finn & Zimmer, 2012; Handelsman et al., 2005; Kuh, 2005) has argued that student engagement is socio-psychological (reflecting on one's affective/cognitive engagement, intra/interpersonal engagement), context-dependent (responsive-ness to environmental conditions such as topic, activity, skills, and tools), and developmental (evolving over time). This suggests that any learning activity is multifaceted and encompasses a number of overlapping forms of engagement. Other researchers (Budhai & Skipwith, 2017; Chickering & Gamson, 1987; Conrad & Donaldson, 2011; Malone & Lepper, 1987; Poll et al., 2014) have provided pedagogical suggestions to foster learner engagement (e.g., encouraging teacher-student communication, peer-peer interaction, active learning, provid-ing timely and constructive feedback, and respecting and being acknowledged by others). Various studies have also correlated student engagement with academic success, student satisfaction, and reduced levels of attrition (Krause & Coates, 2008; Trowler, 2010).

Garrison et al. (2000) and subsequent publications (Cleveland-Innes et al., 2018; Garrison, 2016) have greatly influenced researchers and practitioners with the introduction of the "Community of Inquiry" (COI) framework. This model suggests that three core elements (teaching presence, social presence, and cogni-tive presence) contribute to the educational experience of an online community of learners. A primary goal of education is to develop learners' critical thinking skills that will lead to self-directed learning behaviours. The authors assert that both teaching presence (planning, design, initiation, and discussion of topics and course content) and social presence (open communication, expression of personal characteristics, use of humour, and group cohesiveness) support the development of learners' cognitive presence (exploring, connecting and applying ideas, and resolving problems) through sustained communication. The COI model thus recognises how engagement is critical for learning to occur and provides an ana-lytical framework for investigating teaching, social, and cognitive presences in online educational settings.

Even though empirical support for the COI framework exists, it is not with-out criticism (see Cooper & Scriven, 2017; Jezegou, 2010; Rourke & Kanuka,

2009). The separation of teaching, social, and cognitive forms of presence has prompted further refinement of the model to acknowledge an instructor's social presence (Richardson & Lowenthal, 2017; Sheridan & Kelly, 2010), learning presence (Shea & Bidjerano, 2012; Shea et al., 2012), or the view that social presence is essentially intersubjective (Kehrwald, 2010). One of the aims of this chapter is to explain how researchers have conceptualised social presence and to draw conclusions on how learning is supported through online engagement; therefore, a brief overview of previous definitions of social presence is presented in the next section.

Definitions of social presence

One of the earliest definitions of social presence can be traced to Short, Williams, and Christie's (1976) definition of "technical social presence" as "the degree of salience of another person in an interaction and the consequent salience of an interpersonal relationship" (p. 65). This term originates from the field of communications and media but has been adopted by researchers in education to explain how perception of others' presence impacts learning. Garrison et al's (2000) COI framework defines social presence as "the ability of participants in the COI to project their personal characteristics into the community, thereby presenting themselves to the other participants as 'real people'" (p. 89). The authors cite indicators of social presence (e.g., expressing emotions, humour or one's personality, friendly open exchange of ideas, addressing others by name and being part of the group) and assert that the establishment of social presence facilitates learners' critical reflection and cognitive engagement with discussion topics.

Garrison et al.'s (2000) inclusion of social presence within a model of learning initiated further discussion from other researchers regarding how it is defined and its applicability to online learning contexts. Guichon and Cohen (2014) cite Michinov's (2008) work by referring to three dimensions of social presence: immediacy (reducing psychological distance through physical cues such as gesturing, eye contact, smiling, and head nodding), intimacy (acknowledging other learners' ideas and having a feeling of being understood), and sociability (being able to project one's personality and other aspects of their social self). Unfortunately, some learners in synchronous online EAP classes may not perceive the need to express one or more of these three dimensions. This raises the question of how social presence can be manifested among learners from diverse cultural backgrounds with varying expectations that typically define EAP learning contexts.

Kehrwald (2010) argued that social presence is essentially an intersubjective process of uncovering relations between participants. Some participants may be active initiators and contributors to online discussions, whereas others may have their cameras and microphones off. This reflects their willingness to engage with the instructor, with other students, or with the content, and as a result, impacts their relations with each other. Kehrwald (2010) identified three characteristics of social presence suggesting that it is demonstrative (a sense of others is conditional upon how participants present themselves to others), dynamic (a sense of others can change quickly within a single event depending on the quantity and quality of interactions), and cumulative (a sense of others evolves over a series of online meetings as participants develop a history with one another). Thus, as Kehrwald (2008) suggests varying degrees of social presence can exist. Learners express their agency in terms of how much of themselves they are willing to reveal to others; therefore, instructors are faced with orchestrating an online learning environment that cultivates a willingness to engage. In the following section, I will exemplify how social presence was fostered in an EAP course during the Covid-19 pandemic.

Local practices

The government-mandated lockdown during the Covid-19 pandemic transformed a blended learning environment (online and physical classrooms) into a purely online learning experience at Massey University, New Zealand. For my undergraduate academic writing course, the demographic profile consisted of primarily Chinese international students between the ages of 19 and 23; however, several other regions (South and East Asia, Middle East, South America, Europe) and adult learners returning to school were also represented. One of the aims of the course was to assist learners in developing their academic literacy skills to use in their other courses. Their previous learning experiences within New Zealand or overseas influenced their perceptions of what academic writing entails. For example, a 5.5–6.0 IELTS score enabled students to enter university, but some of students were accustomed to expressing their opinions without evidence from academic sources. This EAP course focused on not only their critical reading and writing skills but also their academic socialisation. In other words, the approximately 80 students enrolled in this first year undergraduate course were learning how to learn at university by acquiring skills and study behaviours (e.g., time and information management) for them to succeed at the tertiary level.

The undergraduate students were three weeks into the 12-week academic writing course when the transition to online learning occurred. Despite additional teaching and technical support provided by the university, academic staff were still entering new territory with how to effectively teach using Zoom. Apart from teaching (e.g., making lecture recordings accessible) and assessment-related changes (e.g., redesigning the final, in-class writing exam to a time-restricted online writing assessment), each lecturer was exploring an unknown path of teaching solely online. The next section will share my experiences of teaching during the pandemic and explain how a focus on social presence is integral for fostering thinking, sharing, and learning.

FIGURE 16.1   Zoom's functions

Strategies for cultivating social presences

Instead of projector screens in a physical classroom, Covid-19 introduced a different set of tools to work with. In my first online lesson, I anticipated that my students would not necessarily know how to effectively use the various functions available on Zoom (see Figure 16.1). It was apparent from the outset that many of my students were adept at using "Stop Video" and "Mute" buttons. When I asked students if they could turn their cameras or microphones on, I began to uncover their reasons for disengagement and understand how they were individually affected by the pandemic. Some students felt embarrassed about their home environment or had to connect while sitting in their cars. Videos could reveal aspects of their private lives that they did not wish to share. Reclusive personalities became even more withdrawn on Zoom, but I was pleased that they at least turned up to class. I explained how they could use "virtual backgrounds" and showed them an example of myself in front of a supermarket aisle with empty toilet paper shelves. I showed how they could insert their name on Zoom for everyone to see so they could feel included during our class discussions. One strategy, both for myself as the lecturer and for the students, was to not only become aware of Zoom's functionalities but also better understand why or how we use them.

The importance of names

As mentioned earlier, social presence relates to an awareness of others. Without seeing faces, it becomes extremely difficult to gauge students' reactions to the content or each other. Several researchers (Guichon & Cohen, 2014; Richardson & Lowenthal, 2017; Satar, 2015; Yamada, 2009) have discussed the importance of having cameras on, since this enables everyone to see non-verbal backchannels (e.g., smiling, laughing, nodding, eye contact, facial expressions, gestures) showing their involvement, immediacy, and degree of comprehension. Researchers have also pointed out that Asian students may be more likely to exhibit reticence and passivity in classroom discourse (Cheng, 2000; Meyer, 2012; Liu & Littlewood, 1997), which materialised in the form of blank video screens on Zoom. While students may feel empowered to disable their audio and video functions, instructors can still cultivate a social presence through engaging with students in other ways. Greeting students when they first appear online, and acknowledging their questions and answers using their names are, for example, ways to build social presence. Referring to students' names also goes hand-in-hand with modelling positive reinforcement. Agreeing with students' contributions or referring to what another student has said provides encouragement and builds rapport. Responding to students' verbal or written comments indicates that their contributions are valued and may increase confidence and lessen students' inhibitions to express themselves. Using names also shows an awareness of the other person as an individual and humanises the experience of teaching and learning. Although acknowledging each other's names is important in traditional face-to-face classrooms, it becomes vital for cultivating social presences in online learning contexts.

Writing aloud

Besides verbal responses and using emoticons (hands clapping, thumbs up) or pen highlighters in Zoom, students can also use the "Chat" function to contribute to the class discussion, respond to other postings, or use "private messaging" to ask face-threatening questions (e.g., requests for an extension). For my writing course, instead of simply verbalising a question or example, I would simultaneously and selectively type on the screen using Zoom's Chat function. For instance, I would often use examples that aim to cultivate social presence in a variety of ways. The example below is a result of two simple sentences (Steve Nash is a two-time NBA MVP and Steve Nash is currently the head coach of the Brooklyn Nets) combined into one sentence:

(1) Steve Nash, a two-time NBA MVP, is currently the head coach of the Brooklyn Nets.

This example is an introduction to sentence combining, embedded phrases, and appositions on a non-academic topic. It not only reveals my interest in a particular sport but also provides an opportunity for students who have a shared interest in basketball or other sports to contribute to an off-topic discussion. With regard to social presence, Richardson and Lowenthal's (2017) point out that, "online students care about getting a sense of who their instructors are and that they are 'real' people and 'there'" (p. 532). By referring to my own topics of interest, my goal is to increase their willingness to communicate and express themselves verbally or in writing. Small talk or talking off-task may seem like an activity reserved only for the start and end of class, but it can be strategically integrated within a lesson. The next example serves a similar albeit different purpose:

(2) Elon Musk, co-founder of SpaceX and Tesla, started Neuralink in 2016.

In example (2), referring to someone that students may be familiar with provides an opportunity for further discussion, but its main purpose is to increase their willingness to take risks in constructing a complex sentence. I would frequently ask who their favourite actors, musicians, athletes, or celebrities are. Taking an interest in their lives provides a wealth of examples to use in the online chat space. Students can also engage in cooperative problem-solving (Newberry, 2005) when an incomplete or incorrect apposition is presented to them. This activity, whether in a breakout room or not, provides a forum where they can gain a better sense of each other and increase their sense of belonging. The last example that follows moves closer to the types of writing that they encounter in their university assignments.

(3) Veerabhadran Ramanathan, a climate change expert, suggested that methane and other sources significantly contribute to global warming.

Example (3) is a typical case where students must refer to authorities, theories, or concepts that the reader or audience may not be familiar with. Students would typically write, "Ramanathan suggested that . . .", which would lead me to ask probing questions: Who is Ramanathan? How does adding "a climate change expert" make the statement more persuasive? By thinking (or writing) aloud, I am essentially trying to teach them how to think as well as write. Another aim is to stress the importance of establishing credibility for the authority figure and convincing the reader. The three examples provided earlier relate to the thinking process behind constructing appositions, but the focus of instruction could lead to other related issues including citations, identifying surnames, or whether authors' titles and professions should be included. The Chat function can be invaluable in any writing course since it creates opportunities to engage with students and foster their confidence in expressing themselves before their peers and instructor. In times of difficulty, cameras and microphones are more likely to be turned off, but their use of Chat can provide an essential means of building rapport and facilitating communication.

A model of social presences

Models of teaching and learning tend to foreground activities, behaviours, or processes where participants are identified as a collective (e.g., teachers, students) but often with little recognition of individuals as real people (e.g., Xin is from Guangdong but has lived in New Zealand for three years and is studying finance). A classroom full of students of similar age, gender, and ethnicity can exhibit a diversity of personalities, skill levels, and experiences. Furthermore, what works for one student may not work for another.

As discussed previously, Kehrwald (2010) views social presence through students' levels of engagement that impact their perceptions of each other and learning experiences. He suggests that learners express their agency, revealing their physical presence (or absence), psychological involvement (how they think or feel), and behavioural involvement (what they say or do). Thus, social presence exists in varying degrees and is essentially intersubjective, reflecting the co-constructed nature of social presence. Referring back to the earlier example with Elon Musk, student X may express their opinion about Tesla cars, whereas student Y may remain silent behind a name visible on a blank screen. Over time, the social presence that emerges with the two students will evolve along different paths. My point here is that conceptualising social presence as a singular construct undermines the individualised nature of teaching and learning. Figure 16.2 shows a model of multiple social presences that foregrounds the individual learner and the intersubjective nature of engagement in a digital learning environment.

In Figure 16.2, for the sake of simplicity, one instructor and three students have attended an online class where most of what is known about each person is displayed or hidden offline. From the very beginning, instructors can quickly identify which students are active contributors, occasional participants, or peripheral observers through their actions (use of greetings, responding to the instructor's question prompts) or inaction (cameras and microphones are turned off). These behaviours are not static as an active contributor may sometimes become a peripheral observer or somewhere in between, depending on the topic, task, or other personal reasons.

The instructor plays a central role in orchestrating a learning environment that acknowledges others' presence and encourages risk-taking (Swan & Shih, 2005). With learner A, the instructor may try to "coax" him or her with greetings (Good morning A, Thank you for joining today's class A) or conversation

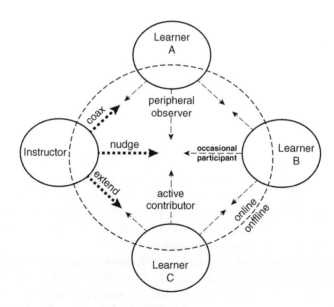

FIGURE 16.2   Social presences in a digital learning environment

starters (What's your major? Do you have any assignments due next week?) and integrate any of learner A's responses into the lesson (Since A is studying economics, why don't we have a look at . . .), thereby acknowledging his or her presence. With learner C, the instructor may focus on "extending" the student's understanding of the content, writing, or language (Great C, can you think of an example of X?; How would you apply X to Y?), or group the student with other learners in a breakout room. The interaction between the instructor and learner C may also serve to model EAP skills and social behaviours for other online participants. Finally, Learner B, the occasional participant, may require a "nudge", sometimes coaxing them into the conversation or at other times, extending their understanding of the EAP content. By finding out more about each student, instructors can select topics and tasks that show a co-awareness of each other as individuals. These examples of instructor-learner engagement represent different types of social presence that evolve over time. While some learners may lack awareness of the peripheral observers, instructors must adopt a policy of inclusiveness and strive to make everyone feel that they are part of the learning group.

Global trends

It is unclear what the future holds for teaching and learning in EAP classrooms. If educational institutions continue along a trajectory of transitioning to online modes of learning, instructors will need further explore ways to encourage their students to be present in online classrooms. Here I would like to raise two issues related to social presence that may impact the nature of instruction for institutions around the world. First, with the rise of social media, many of our students are accustomed to viewing content through YouTube, TikTok, or other apps. The digital learning environments used by educational institutions may appear much less attractive or user-friendly compared to their social media counterparts (Cooper & Scriven, 2017; Peacock & Cowan, 2016). Instructors might need to take a closer look at the tools offered in the digital spaces that we ask students to inhabit, which could lead to innovative ways for both the instructor and the students to jointly build a social presence. This chapter has provided examples using Zoom in an academic writing course. Other institutions may use other tools or a combination of platforms (e.g., VoiceThread, Facebook, WeChat) to engage students synchronously and asynchronously. Regardless of technologies employed in a digital learning environment, it seems vital that they are not only used as repositories of information but also consciously and meaningfully as tools to increase social ties.

The pandemic has created a learning environment where social distancing is expected and isolation can be problematic. Poor bandwidth connections, unproductive home study environments, family commitments, and a host of other issues have only added to the challenges of teaching and learning online. Therefore, a second area of consideration is students' access to support networks. Who can students turn to when things go awry? Social presence is more than fostering an awareness of others. Over a series of online meetings, being present can build positive instructor-student and student-student relationships that reflect trust, approachability, and support. Instructors could actively organise Q&A forums using the institution's online network or suggest the formation of study groups through students' preferred social media. Other support networks (library assistants, health counsellors, student associations) can also raise students' awareness about available help.

Conclusion

The shift to online teaching and learning in EAP has been expedited with the emergence of Covid-19. While instructors upskill and train to teach remotely, learners are adapting to their new learning environments. What has not changed is the view that teaching and learning is a shared experience. Teaching should not be reduced to transmitting knowledge and neither should learning be reduced to downloading content. In order to mitigate the risk that technology dictates how we teach, we must view learning as an evolving series of shared social experiences. The pandemic has physically isolated us from others, but this only magnifies the need to be present and aware of others in online settings. EAP practitioners will nevertheless experience difficulties with learner engagement in their online classrooms. The following suggestions may thus assist with fostering engagement and promoting a sense of community:

- Greet, acknowledge, and compliment students using their real or preferred names
- Extensively use the chat messaging function to encourage camera-shy learners to feel comfortable with contributing to the class discussion
- Write aloud while talking to provide students a chance to comprehend challenging words or concepts
- Weave in personal topics and examples from students or yourself into the pedagogical focus of the lesson
- Extend, nudge, or coax students into the online discussion when the opportunity arises

The act of expressing oneself, exchanging views, and considering the ideas of others all contribute to what makes us human. Kehrwald (2010) aptly stated that social presence acts to "humanise" the experience of online learning (p. 48). If we are to move beyond this turbulent crossroad and embrace new approaches to teaching EAP, we can only benefit from being more cognisant of the social presences that we cultivate in our online classrooms.

Reference list

Anagnostopoulos, D., Basmadjian, K. G., & McCrory, R. S. (2005). The decentered teacher and the construction of social space in the virtual classroom. *Teachers College Record, 107*(8), 1699–1729. https://doi.org/10.1177/016146810510700807

Block, D. (2003). *The social turn in second language acquisition.* Edinburgh University Press.

Budhai, S. S., & Skipwith, K. B. (2017). *Best practices in engaging online learners through active and experiential learning strategies.* Routledge.

Cheng, X. (2000). Asian students' reticence revisited. *System, 28*(3), 435–446. http://dx.doi.org/10.1016/S0346-251X(00)00015-4

Chickering, A. W., & Gamson, Z. F. (1987). Seven principles for good practice in under-graduate education. *AAHE Bulletin*, 3–7. https://files.eric.ed.gov/fulltext/ED282491.pdf

Cleveland-Innes, M., Garrison, D. R., & Vaughan, N. (2018). The community of inquiry theoretical framework: Implications for distance education and beyond. In M. G. Moore & W. C. Diehl (Eds.), *Handbook of distance education* (4th ed., pp. 67–78). Routledge.

Conrad, R. M., & Donaldson, J. A. (2011). *Engaging the online learner: Activities and resources for creative instruction.* Jossey-Bass.

Cooper, T., & Scriven, R. (2017). Communities of Inquiry in curriculum approach to online learning: Strengths and limitations in context. *Australasian Journal of Educational Technology, 33*(4), 22–37. https://doi.org/10.14742/ajet.3026

Finn, J. D., & Zimmer, K. S. (2012). Student engagement: What is it? Why does it matter? In S. L. Christenson, A. L. Reschly, & C. Wylie (Eds.), *Handbook of research on student engagement* (pp. 97–131). Springer.

Firth, A., & Wagner, J. (1997). On discourse, communication, and (some) fundamental concepts in SLA research. *The Modern Language Journal, 81*(iii), 285–300. https://doi.org/10.2307/329302

Garrison, D. R. (2016). *E-learning in the 21st century: A community of inquiry framework for research and practice.* Taylor & Francis Group.

Garrison, D. R., Anderson, T., & Archer, W. (2000). Critical inquiry in a text-based environment: Computer conferencing in higher education. *The Internet and Higher Education, 2*(2–3), 87–105. http://dx.doi.org/10.1016/S1096-7516(00)00016-6

Gass, S. (1997). *Input, interaction, and the second language learner.* Lawrence Erlbaum.

Guichon, N., & Cohen, C. (2014). The impact of the webcam on an online interaction. *The Canadian Modern Language Review/La Revue canadienne des langues vivantes, 70*(3), 331–354. https://doi.org/10.3138/cmlr.2102

Handelsman, M. M., Briggs, W. L., Sullivan, N., & Towler, A. (2005). A measure of college student course engagement. *The Journal of Educational Research, 98*(3), 184–192. https://doi.org/10.3200/JOER.98.3.184-192

Jezegou, A. (2010). Community of Inquiry in e-learning: A critical analysis of the Garrison and Anderson model. *The Journal of Distance Education/Revue de l'Éducation à Distance, Canadian Network for Innovation in Education, 24*(3), 1–18. edutice-00596237. https://edutice.archives-ouvertes.fr/edutice-00596237/document#:~:text=for%20Measuring%20Presence-,in%20e%2Dlearning,of%20a%20community%20of%20inquiry.

Kehrwald, B. (2008). Understanding social presence in text-based online learning environments. *Distance Education, 29*, 89–106. http://dx.doi.org/10.1080/01587910802004860

Kehrwald, B. (2010). Being online: Social presence as subjectivity in online learning. *London Review of Education*, *8*(1), 39–50. https://doi.org/10.1080/14748460903557688

Krause, K-L., & Coates, H. (2008). Students' engagement in first-year university. *Assessment & Evaluation in Higher Education*, *33*(5), 493–505. https://doi.org/10.1080/02602930701698892

Kuh, G. (2005). Student engagement in the first year of college. In M. L. Upcraft, J. N. Gardner, & B. O. Barefoot (Eds.), *Challenging and supporting the first-year student: A handbook for improving the first year of college* (pp. 86–107). Jossey-Bass.

Liu, N. F., & Littlewood, W. (1997). Why do many students appear reluctant to participate in classroom learning discourse? *System*, *25*(3), 371–384. http://dx.doi.org/10.1016/S0346-251X(97)00029-8

Long, M. H. (1996). The role of the linguistic environment in second language acquisition. In W. Ritchie & T. Bhatia (Eds.), *Handbook of second language acquisition* (pp. 413–468). Academic Press.

Malone, T. W., & Lepper, M. R. (1987). Making learning fun: A taxonomy of intrinsic motivations for learning. In R. E. Snow & M. J. Farr (Eds.), *Aptitude, learning, and instruction, volume 3: Conative and affective process analyses* (pp. 223–253). Lawrence Erlbaum.

Meyer, D. (2012). Broadening language learning strategies for Asian EFL students. *Language Education in Asia*, *3*(2), 243–251. http://dx.doi.org/10.5746/LEiA/12/V3/I2/A12/Meyer

Michinov, E. (2008). La distance physique et ses effets dans les e´quipes de travail distribue´es: une analyse psychosociale. *Le Travail Humain*, *71*(1), 1–21. http://dx.doi.org/10.3917/th.711.0001

Newberry, B. (2005). Social presence in distance learning. In C. Howard, J. V. Boettcher, L. Justice, K. Schenk, P. L. Rogers, & G. A. Berg (Eds.), *Encyclopedia of distance learning* (pp. 1634–1640). https://doi.org/10.4018/978-1-59140-555-9.ch248

Norton Pierce, B. (1995). Social Identity, investment, and language learning. *TESOL Quarterly*, *29*(1), 9–31. https://doi.org/10.2307/3587803

Pavlenko, A., & Blackledge, A. (Eds.). (2004). *Negotiation of identities in multilingual contexts*. Multilingual Matters.

Peacock, S., & Cowan, J. (2016). From presences to linked influences within communities of inquiry. *International Review of Research in Open and Distributed Learning*, *17*(5). https://doi.org/10.19173/irrodl.v17i5.2602

Poll, K., Widen, J., & Weller, S. (2014). Six instructional best practices for online engagement and retention. *Journal of Online Doctoral Education*, *1*(1), 56–72. Loyola eCommons. https://ecommons.luc.edu/cgi/viewcontent.cgi?article=1030&context=english_facpubs

Richardson, J. C., & Lowenthal, P. (2017, April 27–28). *Instructor social presence: A neglected component of the Community of Inquiry*. The 13th International Scientific Conference eLearning and Software for Education Bucharest. https://doi.org/10.12753/2066-026X-17-160

Rourke, L., & Kanuka, H. (2009). Learning in Communities of Inquiry: A review of the literature. *Journal of Distance Education*, *23*, 19–48. https://files.eric.ed.gov/fulltext/EJ836030.pdf

Satar, H. M. (2015). Sustaining multimodal language learner interactions online. *CALICO Journal*, *32*(3), 480–507. https://doi.org/10.1558/cj.v32i3.26508

Sfard, A. (1998). On two metaphors for learning and the dangers of choosing just one. *Educational Researcher*, 4–13. https://doi.org/10.2307/1176193

Shea, P., & Bidjerano, T. (2012). Learning presence as a moderator in the community of inquiry model. *Computers & Education*, *59*, 316–326. https://doi.org/10.1016/j.compedu.2012.01.011

Shea, P., Hayes, S., Smith, S. U., Vickers, J., Bidjerano, T., Pickett, A., Gozza-Cohen, M., Wilde, J., & Jian, S. (2012). Learning presence: Additional research on a new conceptual element within the community of inquiry (CoI) framework. *The Internet and Higher Education*, *15*, 89–95. https://doi.org/10.1016/j.iheduc.2011.08.002

Sheridan, K., & Kelly, M. A. (2010). The indicators of instructor presence that are important to students in online courses. *Journal of Online Learning and Teaching*, *6*(4), 767–779. https://jolt.merlot.org/vol6no4/sheridan_1210.htm

Short, J., Williams, E., & Christie, B. (1976). *The social psychology of telecommunications*. John Wiley & Sons.

Storch, N. (2002). Patterns of interaction in ESL pair work. *Language Learning*, *52*(1), 119–158. https://doi.org/10.1111/1467-9922.00179

Swan, K., & Shih, L. F. (2005). On the nature and development of social presence in online course discussions. *Journal of Asynchronous Learning Networks*, *9*(3), 115–136. https://doi.org/10.24059/olj.v9i3.1788

Trowler, V. (2010). Student engagement literature review. *The Higher Education Academy*. www.heacademy.ac.uk/system/files/StudentEngagementLiteratureReview_1.pdf

Yamada, M. (2009). The role of social presence in learner-centered communicative language learning using synchronous computer-mediated communication: Experimental study. *Computers & Education*, *52*(4), 820–833. https://doi.org/10.1016/j.compedu.2008.12.007

PART IV

Assessing students online

Martin Percy

The transition from the physical learning environment to remote delivery through online learning, necessitated by Covid-19, has had a transformative impact on assessment. Many tertiary institutions, which previously practised blended learning, are likely to have seen a slightly less radical transformation, as digital learning environments were prevalent before the pandemic, with written formative and summative assessments submitted via Learning Management Systems. However, the transformation for institutions, which were previously solely based on face-to-face delivery, is likely to have been more dramatic in terms of instrumentation and implementation. Although the technological affordances were already available, the pandemic accentuated the use of digital learning environment-based assessment and focused minds on aspects of reliability, construct validity, practicality, and ethical considerations within such a context, and how such assessments could be operationalised. Much of this is likely to have a long-term impact.

To date, there has been limited research into EAP assessment practises during the pandemic, in terms of both formative and summative assessments. It can be assumed that time constraints, limited experience of online assessment, and how to identify unethical behaviour are likely to be significant issues, although some aspects of online assessment would already be familiar to educators due to the increasing levels of blended learning used within traditional learning environments. However, it should be acknowledged that many institutions have rapidly transitioned straight from high stakes classroom-based assessment to entirely online assessment. Some lecturers' experiences of such practices are included in this section.

The transition to online learning is likely to have led to reflections on a contextually appropriate pedagogy. Connectivism is a learning theory, or arguably a

DOI: 10.4324/9781003283409-21

pedagogical approach, which is grounded in constructivism and acknowledges that technology is an intrinsic component of the learning process as well as a tool for interaction, as knowledge is distributed and communicated via connected networks. Connectivism is therefore likely to be a theoretical framework, which has and will increasingly play a role in informing the design of assessments. An interactive and deep approach to learning is assumed and facilitated by a diverse range of perspectives (Siemens, 2005). Such a process is likely to have been accelerated by the rapid transition to online learning during the pandemic due to the significance afforded to technology within the theoretical construct, and raises questions of security, ethics, technological affordances, and increasing levels of literacy brokering occasioned by more sophisticated technological developments.

The European Council's Common European Framework of Reference (2020) acknowledged the increasing significance of digital technologies by replacing assessment of the discrete skills of reading, writing, listening, and speaking with the communicative activities of reception, interaction, production, and mediation. This has implications for the potential application of the principles of connectivist learning theory. Connectivism differs from social constructivism in that the former previously lacked a conceptualisation of knowledge construction at an interpersonal level (Bates, 2015). Cara Dinneen has recently responded by initiating the revision of EAP assessments as an interactive writing activity and an integrated skills test through the application of connectivist theory, exploiting the technological affordances available.

In their chapter, Tewero Tchekpassi and Tong Zhang focus on their experiences of the challenges faced through the transition from face-to-face to remote synchronous learning, and of providing guided assistance and implementing formative assessments online, whilst engaging students as co-creators of formative assessments. Natalia Smirniova and Irina Shchemeleva also explore the challenges of implementing formative assessments online and the outcomes. Both Dinneen, and Smirniova and Shchemelev acknowledge that the transformations are likely to continue to inform practice in the future. Dinneen concedes that a reversal to previous practices would be regressive. However, both Dinneen, and Tewero and Tong recognise that the accessibility to technology and learners' previous experiences with technology need to be taken into consideration and currently present a challenge. Therefore, training sessions for students on online collaboration may be necessary, as well as scaffolding to facilitate socio-pragmatic and intercultural competences, multiliteracy skills, and to enhance familiarity with the metalanguage of assessment practises.

Zhang Li, Liu Jing, and Yan Guoying, and Pragasit Sitthitiku and Vorakorn-Tuvajitt emphasise that the transition to the online delivery of their programmes led to a greater proportion of their assessment becoming formative and a lesser proportion being summative, necessitating a greater level of focus on the learning process. Sitthitiku and Tuvajitt replaced peer-evaluation processes with self-evaluation and a formal test with a group project. However, although the group project was deemed a success, self-evaluation processes were considered less than satisfactory due to a lack of learner familiarity with the approach and an over dependence on teacher feedback among learners within the local context. However, they conclude that their students did not appear to use the self-reflection guidelines in a manner, which is likely to facilitate personal development or to have a transformative impact on the construction of texts, and that the learners did not appear to take self-evaluation as seriously as peer evaluation. Therefore, critical self-reflection on such practices is likely to prove beneficial.

Summative criterion-based assessments are usually perceived by students to be high stakes tests, and are therefore likely to be taken more seriously. Sitthitiku and Tuvajitt explore how his institution transitioned from the formal test used in the face-to-face learning environment to an online group project, so as to promote collaborative learning and enhance authenticity. Zhang et al. have narrowed down their focus on summative assessment, moving away from their previous textbook orientated examinations to focus on active vocabulary use, argumentative, and analytical writing, although they maintain the essence of the assessment has not changed.

In conclusion, contentious themes regarding transformations in digital EAP assessment are explored in the chapters within this part. The new CEFR descriptors, acknowledging the significance of digital literacy skills, appear to be having an impact on assessment design, necessitated by the pandemic, and the viability of former approaches within the digital environment are being questioned. The transition to online assessment would seem to have led to a shift towards a greater emphasis on formative assessment, focusing increasingly on the learning process, facilitating construct validity, and assuming assessment to be an intrinsic part of the learning process. As the chapters in this part suggest, there are still unresolved and contentious aspects of evaluation strategies of such transformations and their effectiveness.

Reference list

Bates, T. (2015). *Teaching in a digital age: Guidelines for designing teaching and learning for a digital age.* BCcampus Open Textbooks.

Common European Framework of Reference for Languages: Learning, Teaching, Assessment. Cambridge: Cambridge University Press. Council of Europe (2020).

Siemens, G. (2005). Connectivism: A learning theory for the digital age. *International Journal of Instructional Technology and Distance Learning, 2*(1). https://jotamac.typepad.com/jotamacs_weblog/files/Connectivism.pdf

17

COMMUNITY, ENGAGEMENT, AND ACADEMIC INTEGRITY IN ENGLISH PREPARATION PROGRAMMES FOR UNIVERSITY IN AUSTRALIA

Cara Dinneen

Introduction

The Macquarie University English Language Centre (ELC) in Sydney Australia has been preparing students with English as an additional language (EAL) for university study for more than 30 years. Students are typically between the ages of 18 and 25, and from a diverse range of linguistic, educational, and cultural backgrounds predominantly from across the East Asian countries of China, Hong Kong, Japan, Mongolia, Korea, and Taiwan, as well as the Southeast Asian countries of Cambodia, Malaysia, Singapore, Thailand, and Vietnam. Students undertake five to 50 weeks of EAP programmes at the ELC to qualify for direct entry (DE) to a Foundation, Diploma, Undergraduate, or Postgraduate course at Macquarie University.

The ELC's suite of English for Academic Purposes (EAP) programmes use a genre-based literacy pedagogy (Martin & Rose, 2005) to develop students' English language proficiency and awareness of academic genres. The EAP programmes have a textually oriented view of discourse (Hyland, 2009; Paltridge, 2010), which takes account of the sociocultural context of discursive practices and focuses on language features of a range of academic genres that are typically found in higher education assessment tasks such as argumentative essays, research reports, and academic presentations. The pedagogy of these programmes is informed by English language proficiency models of communicative competence (Bachman & Palmer, 1996; Canale & Swain, 1980; Celce-Murcia, 2008; Celce-Murcia et al., 1995), which broadly involve the development of a range of linguistic, socio-cultural, discursive and interactional competences. Lesson design is shaped by social constructivist theories of learning (Vygotsky, 1978) in which knowledge is co-constructed through collaborative learning experiences.

DOI: 10.4324/9781003283409-22

The DE Programme is a ten-week EAP programme for undergraduate and postgraduate EAL students who have the language proficiency equivalent of a Common European Framework of Reference (CEFR) B2+, Academic IELTS 6.0, TOEFL iBT 73, or Pearson Academic 50. On successful completion of the DE programme, students are deemed to have acquired the requisite English language proficiency level for entry to their degree course at Macquarie University without taking a formal language proficiency test. DE programmes come under the Australian Government's English Language Intensive Courses for Overseas Students (ELICOS) Standards, and must have "formal measures in place to ensure that assessment outcomes are comparable to other criteria used for admission to the tertiary education course of study" (Australian Government, 2017, p. 8). Traditionally, assessment in DE programs has been based on assignment work, such as a researched essay, as well as separate skills testing through pen and paper tests, similar to the IELTS constructs of proficiency. This includes listening tests, reading tests, speaking tests, and timed writing in which candidates write from personal experience in response to an essay question prompt.

Prior to the Covid-19 lockdowns of March 2020, the ELC had two streams of DE programmes: one for students undertaking further studies in Business, Accounting and Economics (BAE) and another for Human Sciences, Arts and Science (HAS). In January of 2020, the ELC's curriculum development team was scheduled to redevelop both programmes into one programme to commence in May 2020. Focus group discussions had taken place with academics from target faculties, and former HAS and BAE students and teachers. Additionally, to understand more about the context of language use in contemporary higher education, a review of literature on 21st-century pedagogical assumptions and practices at universities in Australia was undertaken. The research identified that multi-modality and digital learning environments were increasingly prevalent in higher education even prior to the pandemic, and that learning scenarios have broadened from traditional modes of lecture and tutorial to embrace interactive, and collaborative learning such as team-based, project-based, and problem-based learning (Arkoudis et al., 2013). The literature also revealed that assessment practices are changing as academics strive for relevance and authenticity. The application of knowledge in real-life settings and the inclusion of personal reflection, peer review, the development of evaluative judgement, assessment literacy, and feedback literacy (Bearman et al., 2020; Boud & Falchikov, 2007) are increasingly common. Even as we began to plan for implementing curriculum change prior to the Covid-19 pandemic, it was clear that greater consideration of EAL students' socio-pragmatic and intercultural competences, multiliteracy skills, and metaknowledge of assessment practices was needed.

At the time of writing, Australia's international borders remain firmly closed to offshore international students, and remote delivery of EAP programmes is set to continue into 2022 and beyond. The following account of amendments made to the DE programme in response to Covid-19 remote delivery has developed progressively across the last three programme deliveries.

Theoretical influences

Synchronous, asynchronous, and blended learning were all familiar concepts at the time the pandemic struck, but the complete replacement of face-to-face classroom delivery with remote delivery via video conferencing came as a surprise to educators and students globally. This section considers the theories that informed design decisions on the ELC's DE EAP programme and will continue to inform decisions across all its EAP programmes as they continue to diversify and evolve.

The model below illustrates course designers' engagement with theory as they raced to redesign the DE EAP programme in time for the May delivery.

Connectivism

The theory of connectivism (Siemens, 2005) and its nexus of technology and socialisation were influential at the conceptual level in considering the sorts of changes to make for a better student experience. Connectivist theorists such as Downes (2007) and Siemens (2005) hold that because *knowledge today* is distributed broadly across connected networks, via the Internet, *learning today* is about connecting and navigating those information networks. Curriculum developers identified the relevance of this concept for remote delivery and indeed for 21st-century higher education. Connectivism draws some digital parallels to the social constructivism of the EAP classroom because it sees learning as a process of connecting to information sources, which are human (or non-human). The learning process is fuelled by interaction, diversity of opinion, and the ability to see connections between fields, ideas, and concepts (Siemens, 2005). Where connectivism differs from social constructivism is that it holds no particular concept of building knowledge at the intrapersonal level (Bates, 2015). Nonetheless, the principles of connectivism provide a sound conceptual basis for the shaping of digital pedagogy.

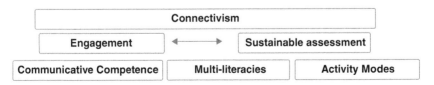

FIGURE 17.1   Engagement with theory

Engagement

Another relevant body of theory lies in understanding student engagement in the digital space. The reality of remote teaching is that students have much less supervision than is the case in a physical classroom environment; consequently, they can disengage from learning more easily. Course designers needed to consider the theoretical dimensions of engagement, generally accepted to be cognition, behaviour, and affect (Fredricks et al., 2004). The creation of tasks that facilitate participants' episodic engagement (Khan & Reinhart, 1990) were constructed, calling on students to employ cognitive, behavioural and affect resources to fulfil the requirements of the task. Wiseman, Kennedy, and Lodge advocate that "high levels of digital task engagement may result in both tangible learning outcomes (conceptual change) and improved learning experience (psychological well being)" (2016, p. 669). Since DE is a high stakes programme, students are typically emotionally invested in passing and can become quite fixated on outcomes, as measured by scores, instead of focusing on conceptual growth, language use, and skill development. It was important, therefore, to design an assessment that rewards *the process* of achieving an outcome, rather than merely grading the final piece of work. Tasks that reward the outcome, the process of achieving the outcome, and a student's contribution to a group or learning community create opportunities for episodic engagement and promote positive learning attributes. In times of isolation and remote delivery, well-designed tasks can also create the need and scaffolding for students to engage with academic texts and each other beyond the scheduled class time.

Sustainable assessment

To promote positive levels of engagement, curriculum developers wanted to utilise sustainable assessment (Boud & Falchikov, 2007; Boud & Soler, 2016) that would serve the needs of the current programme as well as the students' future needs at university. By nature, EAP programmes are needs-based, designed to induct novice academics into the discourse of their chosen fields. DE EAP programmes develop students' communicative competence to facilitate participation in a range of fields; consequently, to design sustainable assessment, course designers must be aware of the language use domains. The literature on 21st-century learning and teaching trends showed broadening cultural diversity, increased interaction and networking (Arkoudis et al., 2013), and a greater need for learner autonomy and self-awareness (Ajjawi et al., 2018; Carless & Boud, 2018) as being key factors that influence language use. Preparatory courses such as DE programmes must develop language within these contexts so that the appropriate knowledge and metaknowledge associated with language, cognition, and socio-pragmatic competences are embedded in the developmental journey. This requires a departure from the EAP traditions of the former DE programmes, which relied primarily on written genres to satisfy the requirements of course assessment, and a shift toward academic discourse socialisation (ADS) (Kobayashi et al., 2017). ADS takes greater account of students' socialisation into academic discourse communities, social networks, and evolving academic genres, such as multimodal practices involving video conference collaborations and academic presentations using digital tools. Recognising the importance of ADS allowed course developers to create assessment with positive washback that enhances engagement.

Due to the high stakes of the DE program, academic integrity was a key consideration in planning assessment. Curriculum developers referred to the work of the Contract Cheating and Assessment Design Taskforce, which had undertaken research across Australian universities between 2016 and 2018 and identified good practice in promoting academic integrity (Bretag et al., 2018). Assessment activities noted as more reliable in this digital era are those that model authentic use of language and skills, are relevant to students' current and future needs, and include the application of knowledge and skills in real-life settings. Bearman et al. (2020) suggest a students' creation of a digital presence through professional online communities is an example of an authentic, real-life task.

In considering ways to diversify the type of writing tasks on the DE programme, curriculum developers were influenced by the Common European Framework of Reference (CEFR) Companion Volume (Council of Europe, 2020), which was developed in response to the Internet's transformation of communication. In this volume, the CEFR has shifted terminology from the traditional four skills of reading, writing, speaking, and listening to four modes of communicative activity: reception, interaction, production, and mediation (see Figure 17.2).

This focus on *language use* places interaction at the centre of learning and establishes the mediation of language, information, and concepts as a goal. This is particularly relevant for EAP training as higher education students are ultimately graded on their ability to mediate and apply concepts and theories. The CEFR Companion Volume includes new descriptors for the mediation of texts, concepts, and communications and in response to increasing digital pedagogy, descriptors for online conversation and discussion as well

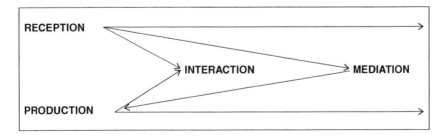

FIGURE 17.2   CEFR communicative activity modes (Council of Europe, 2020, p. 34)

as goal-oriented online transactions and collaboration are also included. The remote delivery of EAP and university programmes of 2020 and 2021 provided ample opportunity to exploit these resources, which proved to be highly instructive and relevant.

Course modifications

Having identified community, interaction, and academic integrity as key considerations, the curriculum development team has implemented three changes to the written assessment, which substantially enriched the course learning outcomes in productive and manageable ways. The first change was a step away from EAP tradition and its reliance on established writing genres towards an ADS approach, which used *interactive writing* as a prominent feature of course design. The second change replaced discrete skills tests with integrated skills test. The third aimed to develop students' metaknowledge by shifting the focus of the traditional researched essay to reward process as well as product. This section considers each of these three developments by describing the change, reflecting on the impact, and considering future directions.

i) Interactive writing

It was felt that because students in lockdown were likely to be experiencing isolation, the use of discussion forums would provide opportunity for engagement beyond the class schedule and the possible formation of friendships. A new *interactive writing* assessment task was created to help students develop functional language and socio-pragmatic skills for managing themselves in weekly written discussion forums. Curriculum developers reasoned that because the pragmatic rules and functional language of informal written interaction have similarities with the spoken interaction required in learning scenarios in higher education, the development of these skills and knowledge would serve the immediate needs of the course as well as students' future needs.

On the discussion forums, peers discussed assigned reading texts in the way they might in university tutorials. Language input was provided and modelled for appropriate ways of agreeing, disagreeing, clarifying concepts, conceding, and accepting other points of view. At the end of a five-week period, students wrote a reflection on their contribution to the learning community by describing and evaluating the *frequency, quality, and range* of their interactions. The reflection was written during class time and students were asked to use screenshots of the forum to demonstrate some of their best interactions. The following samples demonstrate the positive uptake by students who worked strategically to incorporate a range of interactions and increase their mastery of functional language.

Discussion Forum Student Sample 1

> *When I saw ideas I agreed with, I also commented on why I think they are great. Furthermore, I will give some examples to support my opinion.*

> *I agree with you that all nations need to work together at this specific time. In my personal opinion, every nation should share experimental data and urgent materials. Even China invents efficient medicine, she will hyalinize the process and achievement. Consequently, when the new virus appears, it could help other countries have the experience of coping with the crisis.*

It is not uncommon for international students to avoid disagreeing or expressing alternative views in class because they are uncertain of the pragmatic conventions and do not want to offend. The following example demonstrates a student successfully engaging in disagreeing and expressing an opinion.

Discussion Forum Student Sample 2

> *Sometimes, I thought my classmates' ideas have their points, but I had a different view. I would tell them my reasons politely.*

You have a point there, Yuki. I agree that the government needs to help people reduce their dependence on alcohol. However, I am worried that if heavy drinkers could not access alcohol suddenly, they may possibly have withdrawal symptoms. In other words, they might hurt themselves and the people around them. The government should adjust policies for different situations.

Discussion Forum Student Sample 3

> *I also clarify other people's posts. When Han was confused about some of the data in the article, I responded to her confusion and found relevant content in the article to prove it.*

Hi, Han, I understand your confusion. There is no clear explanation for the reason why the rate of children infected with coronavirus is lower than adults, but the article says that only a very small number of children worldwide have been confirmed to have died from the virus. At the same time, a study in Iceland showed that symptomatic children have not been detected with coronavirus, and the article also mentions coronavirus in family gatherings in some countries, such as China and South Korea, the main spreader account for less than 10% of children, although it is not known why and finally, the author also mentions that there was no evidence of secondary transmissions in schools with confirmed cases in Australia. Therefore, I guess the reason why the author wrote this is based on the aforementioned facts.

Reflection on impact

Student writing on the discussion forum reflected a hybrid of formal and informal registers and provided an authentic base for teachers to draw comparisons between registers. In seeking to clarify ideas from the texts, students naturally engaged in the mediation practices of summarising and paraphrasing, which are key learning outcomes of the programme. Teachers were able to scan the discussion forum for good examples of summarising and paraphrasing to show in class and point out to individuals how they could better meet originality requirements.

Teachers commented on the enthusiastic uptake of the discussion form task, "WOW! – have you had a look at some of those conversations? Some of the best (academic) student interactions I've seen" (C. Carpp, personal communication, July 10, 2020). However, many teachers remained unconvinced of the validity of using such a task on a gateway programme. They were concerned that the language used in the discussion forum may have been enhanced by digital tools and as such may not be reflective of the students' actual ability. They also noted that student writing in the reflection itself was somewhat formulaic, taken prescriptively from the model reflection provided as a part of the course materials. As a result, in the subsequent DE programme, the discussion forum activity remained, but in this iteration, small student groups took turns to select an article and prepare some comprehension and language questions about the text for the rest of the class to engage in. The reflective task involved students using Gibbs reflective cycle (Gibbs, 1988) to reflect on an aspect of the first five weeks of class. This could include their contribution to the forum through engagement in discussions, their role in selecting and developing the input for the forum, or some other aspect of the learning and teaching. Students were not required to draw on examples of their interactions in the discussion forum.

Future directions

A possible direction for interactive writing is to broaden the construct of this assessment to integrate listening and speaking components involving weekly podcasts and an asynchronous verbal discussion thread. In this way, the dynamic of contemporary higher education is more meaningfully represented, and students are guided to develop socio-cultural, socio-pragmatic, and linguistic competences that will enhance their higher education experience.

ii) Integrated skills test

The programme's traditional use of separate skills testing in their final exam suite was identified as a detractor from the sustainable assessment goal, and an academic integrity issue when assessed online. To be a more sustainable assessment, it was decided that rather than writing essays on personal experience, students should write from source texts in the way they are required to at university. Concurrently, staff were noting that despite remote invigilation, the short answer and multiple choice questions in listening and reading tests could be efficiently shared among students via social media during the exam. Through trial and error, staff found that digitally competent students could set up a transcription tool to transcribe the listening audio into written text, in live time, which allowed them to use the script to answer comprehension and gap-fill questions. There was also a lack of authenticity in these tests because the question types do not reflect language use in higher education.

In response, an integrated skills test has been established in which students use concepts and ideas from a reading and listening text to respond to an essay prompt. The rating rubric has been changed in two ways. Firstly, the task achievement criterion, now worth 35% of the overall grade, awards students' ability to use key ideas, examples, and explanations from the source texts to answer the essay question. Secondly, a new criterion for *mediation* of language was added to the rating rubric, worth 30%, which evaluates students' ability to summarise and paraphrase from the input sources with acceptable degrees of accuracy and clarity. This focus on students' ability to use the texts, rather than simply displaying comprehension, makes it a much more sustainable assessment.

Reflection on impact

The washback from the integrated skills test has been extremely positive. In the tradition of genre-based pedagogy, curriculum designers have included preparatory materials, which focus on citation methods, paraphrasing, and summary writing through deconstruction and co-construction of model answers. This focus is beneficial preparation for the final exam, the researched essay, and for university study beyond the DE programme. Additionally, the test has helped to curtail some of the cheating behaviours that had been identified in remote delivery of discrete skills tests. There is no opportunity to quickly share answers to the response and if students are able to access translation, transcription, or paraphrasing tools during the exam, these tools are of little use in constructing a relevant response to the essay question within a restricted period of time.

iii) Rewarding process and product

In the digital environment of Covid-19 remote delivery, students have reduced supervision and teacher contact time, and are substantially distanced from the ethical ethos of the institution of study. This makes managing academic integrity a challenge. In response, several changes were made to the researched essay writing process and the way it is assessed.

The first change was made to better manage students' *process* of writing in order to broaden the opportunities for feedback and promote the development of assessment and feedback literacy. There is a growing awareness that for feedback to be a learning centred process, students must know how to engage effectively with the process and utilise the feedback information productively (Boud & Molloy, 2013; Molloy et al., 2020). Firstly, rubric lessons were created in which students used the task rating descriptors to make evaluative judgements about exemplar texts. Students referred back to course notes on language and structure to improve the texts they were evaluating and in so doing, took on the roles of experts, developing their assessment literacy and evaluative judgement skills. Students then used these descriptors to evaluate their own work, and the work of their peers.

Secondly, an expectation was set for students to submit their draft essays for review and feedback from two of the digital academic support services that Macquarie University makes available to its students. These included Studiosity, a support platform which provides expert writing feedback, and Turnitin, a service that checks writing for originality and identifies plagiarism in students' work. Students were rewarded for demonstrating evidence of their responses to feedback between initial drafts and final submissions.

Another change in the researched essay task was made in consideration of students' use of digital tools in their written submissions. Studies have identified that students are using digital translation, paraphrasing, and language enhancement tools to improve the quality of their academic writing (Dinneen, 2021) and it is reasonable to expect a higher rate of accuracy in work that has been submitted digitally. In response, the research essay rating rubrics were amended so that the weightings for grammatical and lexical range and accuracy were reduced from 50% of the overall score down to 20%. As Table 17.1 demonstrates, the NEW criteria awarded a higher weighting to elements of writing that are not enhanced by digital tools, that is, task response, essay structure, coherence and cohesion, and the use of academic style such as nominalisation, hedging, and citation methods.

Reflection on impact

The quality of submissions on this research task was much improved from previous cohorts of students who did not have access to the feedback touchpoints of Studiosity and Turnitin. Teachers noted fewer language errors and far fewer plagiarism issues in the submissions. One teacher noted "So many aspects of this course were welcome – The emphasis on students learning to learn well on their own and through cooperation with each other . . ." (C. Carpp, personal communication, July 10, 2020). Likewise, students saw the usefulness in developing institutional literacy (Miller, 2015) by working with some of the support services that are available to them when they begin their university degree. One teacher summarised her class experience (Anonymous Teacher Survey, 27 July 2020):

> Students in our class were overwhelmingly positive about the usefulness of the course content. Some students commented that they cannot imagine going straight to MQ without having completed this course as they would be completely lost without the skills they learnt at the ELC.

TABLE 17.1 Changes to direct entry researched essay rating rubric

Writing Rating Rubric PREVIOUS Criteria	Weighting	Writing Rating Rubric NEW Criteria	Weighting
Content: development of ideas	20%	Task achievement	20%
Structure: Introduction, conclusion, paragraphs	10%	Structure: introduction, conclusion, paragraphs	10%
Coherence & Cohesion: use of devices	10%	Coherence & Cohesion: use of devices	15%
Vocabulary: range and accuracy	25%	Vocabulary & Grammar: range & accuracy	20%
Grammar: range and accuracy	25%	Academic style: nominalisation, hedging, etc.	10%
Academic style: formal language & structures	5%	Referencing: attributions, in text citations, reference list	10%
Referencing: In-text and reference list	5%	Academic Process: plan, draft, engagement with feedback opportunities	15%

Future directions

In a digitally enabled world, assessment design must be reimagined to better encompass the inter-relationship between assessment and the knowledge that resides in digital tools and applications (Bearman et al., 2020). Students' use of the digital language enhancement tools available to them is inevitable, and it is time to consider ways in which these tools should be brought into the learning and teaching programme. The quality of paraphrasing, for example, produced by paraphrasing tools is problematic for student submissions. The tools do not restructure information in the way of an appropriate paraphrase, but instead, substitute nouns and verbs with synonyms, some of which are inappropriate, or at the very least awkward. Students who decide to use these tools must learn their roles as evaluators of the language produced by the tools, rather than assuming that the machine generates language that is better than their own ability. To achieve this, preparatory EAP programmes should help students to develop a level of mastery as *producers* and *evaluators* of English. Future directions could involve teacher-based action research into EAP students' uses of digital tools and the extent to which the teaching of evaluative judgement aids their mastery of English.

Conclusion

In the quest to promote community, online engagement, and academic integrity, the ELC's curriculum development team has shifted towards integrated skills tasks and testing. The resultant constructive alignment exists not only within the DE English language programme itself, but also in its alignment with the learning and assessment practices in contemporary higher education. The reflections and future directions from each of the changes outlined in this chapter point towards a greater integration of language skills, increased training for interaction among course participants, the strategic development of metaknowledge and purposeful exploitation of digital language enhancement tools. To return to the pen and paper practices of our previous EAP programmes, or to seek only to replicate them on the remote delivery platform would be highly regressive. A progressive EAP programme must have the principles and practices of sustainable assessment at its core and to achieve this, it is important to carefully re-examine the contemporary discourse practices of higher education today and the digital affordances of the 21st-century student.

Reference list

Ajjawi, R., Tai, J. H.-M., Dawson, P., & Boud, D. (2018). *Conceptualising evaluative judgement for sustainable assessment in higher education*. Taylor & Francis.

Arkoudis, S., Watty, K., Baik, C., Yu, X., Borland, H., Chang, S., Lang, I., Lang, J., & Pearce, A. (2013). Finding common ground: Enhancing interaction between domestic and international students in higher education. *Teaching in Higher Education*. https://doi.org/10.1080/13562517.2012.719156

Australian Government. (2017). *ELICOS standards 2018*. www.legislation.gov.au/Details/F2017L01349

Bachman, L. F., & Palmer, A. (1996). *Language testing in practice: Designing and developing useful language tests*. Oxford University Press.

Bates, T. (2015). *Teaching in a digital age: Guidelines for designing teaching and learning for a digital age*. BCcampus Open Textbooks.

Bearman, M., Dawson, P., Ajjawi, R., Tai, J., & Boud, D. (2020). *Re-imagining university assessment in a digital world*. Springer.

Boud, D., & Falchikov, N. (2007). *Rethinking assessment in higher education: Learning for the longer term*. Taylor & Francis.

Boud, D., & Molloy, E. (2013). Rethinking models of feedback for learning: The challenge of design. *Assessment & Evaluation in Higher Education*, 38(6), 698–712. https://doi.org/10.1080/02602938.2012.691462

Boud, D., & Soler, R. (2016). Sustainable assessment revisited. *Assessment & Evaluation in Higher Education*, 41(3) https://doi.org/10.1080/02602938.2015.1018133

Bretag, T., Harper, R., Saddiqui, S., Ellis, C., Newton, P., Rozenberg, P., & van Haeringen, K. (2018). Contract cheating: A survey of Australian university staff. *Studies in Higher Education*, 1–17. https://doi.org/10.1080/03075079.2018.1462789

Canale, M., & Swain, M. (1980). Theoretical bases of communicative approaches to second language teaching and testing. *Applied Linguistics*, *1*, 1–47.

Carless, D., & Boud, D. (2018). The development of student feedback literacy: Enabling uptake of feedback. *Assessment & Evaluation in Higher Education*, *43*(8), 1315–1325. https://doi.org/10.1080/02602938.2018.1463354

Celce-Murcia, M. (2008). Rethinking the role of communicative competence in language teaching. In *Intercultural language use and language learning* (pp. 41–57). Springer.

Celce-Murcia, M., Dörnyei, Z., & Thurrell, S. (1995). Communicative competence: A pedagogically motivated model with content specifications. *Issues in Applied Linguistics*, *6*(2), 5–35.

Council of Europe. (2020). *Common European framework of reference for languages: Learning, teaching, assessment – companion volume*. Council of Europe Publishing.

Dinneen, C. (2021). Students' use of digital translation and paraphrasing tools in written assignments on direct entry English programs. *English Australia Journal*, *37*(1), 40–49. https://eajournal.partica.online/digital/english-australia-journal-371/flipbook/48/

Downes, S. (2007). *What connectivism is*. https://halfanhour.blogspot.com/2007/02/what-connectivism-is.html

Fredricks, J. A., Blumenfeld, P. C., & Paris, A. H. (2004). School engagement: Potential of the concept, state of the evidence. *Review of Educational Research*, *74*(1), 59–109.

Gibbs, G. (1988). *Learning by doing: A guide to teaching and learning methods*. Oxford Further Education Unit.

Hyland, K. (2009). *Academic discourse: English in a global context*. Continuum.

Khan, M. S., & Reinhart, C. M. (1990). Private investment and economic growth in developing countries. *World Development*, *18*(1), 19–27.

Kobayashi, M., Zappa-Hollman, S., & Duff, P. (2017). Academic discourse socialization. *Language Socialization*, *8*, 239–254.

Martin, J. R., & Rose, D. (2005). Designing literacy pedagogy: Scaffolding asymmetries. Continuing discourse on language, 251-280.

Miller, A. (2015). On paper, in person, and online: A multi-literacies framework for university teaching. *Journal of Academic Language and Learning*, *9*(2), A19–A31.

Molloy, E., Boud, D., & Henderson, M. (2020). Developing a learning-centred framework for feedback literacy. *Assessment & Evaluation in Higher Education*, *45*(4), 527–540. https://doi.org/ 10.1080/02602938.2019.1667955

Paltridge, B. (2010). *Discourse analysis*. Continuum International Publishing Group.

Siemens, G. (2005). Connectivism: A learning theory for the digital age. *International Journal of Instructional Technology and Distance Learning*, *2*(1). www.itdl.org/

Vygotsky, L. (1978). *Interaction between learning and development*. Scientific American Books.

Wiseman, P., Kennedy, G., & Lodge, J. (2016). Models for understanding student engagement in digital learning environments. Proceedings of the 33rd International Conference of Innovation, Practice and Research in the Use of Educational Technologies in Tertiary Education. In S. Barker, S. Dawson, A. Pardo, & C. Colvin (Eds.), *Show me the learning. Proceedings ASCILITE 2016 Adelaide* (pp. 666–671).

18

ADAPTING FORMATIVE ASSESSMENT FOR ONLINE ACADEMIC ENGLISH INSTRUCTIONS DURING CHALLENGING CIRCUMSTANCES

Lessons from advanced ESL classroom experiences

Tewero Tchekpassi and Tong Zhang

Introduction

The Covid-19 pandemic has challenged teaching and learning communities. It has been found that the online learning platforms, teachers, students, and resources necessary for effective online teaching were not always ready for the transition (Antoniou, 2021; Chan & Wilson, 2020). Many teachers were compelled to adjust their instructional strategies to address the emerging challenges (Chan & Wilson, 2020; Murphy, 2020). This chapter focuses on the authors' experiences of adapting formative assessment as they transitioned from face-to-face (f2f) to remote instruction. As an instructional strategy, formative assessment helps teachers and students assess students' understanding of instructions, identify students' needs, and provide corresponding synchronous support. In addition to formative assessment, enhancing engagement of learning encourages students' involvement and helps maintain a collaborative learning momentum (Kawase & Parmaxi, 2014).

In seeking to identify strategies to support formative assessment instructions in challenging circumstances, this chapter focuses on the challenges faced and the lessons learned while implementing formative assessment and student engagement; it then discusses the impact on the learning of English for Academic Purposes (EAP). The chapter is divided into five sections. The first section introduces the theoretical framework and centers on formative assessment as an instructional strategy that prepares learners to achieve their goals. This section also draws on student engagement theory to highlight how learners' participation supports

DOI: 10.4324/9781003283409-23

collaborative learning. The second section offers a brief description of the teaching context, emphasizing the challenges that inspired the authors' orientation to formative assessment, as well as the context of the *Academic Literacy* and *Advanced Written Communication* courses. The third and fourth sections detail the instructors' experiences of adapting formative assessment to foster online collaborative learning during the pandemic. Fifth, the chapter presents a discussion, emphasizing the lessons learned and suggests a model of formative assessment for EAP instructions.

Theoretical Framework

Formative assessment relates to student engagement by drawing on learning interactions to assess learners' progress and provide help when needed. This section highlights the strengths of formative assessment alongside student engagement theories. Formative assessment aims to provide predictions about students' progress in the learning process. Defined as the assessment for learning, formative assessment provides insights into the students' current performances and helps teachers adjust instructions to meet identified needs (Black & Wiliam, 2018; Carrillo & Flores, 2020; Leenknecht et al., 2020; OECD/CERI, 2008). By providing the opportunity to assess students' progress and help them learn on an individual basis, formative assessment supports the learning of students with diverse levels of achievements (OECD/CERI, 2008). Black and Wiliam (2009, 2018) suggested that using assessment to support learning involves:

• Clearly defining the learning intentions, ensuring that they are understood, and sharing them with the participants (i.e., teacher, students, peers).
• Introducing tasks that engage students by prompting their responses.
• Providing feedback that clarifies the current status of students' learning.
• Providing the support needed to reach the next learning goal.

In practice, to check students' understanding of a concept or their mastery of a skill, a teacher may assign a task and communicate expectations to the students to prompt their responses (Ruiz-Primo & Furtak, 2007). By analyzing students' responses, the teacher could determine whether students have mastered the skill, or they need additional instructional support to work further on the skill (Antoniou & James, 2014; Leenknecht et al., 2020; Ruiz-Primo & Furtak, 2007). For example, teachers may alter a task to increase student engagement, or ask them to repeat an activity to improve the mastery of the skill. In such a learning environment, teachers and students draw on information gained from interactions to make judgments, which they interpret and use in deciding how to reshape learning instructions (Black & Wiliam, 2009, 2018; Leenknecht et al., 2020). In other words, collaboration plays a critical role in the implementation of formative assessment by placing learner development at the center of instruction and emphasizing the contributions of both teachers and students (Kusairi et al., 2021; Leenknecht et al., 2020).

Student engagement is defined as the extent to which students are curious, interested, focused, optimistic, and passionate in a learning context (Glossary of Educational Research, n.d.). Student engagement is a determinant in whether a learning activity will be successful. The theory of student engagement (TSE) was developed to explain remote learning experiences and design related instructional strategies (Kearsley & Shneiderman, 1998). The application of TSE suggests that interactive and meaningful activities increase student participation and learning, and technology increases students' passion to participate in technology-supported learning activities.

The TSE also suggests that, by valuing students' input in the activity design, students feel included, and this feeling triggers their participation excitement. Additionally, the communities in which students function influence their participation, engagement, and achievement (Bond & Bedenlier, 2019). To clarify further, student engagement is informed by whether students (Fredricks et al., 2016): (a) are cognitively engaged; (b) react to the learning context, teacher, and peers positively; (c) are interested and feel a part of the learning community and processes; and (d) participate, persist, and demonstrate positive behavior. Thus, collaboration increases students' participation enthusiasm, which also applies to formative assessment.

Context of Teaching

The Covid-19 pandemic challenged teachers and students in numerous ways, including increased levels of stress, communication problems, pedagogical contingencies, and a variety of technological disruptions. Hartshorn and McMurry (2020) found that teachers and students valued teaching and learning, but student performance decreased due to the impact of issues of health, food security, loss of income and/or lives, and shortage of diverse household supplies. In a study conducted by Wang and colleagues (Wang et al., 2020), increased stress and anxiety caused by the pandemic produced negative effects on students' academic performance (see also Rundle et al., 2020). Additional findings revealed that in some contexts, English learners could not use technology to satisfactorily meet the course requirements because of deficiencies related to the use of online learning platforms, internet access, and download speed (Asmara, 2020; Atmojo & Nugroho, 2020; Mahyoob, 2020; Piller et al., 2020). Students' home environments also needed adjusting for remote teaching and learning processes (Zhang et al., 2020). Furthermore, Carrillo and Flores (2020) suggested that to create careful conditions for structured online learning experiences, roles should be clearly defined to help establish the processes of curriculum construction, pedagogical practice, assessment, competence building, and professional development.

These findings suggest that implementing engaging instructional and formative assessment strategies could help English teaching and learning processes.

This chapter focuses on the practices of formative assessment in *Academic Literacy* and *Advanced Written Communication*, two EAP courses taught at the American Language Institute (ALI) of Indiana University of Pennsylvania during the Covid-19 pandemic. The ALI program is designed to help English learners who are enrolled or seeking enrollment in a university's program to improve their English proficiency and undergo socialization within American academic culture. Students enrolled at the ALI have been provisionally admitted by the university but are required to improve their English. On the basis of their placement tests, ALI students are beginners, intermediate, and/or advanced learners. ALI also accepts exchange scholars who want to improve their English. Students enrolled in the program during the pandemic (2020–2021) came from many countries, including China, Egypt, Poland, Turkey, Japan, Saudi Arabia, and South Korea. More details about the model of formative assessment used in the two courses are presented below.

Teacher–Student Co-created Formative Assessment

The ALI's *Academic Literacy Course* is designed to introduce international students to American academic culture and promote the exploration of their intended academic majors. The aim of this course is to build students' academic literacy knowledge and skills through working on one research writing project for a semester. During the pandemic, this course was delivered as a synchronous online class via Zoom. As students enrolled in this course came from the United States and other countries, how to effectively communicate with students across different time zones became a vital question for transitioning this course from f2f to online instructions.

To confront the uncertainty of whether students and the instructor can communicate effectively in an emergent online learning environment, the instructor prioritized building an engaging and interactive learning community to support students. Rubrics are often referred to as a scoring device for the instructor to evaluate students' performance. In EAP teaching contexts, rubrics are often created by the instructor, and students have rarely been engaged in the creation process. Recently, research has evidenced that engaging students in the process of rubric creation provides strong instructional value by enhancing the clarity of expectations, fostering students' abilities to take responsibility for their learning, and further enhancing their learning performance (Becker, 2016). In the *Academic Literacy* course, the instructor implemented the teacher–student rubric co-creation as an alternative formative assessment by combining self-assessment and peer-review activities. Via a collaborative learning tool (e.g., Google Jamboard), the instructor adapted the rubric creation for an interactive online learning environment. Below is an example of rubric co-creation guidance for a research presentation assignment:

> Guidance for students: Think of the three samples of student presentations you have reviewed in the last class, as well as your experiences of delivering presentations. What are the things that the writer has been doing well in the sample? What are the things that can be improved? In your small group, discuss the strengths and weaknesses that you and your team members used for assessing the qualities of the student research presentations. In the Google Jamboard, please list at least five strengths and the weaknesses by using the sticky notes.

After receiving the guidance, students formed groups and worked on analyzing student presentation samples. Then, they had small group discussions and shared their ideas on the Google Jamboard – a collaborative digital whiteboard. Next, both the instructor and the students reviewed students' input, reduced repeated information on Jamboard, and wrote the descriptions of the criteria. After the whole class had discussed and agreed on the descriptions of the criteria and distribution of points, the instructor organized the contents of Jamboard into a rubric and shared it with students via e-mail. Then students continued using the rubric formatively to generate and understand the feedback from self-assessment and peer review. Figure 18.1 shows the process of how students and the instructor collaborated on the Jamboard.

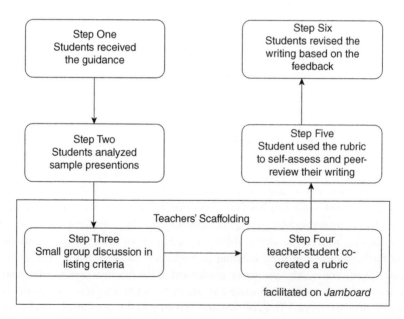

FIGURE 18.1 Process of teacher–student rubric co-creation

By using the co-created rubric as a learning tool, students can generate targeted feedback by referencing the rubric criteria, which further helps them understand the expectations of the assignment. Therefore, the entire process of rubric co-creation and formative feedback generation were connected and integrated into each student's learning process.

Enhancing Student Engagement Through Negotiated Instructional Policies

The *Advanced Written Communication* course, which was delivered through Zoom, e-mail, OneDrive, and the university website, D2L, was designed to help students improve their writing and critical thinking skills. Students received support to improve grammar skills and the use of technology for their writing and presentations. The Covid-19 breakout disrupted the communication processes regulating learning interactions. The following f2f communicative approaches were either suppressed or significantly limited: group interactions, verbal and non-verbal communication, collaborative scaffolding, and collaborative learning of listening, speaking, reading, and writing skills. To address these disruptions, the class negotiated a set of rules to facilitate online interactions.

Created from a set of guiding principles suggested by the instructor and discussed by the class in response to students' concerns for their privacy on Zoom, these policies were also needed to help facilitate collaborative learning through managing turn-taking, maximizing participation, using Zoom video and breakout rooms, implementing accountability, and managing absences. Regarding turn taking, the class agreed that students should contribute to classroom activities by taking turns voluntarily or under the instructor's prompting. Meanwhile, the instructor encouraged every student to participate. Another negotiated policy was that students should turn on their Zoom cameras to help them focus and facilitate collaboration. Nevertheless, students could turn off their cameras whenever they wanted to preserve their privacy. Furthermore, it was agreed that individual writing sessions and small group work should be completed in the Zoom breakout rooms. Also, to maximize interactions, every student should attend class synchronously to participate in collaborative learning. Students who missed class should contact the instructor by e-mail and follow all policies documented in the syllabus. The course materials were made available in D2L with detailed instructions for students who missed class. Additionally, the class discussed the importance of accountability and decided that attendance, class participation, and formative quizzes should count as a part of the course grade, and all group members should participate with feedback. Students who missed the class should request and complete make-up assignments with the help of a tutor. Finally, concerning completion of homework assignments, the class agreed that part of these assignments should be completed in class to avoid overwhelming students.

At the end of each writing session, students were asked to briefly share their progress with the class.

These policies were used to facilitate learning activities, including brainstorming and sharing ideas, analyzing writing samples, drafting, peer review, writing conferences, revisions, reflective writing, oral presentations, and discussions. To help students focus on the writing skills, assignment objectives, checklists, and grading rubrics were provided. Table 18.1 summarizes the instructor's observations of students' reactions to the use of the negotiated policies in the classroom, as well as the responses these reactions elicited. The bottom row of the table presents a summary of the program's formal course evaluations viewed as relevant to the current discussions about the negotiated policies.

As a general observation, students complied with the course policies created with their input. The policies helped students stay engaged and collaboratively practice thinking, listening, speaking, writing, and feedback provision. Additional outcomes of the use of the policies include students' perceptions of the classroom environment as welcoming, a need for instructor flexibility, and the understanding that teacher scaffolding by modeling expectations helps students focus on specific features and skills when they write and analyze their drafts.

Discussion: A Collaborative Model of Formative Assessment for EAP Instructions

Formative assessment has the potential of helping English learners develop their literacy learning skills but fostering students' literacy learning can be challenging. In seeking to explore the strategies that could help students learn formatively when major disruptions affect collaboration opportunities, this chapter centers on the authors' experiences of implementing formative assessment during the Covid-19 pandemic. The chapter suggests that designing formative assessment activities with students' input plays an important role in setting up necessary conditions for collaborative learning and argues that, during challenging circumstances, formative assessment could be promoted through a welcoming classroom environment, collaborative interactional policies, teacher scaffolding, student collaboration, and synchronous feedback.

A welcoming learning environment conducive to sustained collaboration was observed in the synchronous meetings. In circumstances where teachers and students experience difficulties to hold physical meetings, agreed-upon approaches can encourage students to interact, which is useful for the implementation of formative assessment. Promoting anonymity, for instance, could encourage students who feel intimidated by a lack of anonymity in the learning environment to participate in learning tasks (Humiston et al., 2020). Bucholz and Sheffler (2009) argue that establishing a warm classroom environment should be viewed as important as other pedagogical strategies used by teachers.

TABLE 18.1 Students' responses to negotiated instructional policies & elicited instructor replies

Policies	Student responses	Elicited instructor's replies
Taking turns	– Initial low confidence by a few, but class totally complied with turn-taking policy; answered questions, corrected errors, provided and received feedback.	– Continued to managed turns; encouraged participation.
Zoom camera	– Most complied, turned cameras on. – One student stayed off camera.	– Discussed non-compliance at staff meeting. Lesson: reasons might be religious. Continued supporting student off-camera.
Zoom breakout rooms	– Liked brainstorming ideas in breakout rooms; shared with class. – The less confident asked questions in breakout rooms.	– Visited students in breakout rooms; answered questions and encouraged students.
Class attendance	– Majority attended class; those who missed completed make-up assignments; a few needed reminders, encouragement, and deadline extensions.	– Sent emails; encourage students to make up assignments; answered requests for support; worked with tutoring coordinator to help students' make-up work.
Accountability in group work	– Reported group activity collaboratively; made formative and corrective comments on peers' work. – During initial peer-review training, some students asked to learn from the instructor, because others are just learners. – Finally, students committed to accountability policy.	– Praised students for participation and critical thinking; supported agreements and disagreements as a normal process; analyzed samples with class; modeled peer review process to encourage students to provide feedback.
Completing part of homework in class	– All students did individual drafting sessions in the breakout rooms. – Initially, one student expressed desire for large group activities but later, enjoyed drafting individually and receiving support.	– Encouraged students to share progress after each individual drafting session; explained how individual writing could reduce workload.
Formal course evaluation	– All liked course and assessment, attended class, participated, and did classwork; thought instructor treated them well and made class interesting; liked the opportunities to use English and improve skills.	– Thinks: Future instructions should use negotiated policies; student perceptions should be assessed consistently for formative feedback.

Note: This table summarizes the negotiated instructional policies created with students' input, students' reactions to these policies, and the instructor's responses to students' reactions.

Interaction policies can be negotiated to promote participation in the learning activities. However, the nature of the challenges faced by teachers, students, and even parents may require that teachers adapt interactional rules to students on a case-by-case basis. Teacher flexibility could, thus, consist of adapting instructional policies to students' needs emerging from the unexpected circumstances in which they find themselves.

Teacher scaffolding is another key component of formative assessment. Teacher scaffolding includes motivating students to engage with the learning tasks, setting up the boundaries within which tasks are completed, maintaining focus on the learning goals, highlighting the key features of the task, managing frustrations, "modeling solutions to the task" (Gonulal & Loewen, 2018, p. 1), and supervising students as they carry out the tasks toward the learning goals. Whether formative assessment uses instructional policies or co-created rubrics, teacher scaffolding can help English learners develop their literacy skills.

Student collaboration also plays a salient role in supporting formative assessment. As evidenced in the rubric co-construction design and the negotiated instructional policies, students demonstrated a proactive role in contributing ideas through small group activities. This engagement reflects the scholarly discussion (Carless, 2011; Rea-Dickins, 2007) that supports situating students in a collaborative working process to help them communicate with peers and further develop their understanding of the learning expectations.

Besides collaboration, synchronous feedback is critical for ensuring the implementation of formative assessment. In line with Lee and Mak (2018), the students themselves served as resources for generating and understanding feedback in an effective formative assessment design. Through synchronous feedback in an online learning environment, students have immediate support to use feedback formatively to self-regulate their learning in activities such as writing revision.

Critical reflections on the implementation of formative assessment are also provided. Primarily, student engagement should be emphasized in all circumstances. Specifically, to help students engage more enthusiastically and prepare for activities (e.g., peer assessment and feedback), they should be taught how to use rubrics and checklists formatively to assess their peer's writing. To ensure the effectiveness of formative assessment, instructors should check students' learning progress and credit students for showing a collaborative working ethic. In addition, to implement negotiated policies, the instructors' flexibility could be critical for achieving widespread student participation in challenging times. To sum up, a collaborative model of formative assessment requires consistent student input and teacher facilitation to encourage student engagement.

Conclusion

Through revealing the authors' teaching practice of implementing formative assessment in two EAP classrooms, this chapter elucidates the process of conducting formative assessment activities through teacher–student rubric co-construction and negotiated instructional policies with students' input. On the basis of the implementation of a collaborative model of formative assessment for EAP instructions, the chapter concludes that formative assessment supports literacy instructions in three areas. First, clarifying the course expectations can encourage students' persistence in their learning of literacy and writing. Second, engaging students in the design of course policies and teaching activities can spark their participation enthusiasm and help them assimilate instructions. In addition, engaging students in collaborative learning through formative assessment can make the learning process more meaningful during challenging times. Overall, implementing formative assessment in the EAP learning context has been evidenced as conducive to fostering students' learning in an online environment.

The authors' reflections on their formative assessment practices have also revealed that some challenges remain unsolved in online teaching contexts. First, preparing students to collaborate with others remains an ongoing practice. Writing samples, rubrics, and checklists may not be enough to achieve successful scaffolding. Students may need repeated reminders of the learning expectations. Second, implementing formative assessment demands reliable and supportive teacher–student relationships. Teachers should be prepared to answer the following questions related to online instruction: *Are students familiar with learning through formative assessment in EAP classes? In communicating with learners from culturally and linguistically diverse backgrounds in an online learning environment, how do teachers ensure students feel comfortable sharing their ideas?* Third, technology accessibility remains a critical challenge for online collaborative learning. Students may not have reliable internet access, equal access to the learning materials, or the skills required to use online platforms. To address these challenges, having a technology training session for students may be necessary for successful online teaching. For practitioners of EAP and scholars of formative assessment in literacy instruction, this chapter suggests a tangible design of a collaborative model of formative assessment that can be adapted and adopted in other classrooms. The first-hand observation of teaching discussed in this chapter offers such insights.

Reference list

Antoniou, C. (2021). Responding to the COVID-19 challenges: The case of a small EAP team and ways forward. In *Narratives of innovation and resilience: Supporting student learning experiences in challenging times* (p. 68). Renfrew: BALEAP

Antoniou, P., & James, M. (2014). Exploring formative assessment in primary school classrooms: Developing a framework of actions and strategies. *Educational Assessment, Evaluation and Accountability, 26*(2), 153–176. https://doi.org/10.1007/s11092-013-9188-4

Asmara, R. (2020). Teaching English in a virtual classroom using WhatsApp during COVID-19 pandemic. *Language and Education Journal, 5*(1), 16–27. https://doi.org/10.52237/lej.v5i1.152

Atmojo, A. E. P., & Nugroho, A. (2020). EFL classes must go online! Teaching activities and challenges during COVID-19 pandemic in Indonesia. *Register Journal, 13*(1), 49–76. https://doi.org/10.18326/rgt.v13i1.49-76

Becker, A. (2016). Student-generated scoring rubrics: Examining their formative value for improving ESL students' writing performance. *Assessing Writing, 29*, 15–24. https://doi.org/10.1016/j.asw.2016.05.002

Black, P., & Wiliam, D. (2009). Developing the theory of formative assessment. *Educational Assessment, Evaluation and Accountability, 21*(1), 5–31. https://doi.org/10.1007/s11092-008-9068-5

Black, P., & Wiliam, D. (2018). Classroom assessment and pedagogy. *Assessment in Education: Principles, Policy & Practice, 25*(6), 551. https://doi.org/10.1080/0969594x.2018.1441807

Bond, M., & Bedenlier, S. (2019). Facilitating student engagement through educational technology: Towards a conceptual framework. *Journal of Interactive Media in Education, 11*(1), 1–14. https://doi.org/10.5334/jime.528

Bucholz, J. L., & Sheffler, J. L. (2009). Creating a warm and inclusive classroom environment: Planning for all children to feel welcome. *Electronic Journal for Inclusive Education, 2*(4), 1–13. Retrieved from https://corescholar.libraries.wright.edu/cgi/viewcontent.cgi?article=1102&context=ejie

Carless, D. (2011). *From testing to productive student learning: Implementing formative assessment in Confucian-heritage settings.* Routledge.

Carrillo, C., & Flores, M. A. (2020). COVID-19 and teacher education: A literature review of online teaching and learning practices. *European Journal of Teacher Education, 43*(4), 466–487. https://doi.org/10.1080/02619768.2020.1821184

Chan, C. B., & Wilson, O. (2020). Using Chakowa's digitally enhanced learning model to adapt face-to-face EAP materials for online teaching and learning. *International Journal of TESOL Studies.* https://doi.org/10.46451/ijts.2020.09.10

Fredricks, J. A., Filsecker, M., & Lawson, M. A. (2016). Student engagement, context, and adjustment: Addressing definitional, measurement, and methodological issues. *Learning and Instruction, 43*, 1–4. https://doi.org/10.1016/j.learninstruc.2016.02.002

Glossary of Educational Research. (n.d.). *Student engagement.* https://doi.org//www.edglossary.org/student-engagement/

Gonulal, T., & Loewen, S. (2018). Scaffolding technique. In *The TESOL encyclopedia of English language teaching* (pp. 1–5). https://doi.org/10.1002/9781118784235.eelt0180

Hartshorn, K. J., & McMurry, B. L. (2020). The effects of the COVID-19 pandemic on ESL learners and TESOL practitioners in the United States. *International Journal of TESOL Studies, 2*(2), 140–157. https://doi.org/10.46451/ijts.2020.09.11

Humiston, J. P., Marshall, S. M., Hacker, N. L., & Cantu, L. M. (2020). Intentionally creating an inclusive and welcoming climate in the online learning classroom. In *Handbook of research on creating meaningful experiences in online courses* (pp. 173–186). https://doi.org/10.4018/978-1-7998-0115-3.ch012

Kawase, R., & Parmaxi, A. (2014). *Online student engagement as formative assessment.* https://ktisis.cut.ac.cy/handle/10488/3476.

Kearsley, G., & Shneiderman, B. (1998). Engagement theory: A framework for technology-based teaching and learning. *Educational Technology, 38*(5), 20–23.

Kusairi, S., Hardiana, H. A., Swasono, P., Suryadi, A., & Afrieni, Y. (2021). E-formative assessment integration in collaborative inquiry: A strategy to enhance students' conceptual understanding in static fluid concepts. *Jurnal Pendidikan Fisika Indonesia, 17*(1), 13–21.

Lee, I., & Mak, P. (2018). Metacognition and metacognitive instruction in second language writing classrooms. *TESOL Quarterly, 52*(4), 1085–1097.

Leenknecht, M., Wijnia, L., Köhlen, M., Fryer, L., Rikers, R., & Loyens, S. (2021). Formative assessment as practice: The role of students' motivation. *Assessment & Evaluation in Higher Education, 46*(2), 236–255. https://doi.org/10.1080/02602938.2020.1765228

Mahyoob, M. (2020). Challenges of e-Learning during the COVID-19 pandemic experienced by EFL learners. *Arab World English Journal (AWEJ), 11*(4), 351–362. https://doi.org/10.24093/awej/vol11no4.23

Murphy, M. P. A. (2020). COVID-19 and emergency eLearning: Consequences of the securitization of higher education for post-pandemic pedagogy. *Contemporary Security Policy, 41*(3), 492–505. https://doi.org/10.1080/13523260.2020.1761749.

OECD/CERI. (2008). *Assessment for learning formative assessment.* www.oecd.org/site/educeri21st/40600533.pdf

Piller, I., Zhang, J., & Li, J. (2020). Linguistic diversity in a time of crisis: Language challenges of the COVID-19 pandemic. *Multilingua, 39*(5), 503–515. https://doi.org/10.1515/multi-2020-0136

Rea-Dickins, P. (2007). Classroom-based assessment: Possibilities and pitfalls. in J. Cummins & C. Davison (Eds.). *International handbook of English language teaching.* Springer.

Ruiz-Primo, M. A., & Furtak, E. M. (2007). Exploring teachers' informal formative assessment practices and students' understanding in the context of scientific inquiry. *Journal of Research in Science Teaching, 44*(1), 57–84. https://doi.org/10.1002/tea.20163

Rundle, A. G., et al. (2020). COVID-19 – related school closings and risk of weight gain among children. *Obesity, 28*(6), 1008–1009. https://doi.org/10.1002/oby.22813

Wang, C., Pan, R., Wan, X., Tan, Y., Xu, L., Ho, C. S., & Ho, R. C. (2020). Immediate psychological responses and associated factors during the initial stage of the 2019 coronavirus disease (COVID-19) epidemic among the general population in China. *International Journal of Environmental Research and Public Health, 17*(5), 1729. https://doi.org/10.3390/ijerph17051729

Zhang, W., Wang, Y., Yang, L., & Wang, C. (2020). Suspending classes without stopping learning: China's education emergency management policy in the COVID-19 outbreak. *Journal of Risk and Financial Management, 13*, 55–55. https://doi.org/10.3390/jrfm13030055

19

ACADEMIC ENGLISH ASSESSMENT IN TIMES OF A PANDEMIC

The case of a Russian research-intensive University

Irina Shchemeleva and Natalia V. Smirnova

Introduction

The arrival of Covid-19 led to changes in how academic writing in English is assessed, as the use of online technologies became central to all aspects of teaching and learning. Earlier studies in computer-assisted English proficiency assessment have focused primarily on the reliability and validity of assessment tools. As Weir (2005) found, when assessing language ability online, context validity needs to be examined as the use of technology impacts the test-takers' ability to perform. There also needs to be some consideration of the physical/physiological characteristics and the use of technology of the test-takers, in addition to the demands of the task and issues with the administration of the test.

With the increase of technology in language classrooms, assessment was subject to change. Covid-19 forced educators to teach online when there was little time to rethink practices, develop an approach and scaffold assessment (Zhang et al., 2021). In a study similar to ours, Zhang et al. (2021) conducted interviews with EFL instructors to explore assessment from the perspective of the changes which resulted, and the factors which played a significant role in these changes. Their small-scale qualitative study provides an insight into the internal and external factors, which impacted the complex assessment practices, namely, a lack of time to prepare new assessment materials, limited experience in conducting online assessment, and the problem of how to distantly monitor the possible unethical behavior of some students. In our chapter, by drawing on institutional policies, interviews, and survey data, we seek to explore the following questions:

- *What assessment initiatives were made by the university and if these were taken up by the teachers?*

DOI: 10.4324/9781003283409-24

- *How the department of foreign languages (DFL) supported EAP teachers' assessment practices?*
- *How the assessment practices of EFL teachers changed in their views?*

University context

The university we are focusing on is a leading research university in Russia where English is widely used for communication, education, and research. The DFL consists of 70 teachers of English and 25 teachers of other foreign languages. There are 12 members of staff who supervise 12 teams of teachers of Academic English (AE), each working in one university department. Each supervisor, apart from teaching AE, also monitors assessment designs and procedures within the team. No blended learning was practiced before the pandemic, and after the pandemic, teaching AE shifted from a completely physical learning setting to a purely online mode of instruction and learning.

Undergraduate students attend an English for General Purposes (EGP) course during their first year of study and an AE course during their second year of study. They must pass a mid-course exam and an end of year exam in English. During the first year, the exams target EGP skills, while during the second year of studies, students sit two exams in AE. Originally, the IELTS past papers were used and then different exam materials were developed to meet the needs of EAP students. Each exam includes the assessment of four skills, listening, reading, writing, and speaking, and is traditionally classroom based. The examination materials are developed by an internal team of test developers, which are then approved by a partner university in the United Kingdom. By the end of the second year, students have to demonstrate B2+ CEFR proficiency, which enables them to use English for their studies, attend EMI lectures and seminars, and take part in international academic mobility programs run by the university. Assessments (both summative and formative) are included in the syllabus. The types of assessment and the grading rubrics are developed by a team of teachers who hold PhD degrees in EFL pedagogy and/or have a CELTA/DELTA certificate. The most common assessment activities/types are a text comprehension, an essay, a project, and an academic presentation. The teachers can adapt the assessment tool to meet the needs of a particular group and match the students' language proficiency. The university's Learning Management System (LMS) is used to store learning materials and to track students' grades.

The pandemic and online shift in EAP assessment research

Assessment in the English for academic purposes (EAP) domain is generally used to evaluate a learner's language ability or progress. Assessment is an integral part of the teaching – learning process and is central to a students' progress toward increasing the control of their language competencies (Hyland, 2006). This conceptualization of assessment is based on criterion-based judgments about student progress for both formative and summative assessments. Formative assessment helps our teachers scaffold the teaching process, monitor learning, and provide feedback, whereas summative assessment allows them to develop a final summary of one's progress at the end of a module. With the shift to online learning and teaching, the conditions of assessment had to change.

Recent studies have explored various modes and approaches to online assessment both to create richer learning experiences for students and to refine assessment tools. Students overall prefer online assessment as it gives them opportunities for quality learning. Hewson and Charlton (2019) explored whether university students' computer-related attitudes and assessment mode preferences were related to their performance on a course-based online assessment task. They revealed that the attitude of the student toward the online or offline mode of assessment had no effect on performance during assessment. Asoodar et al. (2014) explored how online assessment is linked to a sense of community, which is subjectively perceived by students. For example, in Iran, the fact that Iranian students were able to contribute to online blogs was seen as an important indicator of perceived learning. This study brings online collaboration at the forefront in online learning and assessment. The authors suggest developing a new more collaborative EAP assessment approach in online courses. Similar studies have been conducted which explore assessment via collaborative learning (see Chai & Ding, 2012) and peer assessment (Lin, 2019; Wang et al., 2020).

Previous studies have primarily focused on learners' experiences and needs. There is still little known about the teachers and their understanding of the transformations to online assessment practices. In studies on online assessment, the teacher always performs the facilitator role. Palloff and Pratt (2001) proposed a model for online assessment which regards the importance of groups, tasks, technology, and the facilitator. Now, when online courses are incorporated into the curriculum, the medium of distribution and the organization of the course shape the way the students are evaluated. Not only do the traditional forms of assessment (exams, tests,) give a fragmented picture of the students' performances in online courses (Asoodar et al., 2014), but also the creation of co-constructed knowledge (Morgan & O'Reilly, 1999) becomes the important factor as the teacher plays a key role in deciding how and what to assess.

There is limited research to date, which focuses on teachers' assessment practices during the pandemic. That said, Meccawy et al. (2021) conducted a large-scale study months after the start of emergency online teaching in order to explore online assessment practices focusing on students and faculty perceptions of online assessment in higher education at a university in Saudi Arabia. By drawing on survey data, the study points to one salient issue with online assessment: the problem of cheating. While the study discusses possible measures to solve the problem, the solutions offered only stem from the researchers' interpretations of the results of the study and possible solutions to the problem of unethical behavior of students during assessment.

In our research, our focus on practices allows us to explore the real-life experiences of teachers which are rooted in the local educational contexts, their experiences, and knowledge.

Research aims and data collection method

In order to answer our research questions, we chose to:

1. Analyze the assessment support at institutional level (referred to here as the macro level) and document what support was provided by the university to all the staff, to understand the larger context of the assessment agenda. To do so, we analyzed the announcements circulated by the university administration regarding shifting learning online (37 e-mails).
2. Undertake semi-structured interviews with eight EAP teachers-supervisors about their pre- and post-pandemic assessment experiences and the experiences of the teams they supervise (meso level).
3. Conduct a survey by means of a questionnaire with the goal of generating an understanding of the assessment support provided by the DFL allowing us to focus on the specific support of assessment in teaching AE. We call this the micro level. The survey covered the following clusters of questions: *regular assessment practices before the pandemic (requesting explanations and justifications), assessment practices during the pandemic (what and why), key challenges in assessing online, university and DFL support, other types of support, and lessons learned/reflections.* We sent the survey to 70 EFL and EAP instructors and received 52 replies.

Data analysis

Content analysis was performed on the e-mail data set and the initiatives which were designed to support all the university teaching staff were identified. To analyze the interview data, we performed thematic analysis by identifying the common themes in the teachers' responses. Finally, quantitative analysis was carried out on the survey responses using SPSS. We calculated means and standard deviations to understand what assessment activities teachers neglected, changed, or started to use after the pandemic.

Findings

In this section, we will report the findings of our research.

What assessment initiatives were made by the university and were they taken up by the teachers?

We found that different types of support at the macro level were organized for university staff when teaching shifted online. These involved regular webinars and online workshops that were designed to show practitioners how to teach via various platforms, for example, via Zoom, Webinar, and MS Teams. The workshops demonstrated the possibilities the platforms provided and trained the participants in using these platforms. There were also workshops where those with previous experience in online teaching shared their practices. In the first days of online teaching, there was a special section created for teachers on the university website, which demonstrated useful website links and gave pedagogical/instructional advice for online teaching. Special attention during the organized webinars was paid to online assessment, such as online peer review technologies and online proctoring during exams, as important components of the educational process.

Our interviews with the EAP instructors revealed that they found the webinars partly useful, but none of the participants mentioned feeling they had any support available for their assessment practices. For example, Ekaterina[1] said they helped to assess the possibilities each platform provides for assessment and helped her choose the most suitable one. On the whole, however, the participants described the seminars organized by the university as "not very effective, very general and not very clear" (Natali). Dmitry admits that they had to "find all the answers themselves" despite the fact the webinars were organized by the university. The survey results show that only 36% of the respondents viewed the university support as effective for their online teaching practices. At the same time, the fact that the university exerted no pressure on the teachers' choice of platforms was viewed as highly positive by some interviewees:

> We were given a possibility to choose which platform to use. Choose ourselves. . . . I remember there was no pressure from the university. And it was very good.
>
> *(Natali)*

The university subscription to certain platforms (LMS, MS Teams) was also viewed as important support:

> I'm very thankful to the pandemic for receiving the corporate subscription to Office 365.
>
> *(Dmitry)*

---

[1] All names have been changed to protect the anonymity of the participants.

Overall, it may be said that although the university provided support with regard to technology (in that they provided staff with online platforms), their support was not deemed to be very effective from the EAP instructors' view.

How did the DFL support EAP teachers' assessment practices?

According to the survey data, the DFL as a university division was quick to accommodate the shift to online teaching and organized a series of webinars where the language instructors could practice using various teaching platforms for online teaching and for student assessment. The survey results indicate that 71% of the respondents saw them as being effective and attended these webinars and discussions. In their interviews, the participants claimed that the support provided by the DFL helped them at the initial stage of online teaching when they had to master new platforms and find new assessment forms within a short period of time:

> A lot of seminars were organised. We met practically every day and everyone who had no idea [of] what to do was taught.
>
> *(Anna)*

They believe this type of support helped the EAP instructors with their assessment practices because "more experienced colleagues showed [us] how to use different platforms, how to make tests online. That's how I learned about online testing, about Test Pad" (Natali).

Our survey results indicate that the respondents found the departmental seminars a starting point for them to learn more about online platforms and applications like MS Teams and Zoom and the possibility of using them for online assessments. They claimed they had to spend a lot of time educating themselves on how to use the new platforms. One respondent claimed, "I learnt the ABC of online teaching, but I had to learn a lot by myself" while another wrote, "You can learn something only by trying it yourself".

The teachers asserted that they valued not only the seminars organized by the DFL, but also more importantly the informal discussions with their colleagues. Since "no one understood anything" (Dmitry), everyone felt they were on equal terms in their current experiences (or lack of) when they discussed the new ways of teaching and assessment. This informal sharing of experiences with colleagues on an everyday basis (online meet ups, online chats, e-mail discussions) and via self-organized seminars they organized for each other became an important tool for development. Elena illustrates:

> Informal discussions started. Some colleagues told us about Microsoft forms. We tried it and liked it. We asked them to hold a seminar for us and teach us how to use them.

Ekaterina describes how EAP teachers formed small teams to discuss a particular testing platform and share their experiences of using it:

> In teams of 3–4 people we shared lifehacks, showed what and how can be done, and it helped a lot.

In the survey, 87% of respondents also claimed they saw informal discussions with colleagues as a more effective type of support than the formal support given by the DFL. Yet, four interviewees said they had to learn how to assess students' work online by themselves as they were unable to receive the given support. For example, Margarita says that by the time the DFL seminars were held, she "had already checked everything herself".

How did assessment practices change?

Everyday assessment practices

The survey results revealed the main changes in assessment practices after teaching shifted online. Figure 19.1 shows how the number of EAP teachers who used lexical quizzes decreased from 37% to 19%, while those using dialogue tasks decreased from 82% to 62%, and those who used writing tasks, for example, writing a paragraph, lowered from 100% to 90%. Interestingly, 57.7% of the respondents reported that they did not change the forms of assessment, while

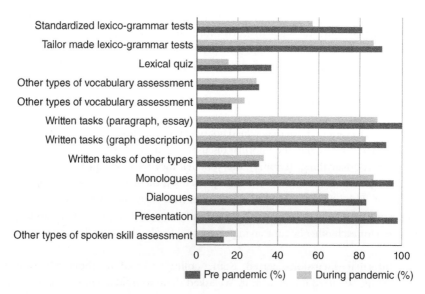

FIGURE 19.1 Pre-pandemic and during pandemic assessment formats at the DFL, HSE University in St. Petersburg

63.5% said that the focus of assessment remained the same. 89.5% of the EAP teachers reported that they followed the same assessment criteria, while 61.5% of the respondents said that the format of assessment had to change.

The interviews signal that the unexpected and forced shift to online assessment in English classrooms has resulted in what is seen by the teachers as significant irrevocable transformations of assessment practices, which will sustain long after the pandemic. Teachers primarily mentioned the importance of new online platforms they had to master, particularly transferring all assessment tasks from paper to an online platform, for example, LMS, MS Teams, OneNote, and Quizlet. The interviewees signaled the main advantages of online testing being that is more time efficient for implementing and processing results, and having more automated processes which control students' work:

> "There's a timer and you can set the time for a certain task, and there're fewer opportunities to cheat".
>
> *(Margarita)*

> "They [online tests] make our life easier. Since we're online, the system should do at least partly some work for us".
>
> *(Natali)*

> "You can see the result immediately, and it's very convenient".
>
> *(questionnaire response)*

> "Online testing saves a lot of time".
>
> *(questionnaire response)*

Both the interviewees and the survey respondents believed that some of the assessment practices they used will sustain long after the pandemic. Forty percent of the participants said that online testing is the practice they are determined to continue when teaching returns face-to-face. They claimed the main advantages of using online platforms for testing were connected to the time spent checking the tests and giving feedback. Online testing was highly valued by both the interviewees and the questionnaire respondents because of its perceived time efficiency. This idea is well articulated by one interviewee who defines "an effective test" as "less time-consuming".

The pandemic appeared to provide new impetus for teachers. Some interviewees admitted that the idea to move all tests online had been with them for many years, but they put it into practice only when they had no other choice:

> "I had this idea for the last 5–6 years because I realized that grading the tests is the major minus in my job. And I had always been thinking about these paper tests. Only the online teaching made me do it".
>
> *(Elena)*

Another interviewee expressed the idea that the pandemic made them use some instruments that existed before but which she had not used. In particular, she was talking about the possibility to record some monologues and presentations and then upload them on the platform for further assessment:

> "This option has always been there, and we knew about it, but never used".
>
> *(Ekaterina)*

Change in assessment focus and content

The data analysis shows that the change in the mode of teaching and the instruments used for assessment resulted in changes in the main content of the assessment. As already mentioned, there is limited research to date, which focuses on teachers' assessment practices during the pandemic. The teachers quickly realized that some traditional assessment methods did not work:

> "We knew almost immediately that something had to be changed".
>
> *(Anna)*

> "It was almost on the first week of online teaching. We had to give a test. We had to find some solution because no one had any experience. We knew that the traditional way was not good".
>
> *(Natali)*

While looking for technical solutions and testing online platforms, some interviewees mentioned that they had altered their traditional offline assessment practices. For example, more productive tasks replaced lexical quizzes and tests:

> "Now I concentrate more on writing tasks and speaking. On productive skills. And online platforms give a range of possibilities for giving feedback. And they allow recordings. The students can see their progress. Even in lexis, in grammar. They show a wider spectrum of students' achievements".
>
> *(Sofia)*

Sofia illustrates that using a Quizlet for vocabulary work allows students to immediately see their progress, making them more engaged in learning. By recording their monologues she says students can now also develop its script, and listen to it once again, so they can develop a deeper understanding of the spoken discourse.

In some cases, interviewees had to seriously reflect on their regular assessment practices:

> "It seems I've changed absolutely everything. I had to make it clear for myself and for the students what I am assessing in my class. And to assess exactly what they have learnt"
>
> *(Ekaterina)*

> "Everything changed 100%. We designed new tasks, we stopped giving tests that take huge amount of time".
>
> *(Anna)*

As a result, according to one survey respondent, "[we developed] a more logical, systematic and consistent process of studying and assessment". The aforementioned analysis, therefore, shows that online teaching assessment changed not only with regard to the instruments used, but more importantly in terms of significantly rethinking our standard assessment practices. Another important finding from our study is that by making the assessment of reading and listening automated, more quality assessment time was given to the writing and speaking assessment.

Giving feedback online

Discussing new assessment practices, several respondents mentioned that the way they gave feedback on writing and speaking tasks had changed:

> "I started giving more feedback on writing and speaking tasks".
>
> *(Sofia)*

> "Now I use different colors, I can always put something on the screen. I've always giving (given) feedback, but now it's more detailed".
>
> *(Margarita)*

According to the participants, these changes became possible for two reasons. The first is that new online instruments significantly increased the spectrum of possibilities for giving feedback and made the process easier. The participants said that new platforms "allow giving extended comments" (Margarita), and make feedback "very clear and structured" and "colorful, precise and detailed" (from the questionnaire). They also noted that with the online instruments, it is "easier to track students' progress" (Ekaterina).

Challenges to online assessment

The participants reported two main difficulties with regard to assessing students online. These were (1) the issue of students' cheating, and (2) the problem of the time the instructors spent on learning how to use new platforms, to design new online materials, and on adapting their assessment practices.

The issue of cheating was immediately raised by the teachers. It was possible because students were at home, doing their assignments without any supervision; therefore, they had the opportunity to cheat. Surprisingly high grades were awarded to students who had previously very poor academic performance. This was evidence enough for the teachers to suspect cheating had occurred. However, the biggest concern for the teachers was proving that there was a case of cheating since they did not have any assessment analytics data. These difficulties were also mentioned in similar research performed by Zhang et al. (2021) during the pandemic.

Sixty-seven percent of the survey respondents named cheating as a negative consequence of online assessment, mentioning "massive cheating that makes it impossible to objectively evaluate the results", "impossibility to make sure that students do their work themselves' and the fact that "you can't prove cheating" (from the questionnaire). As a result, "those who cheat get higher grades. And it's not fair" (from the questionnaire). Students' cheating was also perceived as a problem by the interviewees. They mentioned how they had lot less control over students' work in online teaching compared to face-to-face teaching, and, as a consequence, it was difficult to assess their work:

> "There was some tension that we can't control students' work the same way we used to, when we were in the classroom. We discussed it a lot. Because sometimes you feel that the student can't write it. But such things are improvable".
>
> *(Elena)*

Although the EAP practitioners viewed the students' cheating in the online classroom as a serious problem, they could not offer a solution. Rather, they reached some compromises. For example, they "tried to believe the students" (Natali) and "rely on students' honesty" (Sofia). One reason for that is that they "didn't want to deprive students from their rights", hence the teachers were "looking for some balance, but this balance was difficult to find" (Elena). We might say that the solution of the cheating problem was postponed because it required finding totally new approaches to the organization of the assessment process, which, in turn, is extremely time-consuming.

The issue of time emerged in many interviewees' narratives and in the survey responses. They claimed that "the grading of productive skills requires more time", and that "the teacher is glued to the computer because we have to spend way too much time commenting (on) students' papers" (survey respondents). One respondent wrote that "it demoralizes a lot since you spend a huge amount of time and you can't be sure that students do everything on their own, that they don't cheat" (survey respondent).

Conclusion

The findings of our study echo and extend the earlier findings of Meccawy et al.'s (2021) research on online EAP assessment practices which found that wider educational, social, political and historical contextual factors and experiential (assessment background, training, and practice) factors can impact EFL instructors' practices of assessment. It is evident that the context forms an assessment culture that influences teachers' assessment practices in a local context (development and use of assessment tools). Therefore, experiential factors make teachers use assessment practices they are familiar with, and when new assessment approaches are used, they are forced to learn on the job, making decisions and developing assessments based on their intuition. The main conclusions of our study are the following:

(1) Different initiatives were made at both macro and meso levels. However, they came unnoticed by the EAP instructors mainly due to the need to work within a tight time frame
(2) Informal collaboration and support of colleagues were key to EAP teachers' ability to adapt their assessment practices quickly and efficiently
(3) Assessment practices changed considerably during the pandemic, including assessment activities, online assessment platforms, and assessment focuses. The most valued change was the switch from the paper-based to online tests which saved valuable resources
(4) Many EAP teachers are determined to continue using the assessment practices they acquired during the pandemic, especially the online testing mode
(5) A major concern was student cheating. The problem remains unresolved, primarily because the teachers still lack time to search for viable solutions

Now, having returned to teaching face to face, the future of online assessment lies in the online platforms which support test design and development, allowing us to collect assessment analytics and use the data in various ways. At the same time, such unified platforms create new challenges in how to control the academic honesty of students doing a test (after all they can take screenshots of their answers and send them to peers via chats, who can use their mobile phone to seek help during a test). The problem of cheating, deemed by many as the most negative outcome of online assessment, should be addressed at all the three levels. At the institutional level, there should be more technological support of the assessment for example, having equipment to block mobile phone connections during a test, a university computer for each student, which has no applications to help a student cheat. At the departmental level, it is important to run seminars on how to design assessment tasks so that not only students' progress is checked, but more importantly, students *have no need to cheat*, for example, by developing essay questions, which require an individual point of view, and individual background knowledge and experiences to be reflected in the text. Efforts should also be put into developing online collaborative assessment practices that are found to be effective, (see, e.g., Asoodar et al., 2014), which could undoubtedly lead to higher quality EAP online teaching and assessment practices.

Reference list

Asoodar, M., Atai, M. R., Vaezi, S., & Marandi, S. (2014). Examining effectiveness of communities of practice in online English for academic purposes (EAP) assessment in virtual classes. *Computers and Education, 70*, 291–300. https://doi.org/10.1016/j.compedu.2013.08.016

Chai, S., & Ding, M. (2012). Practical research on the assessment of online collaborative English learning – a case study of blackboard-based course "intercultural communication". In S. K. S. Cheung, J. Fong, L. F. Kwok, K. Li, & R. Kwan (Eds.), *Hybrid learning*. ICHL 2012. Lecture Notes in Computer Science, vol. 7411. Springer.

Hewson, C., & Charlton, J. (2019). An investigation of the validity of course-based online assessment methods: The role of computer-related attitudes and assessment mode preferences. *Journal of Computer Assisted Learning, 35*(1), 51–60. https://doi.org/10.1111/jcal.12310

Hyland, K. (2006). *English for academic purposes. An advanced resource book*. Routledge.

Lin, C. J. (2019). An online peer assessment approach to supporting mind-mapping flipped learning activities for college English writing courses. *Journal of Computers in Education, 6*, 385–415. https://doi.org/10.1007/s40692-019-00144-6

Meccawy, Z., Meccawy, M., & Alsobhi, A. (2021). Assessment in 'survival mode': Student and faculty perceptions of online assessment practices in HE during Covid-19 pandemic. *International Journal for Educational Integrity, 17*(1), 1–24. https://doi.org/10.1007/s40979-021-00083-9

Morgan, C. J., & O'Reilly, M. (1999). *Assessing open and distance learners*. Routledge.

Palloff, R. M., & Pratt, K. (2001). *Lessons from the cyberspace classroom; The realities of online teaching*. John Wiley & Sons.

Wang, J., Gao, R., Guo, X., & Liu, J. (2020). Factors associated with students' attitude change in online peer assessment – a mixed methods study in a graduate-level course. *Assessment & Evaluation in Higher Education, 45*(5), 714–727. https://doi.org/10.1080/02602938.2019.1693493

Weir, C. J. (2005). *Language testing and validation. An evidence-based approach*. Palgrave Macmillan.

Zhang, C., Yan, X., & Wang, J. (2021). EFL teachers' online assessment practices during the covid-19 pandemic: Changes and mediating factors. *The Asia-Pacific Education Researcher, 30*, 499–507. https://doi.org/10.1007/s40299-021-00589-3

20

LANGUAGE TEACHING AND ASSESSMENT AT A CHINESE UNIVERSITY DURING THE PANDEMIC. LESSONS LEARNT AND INNOVATIONS FOR FUTURE PRACTICE

Zhang Li, Liu Jing, and Yan Guoying

Introduction

The year 2020 unfolded in an extraordinary manner which no one could have foreseen. A new virus, reportedly first found in Wuhan, turned out to have been lurking across the world some time before, and consequently spread rapidly. The tempo of life in China and around the world was suddenly put on pause. Lockdowns were imposed to help curb the spread of the virus. Consequently, factories stopped manufacturing, shops were closed, and institutions of learning ceased their educational activities. Yet the consensus was that teaching and learning should be carried out in another way, although many other workplaces were shut down.

However, how to carry out teaching practices which were usually conducted in classrooms before the pandemic became a major concern of practitioners and stakeholders. For online learning to be successful, a good network, easy access to relevant equipment, a reasonable command of necessary software and applications, and support of adequate hardware are all necessary. In addition, a keen awareness of the necessary transformations in teaching, planning, designing, and administering exams was needed to make online teaching/learning possible.

The practices involved in transferring teaching and learning online can also shed light on planning, teaching, and assessment practices. The case study reported in this chapter will examine how the reading and writing courses were conducted remotely in Donghua University, Shanghai, People's Republic of China (DHU),

DOI: 10.4324/9781003283409-25

and how necessary changes were made when evaluating the learners' holistic learning results through summative and formative assessments.

This chapter shares and highlights online teaching during a coronavirus semester at DHU and showcases, at the same time, what most universities and colleges in mainland China have put in place to deal with the turbulent educational situation. The discussion on the feasibility and consideration of blended language teaching and learning in post-coronavirus periods hopes to voice Chinese educators' localized conduct in this new global trend.

Literature review

English for academic purposes (EAP), or Academic English, first appeared by name in the United Kingdom in the 1960s to support overseas learners improve their competence in English language during their disciplinary studies at tertiary level (Cai, 2012). However, in the Chinese teaching and learning context, English is considered a foreign language. Most disciplinary content is still taught in Chinese as a teaching medium language (TML). For the writers of this chapter, College English courses may broadly equate to EAP or Academic English. That means, college English teaching shares academic content and features with EAP and aims at improving learners' competence in the English language.

With the outbreak of Covid-19 at the end of 2019, college English teaching and learning faced great challenges in China. Traditional classroom teaching was no longer possible since most schools and universities decided to close temporarily. Teachers and students were told to stay at home to help control the spread of the virus. Similar recommendations were given in India (Joshi et al., 2020), Iran (Khatoony & Nezhadmehr, 2020), Georgia (Basilaia & Kvavadze, 2020), and many other nations. The solutions to these challenges included turning traditional classroom teaching into distant and online learning, among which language teaching courses were included. Language educators in China have endeavored to explore online teaching long before the pandemic but efforts in this area increased with the Covid-19 outbreak at tertiary level (e.g., Zhao & Lv, 2020; Zhai et al., 2021), in middle schools (e.g., Yi, 2020), as well as in vocational schools (e.g., Yu & Wang, 2020).

Local practices

This section will report on DHU's teaching and assessment during the pandemic. The report focuses on the reading-into-writing integrated courses in DHU as an example.

Teaching reforms

The most difficult teaching circumstance appeared in the Spring semester of 2020, as a sudden shift from traditional classroom teaching to online learning and teaching was necessary due to the closure of the university. Taking reading-into-writing Courses Two and Three in DHU as an example, the participants involved included 81 classes, 1,770 learners, and 20 English teachers. The learners were mostly non-English major college freshmen and sophomores, spread over China, who had to stay in their hometowns to have distant and online learning.

College English courses are compulsory for college study, with two credits awarded for each course. The main learning materials remained the same textbooks – *New Standard College English integrated course 2 and 3* (2nd edition), edited by Simon Greenall (UK) and Prof. Wen Qiufang, jointly published by Macmillan Education and Foreign Language Teaching and Research Press since 2016. The online platform in DHU was the Chaoxing learning platform, which was introduced and arranged to be used by the Dean's Office at the university. The main challenges facing teachers were (a) designing online classroom activities and (b) segmenting the teaching knowledge and teaching objectives into micro lectures and recording them into various mini-videos. Other challenges included (c) the unfamiliarity of online courses and teaching facilities, (d) possible lack of teaching equipment, and (e) poor network connectivity. The preparation periods extended for no more than three weeks before the delayed start of that troubled Spring semester in March. Thus, it was a challenging job for all the participating teachers. Teachers were also advised to borrow Massive Open Online Courses (MOOC) or use online course wares (U campus for the teaching textbook in this case). If teaching videos were difficult to make, then the direct recording of PowerPoint presentations was allowed as a replacement. The teaching team also had to consider possible adjustments to the teaching syllabus and teaching schedule.

During this semester, teachers prepared their teaching recordings, learning requirements, and tasks, as well as texts for the students to peer review in advance and then posted them every fortnight onto the Chaoxing platform. Teachers were welcome to contact their learners before and after the scheduled lecturing dates at a Tencent group meeting or WeChat group meeting. In this sense, similar to what their Indian counterparts experienced, the traditional classroom teaching had become asynchronous. Like their Indian counterparts had experienced (Joshi et al., 2020), many Chinese learners were faced with a lack of basic facilities and external distractions such as time differences, family interruptions, and the like. Chinese teachers also had to struggle with outdated technological applications, ambiguous clarifications regarding online teaching practices, and the lack of confidence in technical integration into their existing courses. Nevertheless, with the implementation of the slogan "classes suspended but learning continues" advocated by the Chinese Ministry of Education, these aforementioned difficulties and challenges were overcome in the end. Teachers pasted teaching notices and U campus learning content previews on Tencent or WeChat groups. During scheduled lecturing hours, they either arranged online collaborative learning, project-based and problem-based learning (PBL), or scaffold learners to do text reading analysis and guided writing with or without Chinese as the TML.

Figure 20.1 represents the teaching process in online courses. From the figure, one can see that teaching practices in that semester showed some features of semi-flipped classes and blended teaching.

Various teachers chose diverse teaching resources, designed different teaching activities, and carried out numerous exercises and tests. Teaching institutions may not have used the same platforms and equipment to provide online teaching, but the primary mode of course delivery was quite similar: providing courses to distant learners via a network.

Changes in assessment

In this section, the focus is on changes in course assessment and evaluating results during the Covid-19 semester. Taking reading-into-writing integrated courses as an example, the first change was the proportion of summative and formative assessment. Traditionally, the assessment weighting for college English courses has been 40% of formative and 60% summative. However, the proportion of formative assessment increased to guide learners and practitioners towards paying more attention to the learning process, especially learners' online learning

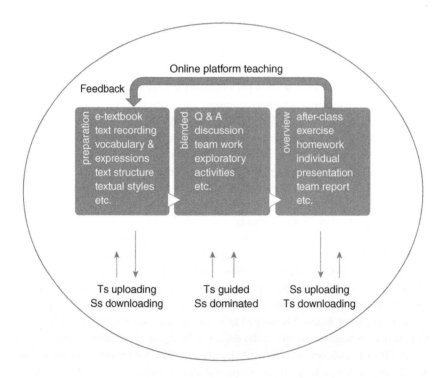

FIGURE 20.1   Teaching/learning process in distant online courses

participation and performance. The final decision of the teaching team concerning this ratio reversed the traditional proportion, so the formative component became 60% and the summative assessment 40%. Obviously, online learning data needs to be considered more closely when evaluating the course's holistic learning/teaching effects. Specifically, online learning data refers to the attendance of students for online discussions, seminars, and tutorials; quantity and quality of exercise and homework uploaded onto the Chaoxing learning platform and learners' watching percentages of recorded mini-lecture videos. Like most other online learning/teaching platforms, the Chaoxing platform has various functional modules such as the uploading section, discussion section, log-in recording area, and in-sessional quizzes and to match users' teaching/learning needs. Teachers may design their own creative testing forms and content to form part of their formative assessment components.

The second change introduced due to the pandemic was the contents being tested in the summative assessment. Previously, teaching teams would design examination papers, print, and hand them out to learners. The contents being tested in that final paper would be textbook-oriented and usual testing items included reading comprehension, vocabulary choices, cloze questions, translation, and writing. During the online learning periods, the principal features of the achievement test remained unchanged. The summative tests focused on learners' mastery of the language points, their text analysis, and understanding the textbook with the highlighted focus on English reading and writing competence. The real summative testing was narrowed down to two parts, which were carried out in two teaching weeks. The first part was vocabulary and phrases. which they were expected to combine into a short paragraph. The second part was devoted to writing. The given topic was a discussion and analysis of a social phenomenon, a typical argumentative writing task of 150–200 words in length.

Finally, the summative online testing procedures were introduced. As mentioned earlier, the final summative test included two parts and was carried out in two teaching weeks. Considering that this was the first attempt of online testing for most participants, both teachers and learners needed to familiarize themselves with the platform and the procedures. Therefore, pre-tests were carried out several times and notices were posted in advance, reminding learners and teachers to prepare necessary electronic equipment and to ensure that the testing environment was operational. In final testing weeks, the teaching team prepared and used more than 20 testing papers as a testing corpus for random sampling. The writing test, for instance, lasted 60 minutes. However, examination monitoring included checking both the learner's identity and qualifications before the start of the test. The whole testing process occurred in real-time with data being transmitted from the learners' cameras onto the screen of the teacher who was monitoring. Figure 20.2 shows a screenshot in a monitoring site at the end of the exam. The students were supposed to take the test on their computer, with their mobile

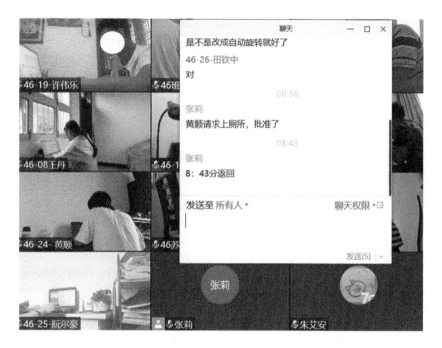

FIGURE 20.2   Screenshot at monitoring end

phones' camera recording them. Before the test, each of the learners signed a letter of commitment and honesty.

The monitoring teachers were asked to record the process to check the students' identities and accreditation. During the testing period, if learners were off-line for no longer than ten minutes, the missing minutes would be added to the remaining testing time manually by the teachers who were monitoring. If students missed. If more than 10 minutes during the testing periods, they would be asked to take part in replacement tests when their connectivity improved.

Global implications

The local teaching and assessment practices at DHU showcase the feasibility of distant and online education at tertiary level. Table 20.1 compares learners' satisfaction data and the learning impact before and during the Covid-19 semester. Results show no obvious changes from the Dean's office view. They would consider dimensions like teachers' commitment, learners' interest triggers, and knowledge mastery. As can be seen, the statistics before and during the pandemic semesters show no significant difference either. The data for the online class are even slightly more favorable than those for the traditional class.

TABLE 20.1 Learners' satisfaction and learning effect

Satisfaction data		Learning effect (mean score)	
Traditional class	Online class	Traditional class	Online class
94.16	96	76.62	77.04

Note: Satisfaction data come from Lily's course 3. All the data would have 100 as a full score.

The practices in the Covid-19 semester also bring out considerations about the advantages and drawbacks of online education. The advantages may include: (a) being free of time and regional limitations; (b) it maximizes the utilization of human and material resources (Zhou, 2020); (c) theoretically, it facilitates equality of education; and (d) it has the potential to trigger learning interest and participation, hence improve the learning effect. On the other hand, online learning could (1) bring an actual increase of learning and teaching time; (2) some learning activities, such as oral English communication and group reports, may be more suitable for the traditional class; and (3) some learners may feel inferior if their network or learning facilities are inadequate.

Therefore, post-coronavirus, education at a tertiary level may provide learners on campus with blended learning/teaching opportunities. According to Bonk and Graham (2005, p. 5), blended learning systems combine face-to-face instruction with computer-mediated instruction. When universities and colleges become open to learners again, courses may undergo the development from traditional classes to online classes, and then to blended classes. The Chaoxing platform and other similar online learning platforms still function as learners' virtual learning places. Teachers can upload the recorded mini-lectures onto those platforms and motivate learners to learn on their own. These recorded videos could turn into Small Private Online Courses (SPOC) tailored to those particular learners.

Teachers may also choose to use MOOC or recommended courseware to match their own offline class teaching. The scheduled and allocated teaching periods could be used as tutoring time, as opportunities to do group reports and presentations, and carry out discussions and Q & A sessions. Hence, the face-to-face, off-line part of blended practices may show flipped or semi-flipped features. Teachers design and guide while learners dominate the off-line learning phase. Learners' questions about early online self-learning on text reading analysis, for example, could be discussed and answered in face-to-face communication in the classroom. Various teaching activities in off-line classes could ensure learners' mastery of certain learning objectives, drill training and fulfilment of output learning tasks. In the end, traditional courses may upgrade into what the Ministry of Education in China called "Golden Hybrid Courses", namely high-quality online and offline blended courses.

Conclusion

By using "reading-into-writing" compulsory courses Two and Three at DHU namely, two compulsory courses, as the subject of a case study, this chapter has described the innovations of teaching and assessment in the English classroom for Chinese university freshmen and sophomores (non-English majors) during the Covid-19 pandemic in 2020.

First, the teaching process and teaching methodology underwent great changes with the demand for online teaching. The Chaoxing learning platform was used to meet the needs of sharing teaching and learning material with the students, and Tencent group meeting and WeChat group meeting applications were applied for telecommunication and online teaching. In order to carry out the innovations, teachers had to set up necessary equipment at home for online teaching, familiarize themselves with such platforms, make short videos, and design PowerPoint for classroom activities and homework for their online classes. It was recommended that teachers design and prepare their materials two weeks before the class started, for the convenience of peer review and students' previews.

Second, the way to assess students' learning had to be adjusted for online teaching during the Covid-19 phase. The ratio for college English series courses used to be 40% formative assessment and 60% summative assessment before the pandemic. With the adaptation of teaching processes and methodology brought about by the pandemic, the formative assessment percentage was adjusted accordingly to match the real teaching and learning process and increased to 60%. Therefore, summative assessment was reduced to 40% with a new focus on learners' mastery of the language points, text analysis, and text understanding, which highlights their English reading and writing competence. Online monitoring techniques for the final summative test were also introduced in the chapter to ensure the strictness and fairness of the final test.

Despite all the challenges and difficulties during the pandemic, teaching was carried out smoothly and satisfactorily. A survey on learners' satisfaction and learning during that semester shows that students' degree of satisfaction and effect of learning were slightly higher than in the pre-pandemic era.

The case study reported in this chapter may guide practitioners in China and other teaching/learning contexts in using blended learning/teaching method post-coronavirus courses that teach English as a second language and to scaffold learners' academic study, by integrating the advantages of traditional classroom teaching and online teaching. Ultimately, the teaching experiences gained from the pandemic semester and the endeavors to carry out blended teaching in the post-coronavirus periods may develop teaching and learning under both normal and difficult circumstances.

Acknowledgment

The writing of this chapter received the support from English 3, a key course project at Shanghai Municipal Level under project number "SKC-18".

Reference list

Basilaia, G., & Kvavadze, D., (2020). Transition to online education in schools during a SARS-CoV-2 Coronavirus (COVID-19) pandemic in Georgia. *Pedagogical Research*, *5*(4). Article em0060. https://doi.org/10.29333/pr/7937

Bonk, C. J., & Graham, C. (2005). *The handbook of blended learning: Global perspectives, local designs*. John Wiley & Sons.

Cai, J. (2012). *A way out for EFL at tertiary level education in mainland China*. Shanghai Jiaotong University Press. 蔡基刚,《中国大学英语教学路在何方》, 上海:上海交通大学出版社

Joshi, A., Vinay, M., & Bhaskar, P. (2020). Impact of coronavirus pandemic on the Indian education sector: Perspectives of teachers on online teaching and assessments. *Interactive Technology and Smart Education*. https://doi.org/10.1108/ITSE-06-2020-0087

Khatoony, S., & Nezhadmehr, M. (2020). EFL teachers' challenges in integration of technology for online classrooms during Coronavirus (COVID-19) pandemic in Iran. *AJELP: Asian Journal of English Language and Pedagogy*, *8*(2), 89–104. https://doi.org/10.37134/ajelp.vol8.2.7.2020

Yi, B. (2020). An exploration and application of middle school English micro-lecture teaching in Covid-19 situation, *View Point*, *000*(003), 1–1. 易波 (2020) , 基于新冠疫情下初中英语微课教学的拓展与应用,《视界观》, *000*(003), 1–1.

Yu, M., & Wang, Y. (2020). (2017). An exploration of college English teaching theories and practice based on e-teaching mode- Strategies of college English teaching in Covid-9. *English Teacher*, *20*(17), 101–103 + 116. 余敏军 , 王月 (2020) , 基于信息化教学模式的高校英语教学理论与实践探讨 – 新型冠状病毒肺炎疫情背景下高校英语教学应对策略,《英语教师》, *20*(17), 101–103 + 116.

Zhai, S., Shi, P., & Zhao, Y. (2021). An analysis of blended teaching effect for English majors in pandemic situations. *Progress in Education*, *11*(2), 9. 柴楣, 史培媛, 赵燕凤 (2021), 新冠疫情下英语专业混合式教学效果探析,《教育进展》, *11*(2), 9.

Zhao, C., & Lv, Y. (2020). Problems and solutions to college English online teaching during the Covid-19. *Jiangsu Foreign Language Teaching and Research*, *75*(03), 3–5 + 88. 赵才华, 吕岩 (2020), 新冠疫情期间大学英语线上教学的问题与对策,《江苏外语教学研究》, *75*(03), 3–5 + 88.

Zhou, J. (2020). An analysis of advantages and disadvantages of computerized online teaching and its strategies. *Tianjin Education*, (24). 周娟, (2020), 计算机线上教学优劣点分析及对策研究,《天津教育》(24).

21

TEACHERS' REFLECTIONS ON ALTERNATIVE ASSESSMENT AND COLLABORATIVE LEARNING IN AN EFL ACADEMIC WRITING CLASS IN THAILAND DURING THE COVID-19 PANDEMIC

A case study

Pragasit Sitthitikul and Vorakorn Tuvajitt

Introduction

In response to the policy on physical distancing in Thailand that arose from the spread of the Covid-19 virus, the mode of instruction changed from traditional face-to-face delivery to remote learning, also referred to as distance-learning, distance education, e-learning, online learning, or emergency learning (Kitishat et al., 2020; Moser et al., 2020). Teachers and students found themselves engaged in different online learning platforms such as Zoom, Google Classroom, and Microsoft-Teams. In March 2020, the Thai government announced a nationwide lockdown to mitigate the spread of the coronavirus, leading to drastic changes across society. The education sector was no exception as it looked to remote teaching and learning methods to provide academic continuity.

Online learning has become increasingly popular in higher education, and 21st-century students are familiar with the use of technology to enhance learning (Alghammas, 2020). Nevertheless, online delivery as a default mode poses challenges to many teachers, although Anderson (2011) contends that the environment of learning and teaching online remains similar to traditional in-class instruction, but with goals that should relate to facilitating effective learning rather than just emulating a classroom-like learning environment. This led the authors to believe that transforming classes from on-site to online was not simply "a change of venue". Designing instruction that conveys effective learning and assessment was a concern, alongside finding effective assessment tasks that would be appropriate for an online setting. The chapter starts by describing the context

DOI: 10.4324/9781003283409-26

of the study, then reviews the related literature, before learning and assessment methods are explored for the online class. Following this, practitioner reflections on the outcomes are discussed with the aim of finding the most suitable learning and assessment methods for online academic English writing classes, along with suggestions for future studies.

The case study

Our case study was set in an Academic English course at a university in Thailand. Switching to an online mode, several challenges occurred. For example, the absence of face-to-face supervision from the teachers increased students' reliance on themselves, which is less common among Thai students. This increased self-reliance increased pressure on students and sometimes made it harder for them to meet the learning goals. Another issue was the lack of social interaction, meaning the students found it difficult to work and learn collaboratively, which is vital for their progress. Hence, the authors tried to address these issues by implementing a new learning and assessment approach.

The course lasted for 16 weeks. There were a total of 85 students from different disciplines, namely; business administration, business, arts, science and technology, communication, and engineering. Most of the students were Thai, with the remainder Chinese, Vietnamese, or Filipino. The class met three times a week, totaling four and a half hours per week. While all four language skills were taught, this study focuses predominantly on writing, as it formed a major proportion of the course. The classes were conducted via Zoom with all assignments provided and submitted through Google Classroom.

Recent research indicates several challenges associated with online language teaching during Covid-19: students' lack of motivation, technical constraints, and teachers' and learners' attitudes (Matvienko et al., 2021; Sa'di et al., 2021). Despite these potential setbacks, opportunities for teachers and researchers have been found. As Hodges et al. (2020) assert, the success of online learning relies on careful instructional design and planning. Hence, the authors introduced a new assessment and learning method: the use of self-evaluation on their writing and the collaborative group report.

Before switching to the online mode, the assessment methods were mainly summative, for example, pen-and-pencil and timed writing tests. Peer evaluation was also a common assessment tool for writing assignments. To illustrate the process, students were either randomly paired or could choose a partner, and they then exchanged their texts to evaluate. Areas of evaluation included surface-level elements (e.g., grammar and spelling) alongside effective communication of content. According to Roscoe and Chi (2007), peer evaluation, by engaging in a cognitively demanding activity such as writing, benefits students who assess their classmates' work through understanding subject matter and writing skills.

However, peer evaluation became a less viable option in the online class and was then replaced by self-evaluation. One reason was that formative assessments are recommended (Rapanta et al., 2020). Another reason for the move to self-evaluation was its suitability for distance learning and its contribution to the development of autonomy. Online classrooms, unlike physical classrooms in which teachers regularly interact face-to-face with students, can be isolating and time-consuming (Dema & Sinwongsuwat, 2020).

Another new learning opportunity arose from the introduction of a group report project. The previous assessment for the report writing unit had been a timed test taken individually, but the test was replaced by a group project for the online version. The rationale behind this was that the authors took it as an opportunity for the students to embrace collaborative learning and produce more authentic work instead of depending solely on online examinations.

After deciding the changes, the authors observed and reflected on the impact of the new assessment and learning methods. Engaging in critical reflection was a means to challenge assumptions and question the practice so the practitioners could alter deeply rooted personal beliefs on teaching and apply them (Larrivee, 2000) to improve teaching and learning.

Literature review

This section presents relevant literature, starting with reflection and reflective practice, which laid the ground for the data collection in the study. This is followed by a discussion of the alternative assessment and collaborative learning that provided solutions to the challenges in this study.

Reflection and reflective practice

In the face of the dynamic and complex nature of today's classroom, particularly the virtual one during the Covid-19 pandemic, teachers must adjust their roles to align with the changes (Larrivee, 2000). They are expected to adjust from having power *over* the learners to sharing power *with* learners. Thus, there are demands for teachers to embrace different roles, such as being a social mediator, learning facilitator, and reflective practitioner.

According to Schön (1991), teacher reflection is an epistemology of practice. Reflection embraces two aspects: reflection-in-action and reflection-on-action. Reflection-in-action refers to reflection during the act, in this online context, it refers to what takes place during the lesson, and it allows the practitioners to rationalize events as they happened and respond to them. In contrast, reflection-on-action happens after the event and in greater depth. This second aspect opened more extensive opportunities to reflect on the causes and explore options for future improvement.

According to the literature, there are several reasons why reflective practice is becoming increasingly recognized as essential in good teaching. Reflection, as argued by Loughran (2002), is a process that helps practitioners make better sense of the information at hand. Additionally, better understanding students' views allows greater opportunities for teachers to reflect back on their own teaching. In this regard, Dewey (1933), cited in Loughran (2002), states that reflective practice is a way for teachers to use their skills to help students learn in meaningful ways, and can lead to greater understanding of students' learning. This approach is supported by Leitch and Day (2000), who consider good teaching to be reliant on an ongoing evaluation of how students learn. Furthermore, understanding their practices helps teachers bridge a dichotomous view of teaching and learning as two opposing entities.

Alternative assessment

Assessment has sometimes been viewed as being separated from teaching. Hyland (2003), however, opposed such a viewpoint as not accurately reflecting the true nature of language pedagogy. In fact, teaching and assessment are intertwined. Besides, beyond the general perception of assessment as part of evaluating students' performance, it is an integral part of learning. Such integration means that assessment can and should be utilized, not only to foster student learning but also to enhance specific aspects of learning necessary for success on the course and in their lives. To carry out effective learning, language educators need to implement and develop a variety of assessment methods, either formative, summative, or both, particularly for higher order concepts (Hoyt, 2005). It can then be concluded that, in the process of learning, assessments can provide a succinct picture of students' learning progress and status (Heng & Vethamani, 2005). Due to the varied nature of language learning, there have been calls for a wider range of assessment methods, such as checklists, journals, logs, self-evaluation, portfolios, self-evaluation, and peer assessment (Huerta-Macias, 1995, cited in Brown and Hudson 1998).

Self-evaluation

This case study examines how self-evaluation was employed as an assessment mechanism. Self-assessment can be defined as "procedures" by which the learners themselves evaluate their language skills and knowledge (Bailey, 1998, p. 227, cited in Matsuno, 2009). Brown and Abeywickrama (2010) stated that theoretical justification from many principles of language acquisition are required. For instance, the principle of learning autonomy is a pillar of successful learning, and it is believed that the ability to set one's goal in learning and then assess progress, drives the development of intrinsic motivation (*ibid*). It should be noted that successful learners will develop the ability to monitor their performance only when they autonomously master the art of self-evaluation (Ekbatani & Pearson, 2000, cited in Brown & Abeywickrama, 2010).

Collaborative learning

Collaborative learning refers to an educational approach that revolves around groups of learners who work together to solve a problem (Laal & Laal, 2012) and a set of methods which enable students to work together to achieve a learning goal (Johnson & Johnson, 2009). Vellanki and Bandu (2021) summarize the two reasons for adopting online collaborative tasks in learning as (1) emphasizing real-life language through meaningful tasks and (2) being student-centered. When the task is interactive, social engagement and collaboration are promoted. On top of that, individual students can develop an ability to seek social assistance rather than learning in isolation. In other words, a communal aim with a common goal is a means for students to develop their autonomous learning skills through social interaction (Cheng, 2019). As previoulsy mentioned, in our online learning mode, students could not generally find the opportunity to make use of social interaction to meet the learning goals. The authors therefore found it necessary to promote collaborative learning through a communal task.

The implementation of the new assessment and instructional methods

After introducing the text and its language features through lectures, discussion, and text modeling, a writing assignment and a checklist for self-evaluation *(see Appendix A)* was provided via Google Classroom. As stated by Jones and Saville (2016) and Anderson (2011), effective teaching demands explicit and detailed discussion of the criteria that learning will be assessed by. In this online setting, before the students started their work, the teachers explained each item on the checklist to ensure they understood.

The checklist was divided into two sections: a yes/no response section and the open-ended part. The first section was a list of statements highlighting key points focusing on the following areas: (1) language use and language features; (2) the content and knowledge of the subject matter; (3) organization – coherence, cohesiveness, and structure. The second part was comprised of open-ended response items to encourage a plan for revision

The group project

In lieu of the individual timed writing test in the Report Writing unit, groups of four students were assigned a project. Each member of the group had a specified role, for example, researcher, evaluator, contact person with the teachers, and editor. The teachers took the role of advisor throughout the project. The students selected a topic of interest and researched information from trustworthy sources to create a short report. After having their proposed topic approved by the teachers, the students had four days to complete the report.

Data collection and analysis

This section presents the data collection and analysis procedure for the outcomes of the plan. During the implementation of the planned teaching and learning methods, the authors closely observed the students' reactions and responses. To ensure essential data were accurately and comprehensively grasped, teaching notes were kept for retrospective reflection. The students' final written submissions were examined to see if they had utilized self-evaluation in improving their texts. For example, in a case of report writing, if a student checked "yes" for the item "A clear and effective problem statement is given", the teachers would check if this had been provided as claimed. At the same time, the open-ended part was expected to reveal how students planned to revise their texts in the future. Like the previous part, the teachers would examine the students' final work and see whether they had applied the revision as planned. If the student had not, they were asked to revise the text again.

As for the report group project, empirical data on the effectiveness of the method came from the students' scores against a set grading rubric. To ascertain the trustworthiness and fairness of the scoring, all the reports and scores were double marked for consistency and accuracy. In addition, the authors collected data from students during the process of making the report, which included questions, concerns, and complaints. The information from both the self-evaluation and group report provided source material for the authors to critically reflect on the efficacy, strengths, and weakness of these pedagogical approaches.

Findings, discussions, and recommendations

Findings

The overall result of the use of self-evaluation as an assessment method was less than satisfying. When examining the students' responses on the checklist against the actual work, many mismatches were found. For example, a student marked "yes" for the item "The topic sentence is clear with a controlling idea" (from opinion writing). In the actual work, the topic sentence was "*The government will construct the nuclear power plant*". Another example was from the statement "The flow of information is good". While some students marked "yes", the actual work contained no logical pattern of organization.

Similar problems were found from the open-ended section of the checklist. Most students' responses had limited insight, often primarily limited to the brief prompts in the reflection notes, and the responses were vague. For instance, for the item "I plan to improve my work by . . . ", a number of students wrote *"check the grammar"*. Nevertheless, when the authors looked at the corresponding work, grammatical mistakes were widespread, and there was little evidence of revision. This shows that the students either did not fully invest in revising the grammar as claimed, or they still lacked the ability to adequately correct it themselves. Moreover, many students did not make use of the assessment checklist at all.

On the other hand, the group project and its use of collaborative learning strategies yielded an active and motivating learning environment. The students tended to productively discuss their own assignments to formulate ideas and orally provide feedback on their peer's ideas. From the authors' observations during the monitoring, students worked remotely using personal communication applications such as Line or WhatsApp and wrote the report together on the shared Google Document. Thus, the use of collaborative activities will still be utilized in the next cycle.

The reports were satisfactory. The final products showed the quality of having the correct format, appropriate language features, fewer grammatical mistakes, and more substantive content. The authors conclude that collaborative work contributed to enabling students improve their writing ability when working together. In addition, online communication proved to be a convenient way for students to work together, without the need to travel.

Discussion

From the perspective of reflective practitioners, the use of self-evaluation by the students was not successful overall. The authors hypothesized that there could be two reasons. The first factor is the lack of experience Asian students have with being autonomous. Asian students are reliant on the teacher's feedback and judgment. The idea is supported by Chang and Geary (2015) and Meesong and Jaroongkhongdach (2016), who claim that Asian students are passive and not well-equipped to learn autonomously. The second factor was the lack of training due to time constraints on applying the self-evaluation checklist to a sample. The collaborative group project, however, demonstrated a high level of efficacy. In line with Dowse and van Rensburg (2015) and Johnson et al. (1998), the use of collaborative learning benefited the students in improving their English, gaining new ideas and perspectives, and organizing their texts more effectively.

The authors reflected that it was important that the group project assignment was more authentic and could represent the social aspect of writing, which requires time to generate ideas and refine texts, unlike in the timed test. The students put great effort into the completion of the work as it represented a large portion of the coursework marks. This also showed the reality of how the students are driven by grades, exams, and products of learning. Lam (2013) and Lee (2014) have pointed out that this is common in an exam-based educational culture such as the Thai setting.

Recommendations

The authors' reflection on the application of self-evaluation to writing and collaborative learning projects in a pandemic provides an example for teachers to systematically collect data about their work to make informed decisions regarding their practices (Farrell, 2012). Seeing the merits, shortcomings, and challenges which emerged from this case study, the authors then reflected further on ways to improve their teaching practice. The Asian learners in this case would benefit from increased support in becoming more autonomous. Otherwise, they could find it difficult to cope with contemporary educational practices that demand greater independence and able to judge their own abilities in the process of arriving at solutions to the problems identified (Nwosu & Okoye, 2014). Practice sessions on utilizing the self-evaluation mechanisms are, therefore, likely to be beneficial, as mentioned by Saito (2008) and Saito and Fujita (2004).

It is recommended that collaborative learning and formative assessment is included in EFL writing classes, regardless of the learning mode. Also, work that represents the nature of writing can enable the students to see the actual process of involved (Hyland, 2003). During difficult times, the use of other alternative forms of assessment should be integrated into the teaching and learning of EFL academic writing. For example, teachers should make use of other online learning applications such as Kahoot! and Moodle as well as encourage peer assessment and online writing portfolios.

Conclusion

The Covid-19 pandemic marked a turning point for teaching and learning. The changes necessitated by the lockdown and school closures imposed many changes on institutions, teachers, and learners. Seeing it as a source of opportunities, it also gave practitioners a chance to find pedagogical approaches that are more suitable for the situation. The "new normal" world enables teachers to re-examinine their beliefs and approaches toward their practices. From this case study, although not all changes in the assessment of the writing proved to be effective, it was still found that reflection provides the key to improving teaching practice. Therefore, reflective practice by teachers is undoubtedly a useful way to deal with teaching challenges posed by similar situations in the future, and the insights from this case study may be transferable to other EFL academic writing classes, both physical and online.

Reference list

Alghammas, A. (2020). Online language assessment during Covid-19 pandemic: university faculty members' perception and practices. *Asian EFL Journal Research Articles*, *21*(4.4), 169–195.

Anderson, T. (2011). *The theory and practice of online learning* (2nd ed.). Athabasca University Press.

Brown, H. D., & Abeywickrama, P. (2010). *Language assessment principles and classroom practices*. Pearson Longman.

Brown, J. D., & Hudson, T. (1998). The alternatives in language assessment. *TESOL Quarterly, 32*(4), 635–675. https://doi.org/10.2307/3587999

Chang, L. Y., & Geary, M. P. (2015). Promoting the autonomy of Taiwanese EFL learners in higher education by using self-assessment learning logs. *Studies in English Language Teaching, 3*(4). http://www.scholink.org/ojs/index.php/selt

Cheng, J. (2019). *An investigation of learner autonomy among EFL students in mainland Chinese universities* [Doctoral dissertation, Universiti Tunku Abdul Rahman]. http://eprints.utar.edu.my/3183/1/15AAD06788_Cheng_Jianfeng_PhD_Thesis.pdf.

Dema, C., & Sinwongsuwat, K. (2020). Enhancing EFL students' autonomous learning of English conversation during COVID-19 via language-in-talk log assignments. *Education Quarterly Reviews, 3*(4). https://doi.org/10.31014/aior.1993.03.04.165

Dowse, C., & Van Rensburg, W. (2015). A hundred times we learned from one another: Collaborative learning in an academic writing workshop. *South African Journal of Education, 35*(1), 1–12.

Farrell, T. S. C. (2012). Reflecting on reflective practice: (Re)visiting Dewey and Schön. *TESOL Journal, 3*, 7–16. https://doi.org/10.1002/tesj.10.

Heng, C. H., & Vethamani, M. E. (2005). *ELT concerns in assessment*. Sasbadi SDN. BHD.

Hodges, C., Moore, S., Lockee, B., Trust, T., & Bond, A. (2020). *The difference between emergency remote teaching and online learning*. ResearchGate. https://er.educause.edu/articles/2020/3/the- difference- between-emergency-remote-teaching-and-online-learning.

Hoyt, K. (2005). Assessment impact on instruction. In *New vision in action*. National Assessment Summit.

Hyland, K. (2003). *Second language writing*. Cambridge University Press.

Johnson, D. W., Johnson, F., & Smith, K.A. (1998). Cooperative learning returns to college: What evidence is there that it works?. *Change, 30*(4), 26–35.

Johnson, D. W., & Johnson, F. (2009). *Joining together: Group theory and group skills* (10th ed.). Allyn & Bacon.

Jones, N., & Saville, N. (2016). *Learning oriented assessment: A systemic approach* (Vol. 45). Cambridge University Press.

Kitishat, A. R., Al Omar, K. H., & Al Momani, M. A. K. (2020). The Covid-19 crisis and distance learning: E-teaching of language between realities and challenges: *The Asian ESP Journal, 16*(5.1).

Laal, M., & Laal, M. (2012). Collaborative learning: What is it? *Procedia-Social and Behaviour Sciences, 31*, 491–495. https://doi.org/10.1016/j.sbspro.2011.12.092

Lam, R. (2013). The relationship between assessment types and text revision. *ELT Journal, 67*, 446-458. https://doi.org/10.1093/elt/cct034.

Larrivee, B. (2000). Transforming teaching practice: Becoming the critically reflective teacher. *Reflective Practice, 1*(3), 239–307. https://doi.org/10.1080/713693162

Lee, I. (2014). Revising teacher feedback in EFL writing from sociocultural perspective. *TESOL Quarterly*, TESOL International Association, *48*(1), 201–123.

Leitch, R. & Day, C. (2000). Action research and reflective practice: Towards a holistic view. *Educational Action Research, 8*, 179–193. https://doi.org/10.1080/09650790000200108

Loughran, J. (2002). Effective reflective practice: In search of meaning in learning about teaching. *Journal of Teacher Education, 53*, 33–43.

Matsuno, S. (2009). Self-, peer-, and teacher-assessments in Japanese university EFL writing classrooms. *Language Testing, 26*(1), 75–100. https://doi.org/10.1177%2F0265532208097337

Matvienko, O., Kuzmina, S., Glazunova, T., Yamchynska, T., Starlin, C., & Foo, S. (2021). The legacy of a pandemic: Lessons learned and . . . being learned. *Journal of Interdisciplinary Education, 17*(1), 14–29.

Meesong, K., & Jaroongkhongdach, W. (2016). Autonomous language learning: Thai undergraduate students' behaviour. *Thai TESOL Journal, 29*(2), 156–186. https://doi.org/10.1177%2F0265532208097337

Moser, K. M., Wei, T., & Brenner, D. (2021). Remote teaching during COVID-19: Implications from a national survey of language educators. *System, 97.* https://doi.org/10.1016/j.system.2020.102431.

Nwosu, K. C., & Okoye, R. O. (2014). Students' Self-efficacy and self-Rating scores as predictors of their academic achievement, *Journal of Educational and Social Research, 4*(3), 223. https://www.richtmann.org/journal/index.php/jesr/article/view/2716

Rapanta, C., Botturi, L., Goodyear, P., Guàrdia, L., & Koole, M. (2020). Online university teaching during and after the Covid-19 crisis: Refocusing teacher presence and learning activity. *Post Digital Science and Education, 2*(3), 923–945. https://doi.org/10.1007/s42438-020-00155-y

Roscoe, R. D., & Chi, M. T. H. (2007). Understanding tutor learning: Knowledge-building and knowledge-telling in peer tutors' explanations and questions. *Review of Educational Research.* 77(4), 534–574. https://doi.org/10.3102%2F0034654307309920

Saito, H. (2008). EFL classroom peer assessment: Training effects on rating and commenting, *Language Testing*, 25 (4), 553-581. Sage.

Saito, H., & Fujita, T. (2004). Characteristics and user acceptance of peer rating in EFL writing classrooms. *Language Teaching, 8*, 31–54. https://doi.org/10.1191%2F1362168804lr133oa

Schön, D. A. (1991). *The reflective practitioners: How professionals think in action.* Routledge. https://doi.org/10.4324/9781315237473

Vellanki, S. S, and Bandu, S. (2021). Engaging students online with technology-mediated task-based language teaching. *Arab World English Journal.* Special Issue on Covid 19 Challenges, 127–136. https://dx.doi.org/10.24093/awej/covid.8

Appendix A

Self-evaluation checklist

Assignment _____ Exercise _____

Date _____

Name: _____

_____

Part 1:

Instructions: Use this checklist against your answer to the questions from the reading passage. Carefully think of each item and mark your response honestly. The purpose of this checklist is to help you see both your strengths and weaknesses.

Comprehension (Paragraph 1)

	Yes	No	Note
• The topic sentence contains the subject mentioned in the question.			
• There is a controlling idea in the topic sentence.			
• All important information is written. If not, what should be added is/are . . .			
• I write in my own words or paraphrase more than copying from the text.			
• I use numbers, names, and/or other facts sufficiently and appropriately.			

(Continued)

Quality of ideas in the argument (Paragraph2)

- I clearly show my standpoint in the topic sentence.
- There are enough supporting arguments for my opinion (at least two to three ideas).
- The opinion is well supported with specific details and/or examples such as facts, numbers, and/or names.
- I use my original ideas rather than getting them from the text to use as supports.
- In general, all the ideas are clear.
- The supporting ideas are different from those in the first paragraph.
- I make strong arguments with good choice of words.
- I sound confident with my opinion.

Quality of word choice

- The word choice is appropriate with the context (clear and accurate).
- The word choice is appropriate with the level.
- I focus on using the noun or noun phrases.

Organization

- The ideas are well connected with cohesive devices (transition, conjunction).
- The use of key nouns and pronouns is correct and consistent.
- The flow of information is logical with the most important idea highlighted.
- Pronouns are properly and correctly used (with consistency).

Grammar (please read the work aloud to see where to stop or pause for periods, question marks, and commas.)

- Proper nouns begin with capital letters.
- Sentences are complete thoughts and contain a noun and a verb.
- There are no run-on sentences/fragments.
- The spelling is correct.
- The work contains many grammatical mistakes (point out the mistakes that happen more than once).

- On the scale of 10, I think this work (draft 1) earns _____ marks

Open Feedback:

1. What I like about this work

_____

2. I plan to make the next draft better by

_____

Part 2: Revision – Answer this part only when you have revised your work.

_____

After revising, the new version is better than the first one _____ YES _____ NO

_____

_____

What I have learned from this assignment

_____

_____

INTERNATIONAL PERSPECTIVES ON ACADEMIC ENGLISH IN TURBULENT TIMES

An afterword

Julio Gimenez

Introduction

As the chapters in this edited collection demonstrate, the global pandemic has had a considerable impact on Academic English at universities around the world. The areas that have experienced the most impact include technical capability and readiness, pedagogic adaptations to online teaching, existing working patterns, and assessing learning. The 21 chapters in the collection offer examples of how academic English practitioners, in a range of different higher education contexts, rapidly and effectively responded to the challenges posed by the pandemic in these areas.

This final chapter presents a summary of the key responses provided in the chapters with a view of offering readers a resource to refer to should we find ourselves facing similar challenges in the future. Following the thematic organisation of the collection, the summary has been divided into four sections: technological and pedagogic responses, adaptations to online teaching, collaborative efforts, and assessment of online learning.

Technological and pedagogic responses

The need for rapid responses to the pandemic has demanded adapting existing, as well as adopting, new technological capabilities and pedagogic practices. As many of the chapters in the collection demonstrate, these demands can be met by:

- increasing and updating the technical capabilities of universities so that technical infrastructure is developed, through which teaching can be effectively delivered online and practitioners and students can be supported in the development of digital literacies (Akhmedjanova and Akhmedova, Ch. 11;

DOI: 10.4324/9781003283409-27

Alhasani (Dubali), Ch. 10; Donovan, Ch. 2; Knežević, Ch. 3; Manasreh, Raza and Sarfraz, Ch. 4; Rodas, Ch. 14)

- re-designing existing courses by following design models, such as the Backward Design, that seem more suited for designing online (EAP) courses (Bolster and Levrai, Ch.1; Deroey and Skipp, Ch. 7) and materials (Wette, Ch. 6), while also taking the students' academic, social, and affective needs into account (Mežek and Kaufhold, Ch. 5; Wette, Ch. 6)
- encouraging dialogue among all stakeholders involved (e.g., the university, departments, colleagues, students) in order to enhance collaborative learning (Bolster and Levrai, Ch. 1; Deroey and Skipp, Ch. 7; Donovan, Ch. 2; Knežević, Ch. 3; Mežek and Kaufhold, Ch. 5) so that collective responses to the crisis are produced (Bolster and Levrai, Ch. 1)
- taking into account not only the physical but also the mental well-being of all stakeholders (Bolster and Levrai, Ch. 1)
- organising effective professional development events for academic English practitioners in an attempt to develop resilience and enhance their ability to face and respond to disruptive events (Akhmedjanova and Akhmedova, Ch. 11; Donovan, Ch. 2; Manasreh et al., Ch. 4; Mežek and Kaufhold, Ch. 5; Pereira-Rocha, Ch. 8).

Adaptations to online teaching

Transitioning from face-to-face to online teaching also requires adaptations to existing teaching practices. The chapters in the volume show some key adaptations that contributors put in place by:

- providing opportunities for vibrant, flexible, and personalised learning, including pastoral and academic support by means of virtual office hours and/or consultations (Colombo, Ch. 9; Pereira-Rocha, Ch. 8; Steyne, Simon, Kam, Timár and Beneš, Ch. 13) through the content and mode of delivery (e.g., face-to-face, blended or online) of the courses (Alhasani (Dubali), Ch. 10; Caplan, Ch. 12; Deroey and Skipp, Ch. 7; Ishii, Ch. 16; Lennon, Trávníková, Hradilová and Štěpánek, Ch. 15)
- encouraging interactive participation, peer feedback, and activities that lead to collaborative learning (Bolster and Levrai, Ch. 1; Colombo, Ch. 9; Deroey and Skipp, Ch. 7; Mežek and Kaufhold, Ch. 5; Sitthitikul and Tuvajitt, Ch. 21; Steyne et al., Ch. 13)
- increasing the amount of writing practice during online delivery so as to provide opportunities for real-time feedback and to minimise time demands (Colombo, Ch. 9; Deroey and Skipp, Ch. 7; Pereira-Rocha, Ch. 8; Rodas, Ch. 14)
- monitoring the online time required of practitioners and students to minimise screen time and online fatigue (Colombo, Ch. 9; Deroey and Skipp, Ch. 7; Pereira-Rocha, Ch. 8; Steyne et al., Ch. 13).

Collaborative efforts

Together with technological and pedagogical adaptations, teaching academic English in turbulent times also demands a higher degree of collaboration among all stakeholders. In fact, collaboration of different types and by different stakeholders has been mentioned in most of the 21 chapters. The contributors to the collection have exemplified their efforts at encouraging collaboration by:

- providing opportunities for academic English practitioners to collaborate by sharing their previous experiences and expertise in online teaching and materials design (Bolster and Levrai, Ch. 1; Colombo, Ch. 9; Deroey and Skipp, Ch. 7; Mežek and Kaufhold, Ch. 5; Shchemeleva and Smirnova, Ch. 19; Steyne et al., Ch. 13)
- creating a learning environment for all stakeholders that fosters collegial interactions based on openness and trust (Colombo, Ch. 9; Rodas, Ch. 14; Shchemeleva and Smirnova, Ch. 19)
- fostering social connections through collaborative activities which can be supported and developed through technology (Ishii, Ch. 16; Lennon et al., Ch. 15).

Assessment of online learning

Changing face-to-face teaching to online delivery also demands changes to assessment. The chapters in the volume show that assessing online learning can be better realised by:

- creating new forms of assessment which integrate and require several skills altogether (Dinneen, Ch. 17) in not only receptive but also productive modes (Li, Jing and Guoying, Ch. 20; Pereira-Rocha, Ch. 8; Sitthitikul and Tuvajitt, Ch. 21)
- providing opportunities for learners to utilise their digital literacies skills to complete assessment tasks (Dinneen, Ch. 17)
- rethinking the role and function of formative assessment as it has come to play a more central role in assessing online learning (Li et al., Ch. 20; Pereira-Rocha, Ch. 8; Steyne et al., Ch. 13; Shchemeleva and Smirnova, Ch. 19; Sitthitikul and Tuvajitt, Ch. 21; Tchekpassi and Zhang, Ch. 18).

Conclusion

The responses summarised in this chapter exemplify the resourcefulness and creativity of academic English practitioners in responding to the challenges of teaching Academic English during the Covid-19 global pandemic. They also show their determination, dedication, and passion for the profession and, in particular, for their students to enable Academic English to continue, despite the turbulent times. We hope the experiences shared in this collection and summarised here will help other practitioners feel more adequately prepared for similar challenges in the future.

INDEX